PROMOTING WALKING AND CYCLING

New perspectives on sustainable travel

Colin Pooley

with

Tim Jones, Miles Tight, Dave Horton, Griet Scheldeman, Caroline Mullen, Ann Jopson, Emanuele Strano

First published in Great Britain in 2013 by

Policy Press
University of Bristol
6th Floor
Howard House
Queen's Avenue
Clifton
Bristol BS8 1SD
UK
t: +44 (0)117 331 5020
f: +44 (0)117 331 5367
pp-info@bristol.ac.uk
www.policypress.co.uk

North America office:
Policy Press
c/o The University of Chicago Press
1427 East 60th Street
Chicago, IL 60637, USA
t: +1 773 702 7700
f: +1 773-702-9756
sales@press.uchicago.edu
www.press.uchicago.edu

© Policy Press 2013

British Library Cataloguing in Publication Data
A catalogue record for this book is available from the British Library

Library of Congress Cataloging-in-Publication Data
A catalog record for this book has been requested

ISBN 978 1 44731 008 2 paperback
ISBN 978 1 44731 007 5 hardcover

The right of Colin Pooley, Tim Jones, Miles Tight, Dave Horton, Griet Scheldeman,
Caroline Mullen, Ann Jopson and Emanuele Strano to be identified as authors of this work
has been asserted by them in accordance with the Copyright, Designs and Patents Act 1988.

Cover design by Qube Design Associates, Bristol
Front cover: image kindly supplied by www.alamy.com
Printed and bound in Great Britain by Berforts Information Press
Policy Press uses environmentally responsible print suppliers

Contents

Lists of maps, tables and boxes

Boxes

About the authors

Dave Horton is a sociologist and writer based in Lancaster, UK. His research is focused on the environment, culture, everyday life, politics, social movements and mobility. However, his main interest and passion is cycling. Dave worked on the Understanding Walking and Cycling (UWAC) research project 2008–11 with particular responsibility for the qualitative and ethnographic research, and is a founder member of the Cycling and Society Research Group. His publications include *Cycling and Society* (Ashgate, 2007), which he co-edited with Paul Rosen and Peter Cox. He writes about cycling for both the academic and popular press and blogs at http://thinkingaboutcycling.wordpress.com.

Tim Jones is a research fellow dividing his time between the Faculty of Technology Design and Environment at Oxford Brookes University and the Transport Studies Unit at the University of Oxford, UK. His research is primarily focused on walking and cycling for short journeys in urban areas, and the application of multiple methods to understand taken-for-granted practices. He was a co-investigator on the UWAC project 2008–11, taking particular responsibility for analysis of the built environment and for the Q Methodology. He was a former member of the National Institute for Health and Clinical Excellence Programme Development Group for Walking and Cycling and is a current member of the government's Cycling Stakeholder Forum.

Ann Jopson is a research fellow at the Institute for Transport Studies, University of Leeds. Her expertise includes travel behaviour psychology, transport planning and policy (including land use), with a particular emphasis on attitudinal and behavioural measures and the social aspects of transport. She worked on the UWAC project 2008–11 with particular responsibility for the development of the questionnaire survey and for its analysis using the Theory of Planned Behaviour.

Caroline Mullen is a research officer at the Institute for Transport Studies, University of Leeds, UK. She works on ethics, political philosophy and governance in transport, environment and health. Current research includes governance and carbon reduction, and investigating implications of equality for sustainability, especially for walking and cycling. Her PhD, from the University of Manchester, was on moral defensibility of transport-related risk and harms. Her publications include H. Widdows and C. Mullen (eds) *The Governance of Genetic Information: Who Decides?* (2009, Cambridge University Press), and 'Mobility (transport)' in R. Chadwick, *Encyclopedia of Applied Ethics*, 2nd edition (2012, Academic Press, pp 137–44).

Colin Pooley is Emeritus Professor of Social and Historical Geography in The Lancaster Environment Centre, Lancaster University, UK. His research focuses on the social geography of Britain and continental Europe since around 1800, with recent projects focused on residential migration, travel to work and other aspects of everyday mobility, including walking and cycling. He has published approximately 100 refereed journal articles and book chapters and 12 books, including *Migration and Mobility in Britain Since the Eighteenth Century* (1998, University College London Press) and *A Mobile Century? Changes in Everyday Mobility in Britain in the Twentieth Century* (2005, Ashgate).

Griet Scheldeman is a social anthropologist working in the UK and Europe. Her research interests centre on perceptive and creative processes in the relationships between people and their environments. With Dave Horton, Griet conducted the ethnographic component of the walking and cycling project. She has published on adolescents' lives with insulin pumps, and on urban walking, including 'Beyond A to B' in T. Ingold, *Redrawing Anthropology* (2011, Ashgate) and 'Gliding effortlessly through life?' in W. Gunn and J. Donovan, *Design Anthropology* (2012, Ashgate). Funded by a postdoctoral grant from the Norwegian Research Council she is currently investigating creativity in Arctic scientists' field practices.

Emanuele Strano is a PhD student at the Laboratory of Geographic Information System at the Federal Polytechnic of Lausanne, Switzerland, and has degrees from the Polytechnic of Milan, Italy, and the University of Strathclyde, Glasgow, UK. His research is focused on quantitative analysis of urbanization processes including the use of complex networks and remote sensing, and on the interface between urban planning, urban design and advanced spatial analysis. Emanuele has published in peer-reviewed journals such as *Urban Studies, Environment and Planning B* and *Nature Scientific Report*. He was responsible for the spatial analysis reported in Chapter Five.

Miles Tight is Professor of Transport, Energy and Environment at the School of Civil Engineering, University of Birmingham, UK. He has undertaken research on sustainable transport for over 25 years, including leading projects funded by the Tyndall Centre for Climate Change Research on reducing transport carbon emissions in London and examining local authority transport initiatives for the Department for Transport. Current and recent projects include the EPSRC-funded Step-Change project and Visions2030: Visions of the role of walking and cycling in 2030. He was a co-investigator on the UWAC project 2008–11 and took particular responsibility for the questionnaire research.

Acknowledgements

Thanks to all the people who willingly gave up their time to be interviewed, to be accompanied and to be observed during their daily journeys. Additional research assistance on the project was provided by Alison Chisholm (Oxford Brookes University), Helen Harwatt, Helen Muir, Tony Whiteing, Matthew Page (all at Leeds) and Emma Bill who undertook a work placement with us while undertaking an MSc course at the University of Plymouth. Sheila Constantine (Lancaster) was project administrator and played an essential role in keeping track of the different strands of work. Assistance with coding and data entry was provided by Anna Tarrant, Emily Bowes and Michaela Edwards (all at Lancaster) and figures were prepared for publication by Gemma Davies and Simon Chew (Lancaster Environment Centre). Research for this project was funded by the EPSRC (research grant EP/G00045X/1) following an approach from Sustrans to develop a small portfolio of projects on walking and cycling linked to the Sustrans Connect2 initiative. We were fortunate in having an active and engaged advisory board drawn from a wide range of organisations: many thanks to all those that attended and contributed to our advisory board meetings. Finally, thanks to Emily Watt, Laura Greaves and all the staff at Policy Press for their careful work on the production of the manuscript.

Preface

Travel is an essential part of everyday life and under normal circumstances it is undertaken without a great deal of thought. Only when our usual travel routines are disrupted for some reason do we need to reappraise travel options and make new choices. For most people in Britain the normal travel routine is to jump into a car and drive to a local destination, and if the car is not their main travel mode at present it is often the one to which people aspire. In this book we argue that there are other travel options and that in particular walking and cycling – either on their own or as part of a multi-mode trip including public transport – can play an important role in everyday travel for short trips in urban areas. Our aim is to explain how and why walking and cycling are not the first choice means of transport for most people, and to propose policy strategies that could shift more short everyday travel away from cars and towards walking and cycling.

The research project that forms the core of this book originated from an EPSRC (Engineering and Physical Sciences Research Council) research event (called a 'sandpit') at which selected academics from a range of disciplinary backgrounds were invited to examine critically issues of sustainable transport and especially walking and cycling in Britain. The initiative had been started by Sustrans – a national body that promotes sustainable transport – and was linked to its Connect2 programme that is providing improved pedestrian and cycle infrastructure in some 60 communities around Britain. In due course the EPSRC agreed to fund three peer-reviewed research projects of which the Understanding Walking and Cycling (UWAC) project reported in this book was one. Research took place between October 2008 and September 2011 and involved academics based at the universities of Lancaster, Oxford Brookes, Leeds and (latterly) Birmingham.

Constructing a multi-disciplinary research team spread across three institutions was a challenging, exciting and very productive process. Most of the research team had not worked together prior to the project and we brought with us a range of different skills and perspectives. Throughout the project we have been learning from each other and have all sought to engage actively with the whole project rather than focusing only on those aspects with which we were individually most concerned. In this way we have sought to generate a genuine dialogue between the quantitative, spatial and qualitative methods employed. Between us we routinely use most forms of everyday transport: most (though not all of us) drive at some time, we all walk for some journeys and most of us cycle on some occasions (some more enthusiastically than others). Overall, we probably travel more sustainably than the majority of the UK population but we are not otherwise atypical. We have all been engaged with the production of this book, with everyone reading and commenting on each chapter. Principal authorship is as follows: Colin Pooley wrote the first drafts of Chapters One to Four, Seven, Nine and Ten, and took overall responsibility for final editing; Tim Jones wrote Chapter Five; Miles

Tight was responsible for Chapter Six and Dave Horton wrote Chapter Eight. Personally, it has been a real privilege to work with such a committed team of expert colleagues and I thank everyone for their commitment to the research.

At the outset of the project we were determined to produce more than a piece of academic research that spoke only to a small number of university-based experts. Throughout the research process we have deliberately tried to engage with policy and have sought to link our research findings to current policy agendas. In this spirit we deliberately use this book to move beyond the presentation of research results (in section II) to set out (in section III) a series of policy strategies that we feel follow directly from our research findings and which, if implemented, could transform the environment for walking and cycling in British towns and cities. We cannot determine what policy makers will do with our research but we hope that, at the very least, the legacy of the project will be to stimulate further informed debate and discussion about sustainable urban transport in the UK and, it is hoped, will lead to the development of urban environments across the country that are welcoming to both pedestrians and cyclists, and in which travelling on foot or by bike is considered to be the obvious and normal means of undertaking many short journeys.

Colin Pooley
Lancaster, August 2012

Section I

CONTEXT

ONE

Setting the scene and defining the problem

Setting the scene

Mobility is something that we mostly take for granted until it is restricted in some way. The ability to travel more-or-less when and where we like – within everyday social, economic and domestic restrictions – is an assumed part of twenty-first century life in most parts of the world. Only when we are deprived of mobility, perhaps through illness or incapacity; because of external factors such as severe weather; or, more rarely, through incarceration do we begin to appreciate the importance of being able to move reasonably freely in our daily lives. Even in the most extreme examples of restriction some mobility is usually possible. A nurse may move a bed or chair of a hospital patient to the window or outside to vary the patient's environment (Gesler, 1992, 2005); most prisoners will have some periods of exercise outside their cell, and can move around inside where personal space may take on special meanings (Baer, 2005); internet access can provide even the most immobile person with virtual mobility to almost any location (Kitchin, 1998; Dodge and Kitchin, 2001); and, excluding people in a state of unconsciousness, we can all move around mentally allowing us to visit other real and imagined worlds. Mobility thus takes many different forms and is an essential and embedded part of everyday life. This book focuses mainly on the most common form of physical mobility: short trips in urban areas that are required in order to carry out everyday tasks such as going to work or school, shopping, or leisure and social activities. Its focus is mainly on twenty-first century England but set within a broader historical and geographical context that allows comparisons to be made with other times and places. It does not examine the movement of goods or ideas though these all form part of the wider nexus of global mobilities.

Sustainability is a concept which, like mobility, is both ubiquitous and vague. A literal definition refers to the ability to maintain or carry on an activity and, in the twenty-first century, the term is most commonly employed in the context of the environment where sustainability implies resource use that does not damage the environment, which is equitable, and which does not compromise future generations (Peake and Smith, 2009; Stern, 2010). Equally important is the linked concept of social sustainability, which requires the development of societal structures (economic, social, cultural) that minimise social and economic inequalities and maximise human welfare (Dillard et al, 2009; Moran, 2010; Dempsey et al, 2011). Mobility is clearly central to concepts of both environmental and social sustainability. All forms of mobility utilise resources, have the potential to damage the environment and to produce social and economic inequalities in access and use (Banister, 2005, 2007; Cox, 2010). Fast and expensive forms of transport with high construction, infrastructure and energy costs (air travel, roads, high speed trains) are obviously the least environmentally, economically and socially sustainable whereas low impact and low cost modes of travel such as cycling or walking are more sustainable. However, even these forms of transport are not cost free. There are the resource costs of producing and disposing of bicycles, and of creating the urban infrastructure (cycle lanes, footpaths) to accommodate cyclists and pedestrians, while both walking and cycling can cause environmental damage in fragile ecosystems (for instance off-road walking or cycling). Although more socially equitable than most other forms of transport, not everyone can afford to own a bicycle and not everyone has the physical capacity to walk or cycle any distance. Even virtual mobility can compromise both environmental and social sustainability. The construction, use, and disposal of IT equipment can create substantial environmental problems, a simple internet search utilises significant energy, and access to computers and high-speed broadband remains socially and spatially unequal (Dodge and Kitchin, 2001; Clark, 2011). This book uses evidence from a major research project to develop an argument explaining why current attempts to increase walking and cycling in Britain are relatively unsuccessful, and to propose why and how walking and cycling could more successfully be promoted as everyday forms of transport in urban areas in the UK. However, even these forms of transport do not overcome all issues of social and environmental sustainability.

Because much everyday mobility is either routine and unremarkable, or spontaneous and ephemeral, collecting accurate information on everyday travel behaviour is difficult. The British National Travel Survey (NTS) collects reasonably detailed information on a regular basis, but is unlikely to capture all journeys or the full complexity that some multi-mode trips encapsulate. Inevitably there will be some simplification in both the construction of and response to any survey (Rofique et al, 2011) but the NTS provides a robust overview of travel patterns in Britain. The most recent data show that overall physical mobility in Britain has declined slightly over the past 15 years. In 2010 respondents made on average 960 trips per year (a 12% fall since 1995/97), covering a distance of 6,726 miles (10, 825 km) which was 7% less than the 2005 peak, and spending 367 hours per year travelling (two hours less than in 1995/7). Thus in a typical day someone in Britain makes between two and three separate trips, covers just over 18 miles (29 km) and spends about an hour travelling. However, both average trip length (seven miles (11 km) in 2010) and mean trip duration (22.9 minutes) have increased slightly since 1995/7. We are travelling less frequently and less far in total, but individual journeys have become a little longer in both time and distance (DfT, 2011a).

Travel can be divided between those journeys which we are required to undertake in order to live an economically and socially functioning life (for adults mostly commuting, travel for business and some shopping), and those discretionary trips which we choose to take for leisure and pleasure. In Britain in 2010, visiting friends and leisure travel combined comprised both the largest proportion of trips (30% of all journeys) and the greatest distance (40% of total distance travelled). Travel for commuting and business made up 19% of all trips and 30% of distance, with shopping (a combination of necessity and leisure) accounting for 20% of all trips and 12% of total distance. It can be argued that the decline in the number of journeys undertaken and the total distance travelled could be due to the increased use of virtual mobility as the internet reduces the need to travel both to visit friends (through the use of e-mail and social media) and, with the increase in on-line shopping, to travel to shops. This is borne out by the fact that travel for shopping decreased by 18% between 1995/97 and 2010, and travel to visit friends decreased by 22% (DfT, 2011a).

However, despite these trends physical travel remains important, and is strongly dominated by the private car which accounted for 64% of all trips and 78% of distance travelled in Britain in 2010. In terms of number of trips, walking was the next most important category (22%) followed by public transport (10%) and cycling (2%). However, as measured by distance travelled public transport was the more important mode (13%) compared to walking (3%) and cycling (1%). Some 77% of British households have access to at least one car and the private car is the ubiquitous and usual form of transport for most people in Britain. This is emphasised if we look only at very short trips where although the majority (77%) were on foot, 20% of journeys of less than one mile (1.6 km) in distance were undertaken by car. The NTS provides only very basic information on spatial variations in travel patterns, but the most notable differences are between urban and rural areas and, especially, between London and the rest of the country. In London, only 41% of all trips are undertaken by car with 31% on public transport and 25% on foot. It can be argued that a combination of good (by British standards) public transport, limited road space and congestion charging produce slightly more sustainable travel patterns in London than elsewhere in Britain. The NTS also provides limited information by age, gender and social group, but it is clear that the travel modes of children do differ substantially from those of adults. For instance, primary school children are more likely to walk to school (47% of all school journeys) than travel by car with an adult (43%). For secondary school children walking declines, but at 36% remains the single most important means of travel followed by local buses (26%) and the car (24%) (DfT, 2011a).

When compared to other north–west European countries everyday travel in Britain is more car-dominated than most comparators and cycling, in particular, is much less important. Thus while levels of walking are similar in most north–west European countries, the 2% of all trips undertaken by bike in Britain compares to 9% in Finland and Sweden, 10% in Germany, 18% in Denmark and 26% in The Netherlands (Pucher and Buehler, 2010; Buehler et al, 2011). If walking and cycling together are viewed as the most socially and environmentally sustainable means of travelling for short trips, then while in Britain just 24% of all journeys are undertaken sustainably, a figure which is similar to that in Belgium and France and well above that for the USA (12%); in Germany and much of Scandinavia the figure is over 30%, while in The Netherlands walking and cycling combined account for 51% of all trips. Clearly Britain has a long way to go to catch up with levels of sustainable urban mobility found in many comparable north–west European countries.

Mobility provides people with essential opportunities for work, leisure and social interaction: without it society could not function. Like most things we need and value, however, it also brings problems. These are well known, but include social exclusion due to lack of transport and access to facilities (Hine, 2003, 2012; Lucas, 2004, 2006, 2012; Lucas and Stanley, 2009; Preston and Raje, 2007); unsustainable resource use and excessive carbon emissions (DECC, 2012a, 2012b); congestion, pollution and associated ill-health (Briggs et al, 2000, 2008; Goodwin, 2004; Mitchell and Maher, 2009; Migliore et al, 2009; COMEAP, 2010; Ogilvie et al, 2004, 2007). One final consequence of the way in which we travel in Britain today is the lack of choice that many people feel they have. Because public transport is often perceived to be poor, and cycling and walking may be assumed to be risky or too strenuous, together with the fact that many people live distant from their place of work and acceptable services and shops, most families feel that car use becomes their only option. Thus people who may have a personal preference not to travel by car, or those who find it hard to afford to run a car, feel constrained to do so because they feel that there is no alternative given the ways in which British urban areas are configured (with motor vehicles dominant and pedestrians and cyclists marginalised) and public transport is structured. Lack of choice is likely to be most obvious in rural areas where public transport is very poor and there may be significant forced car use, but the dominance of the motor car through the 'system of automobility' (Urry, 2004) can also create forced car use in urban areas where although alternatives are in theory available they may not be deemed acceptable.

The foregoing discussion raises a series of key questions about everyday travel in Britain today, and the role of sustainable forms of mobility such as walking and cycling, which we cover in this book. First, it is necessary to establish the ways in which sustainable mobility – especially walking and cycling – are being promoted and developed in Britain today. This will be examined in the remainder of this chapter. Second, there is need to assess the extent to which everyday travel in Britain is similar to or different from other places, and to explain why such differences occur. This is done through brief reviews of the historical evolution of transport modes in Britain and an assessment of British travel experiences within an international context. Third, we focus on data drawn from a research project carried out in four case study towns (Leeds, Leicester, Worcester, Lancaster) to examine in detail why levels of sustainable travel (and especially walking and cycling) remain so low in Britain today despite considerable efforts to promote what is often termed active travel. Fourth, we use these data to identify the key constraints to more sustainable mobility and suggest ways in which future policy may tackle such problems. Finally, we step back from the detailed research to assess critically the potential for using walking and cycling to increase sustainable travel in Britain: what can reasonably be achieved and what is unlikely to change?

Promoting sustainable mobility in Britain

There is a wide range of organisations in the UK that have committed themselves to campaigning at both local and national levels for more sustainable forms of transport. Table 1.1 summarises key characteristics of a selection of relevant organisations. Some of these groups, such as Sustrans, have had notable success in winning funding and influencing government policy. In terms of both visibility and (limited) success in influencing policy it can be argued that cycle campaigners (such as the CTC) have been much more prominent than those organisations concerned with improving conditions for pedestrians and increasing levels of walking. However, despite some signs of change in specific localities such as

Table 1.1: Selected organisations promoting walking and/or cycling

Organisation	Date of formation*	Summary of aims	Key activities
Sustrans	1977	Originally promotion of cycling, especially long-distance routes, now all forms of sustainable travel	Wide range of campaigns and programmes *including Travel Smart, Active Travel, Liveable Neighbourhoods, Safe Routes to Schools*, and the *Connect2* programme that is providing over 60 schemes to improve access and safety for pedestrians and cyclists
CTC (Cyclists' Touring Club)	1878	To protect and promote the rights of cyclists	Programmes such as *Cycle Proficiency Scheme, National Cycling Strategy* (1996), *Cyclists' Defence Fund.* Currently has c60,000 members
Cycling England	2005–11	To work with government departments and cycling organisations to promote cycling and allocate DfT funding. From 2011 activities transferred to the DfT's Local Sustainable Transport Fund	Responsible for developing the *Bikeability* scheme and the *Cycle Demonstration Towns and Cities Programme*; a total of 18 communities gained funding to promote cycling
Living Streets	1929	To create safe, attractive and enjoyable streets where people want to walk	Many campaigns, especially with local groups, including the Walk to School initiative

(continued)

7

Table 1.1: Selected organisations promoting walking and/or cycling (continued)

Organisation	Date of formation*	Summary of aims	Key activities
Walk 21	2000	To create communities where people feel comfortable walking	Various campaigns and, principally, an annual conference
Campaign for Better Transport	c1972	To create communities with excellent public transport and high levels of walking and cycling	A wide range of campaigns including *Save our Buses*, *Railways Fit for the Future* and *Roads to Nowhere*
Slower Speeds Initiative	1998	To raise awareness of dangers of inappropriate traffic speed	Various campaigns including *20's Plenty* which aims to reduce speed limits to 20mph in most urban areas
Cycling Embassy of Great Britain	2011	To promote cycling across Britain	Campaigns to make cycling safe and easy, especially through the promotion of segregated cycle routes
Cycle Training UK	1998	To promote cycling as a sustainable form of transport	Principally through the provision of cycle training for adults and children to enable people to ride confidently
The Bicycle Association	1890	To promote the bicycle industry and cycling	Various campaigns including the BikeHub website
London Cycling Campaign**	1978	To promote cycling in London	Campaigns for improved cycle infrastructure

*Sometimes under a different name

** Many other towns and cities also have active local organisations

Source: Principally organisation web sites (see bibliography for details)

central London, there is little evidence at the national level that rates of cycling in Britain have increased significantly since publication of the National Cycling Strategy in 1996. For instance, according to the National Travel Survey (DfT, 2011a) in 1995/97 cycling accounted for 1.7% of all trips whereas in 2010 this figure had dropped slightly to 1.6%. The best that can be argued is that campaigns to increase cycling have prevented any significant decline in levels of bicycle travel, and have secured some increases in selected locations. In contrast, walking, with much lower levels of nationally visible active promotion, has declined from 26.9% of all trips in 1995/7 to 21.9% in 2010.

There are numerous examples from recent years where various campaign groups have been successful in influencing government policy on walking and cycling, leading to many worthwhile interventions. However, despite these gains, there remain multiple contradictions embedded within the transport policies of the British government. In short, while successive governments have stated their support for more sustainable mobility, and have demonstrated the environmental, health and social benefits that can be gained from increased levels of walking and cycling, they have done little to restrict car use and have often promoted less sustainable forms of travel alongside a declared commitment to change. Such mixed messages are, at best, confusing, but given the existing dominance of car travel within British society and economy, and the assumption that economic growth is synonymous with increasing the opportunities for high speed travel by road, rail and air, it is almost inevitable that motorised transport of all kinds will continue to dominate. The tensions between the aims of economic growth and sustainability are captured nicely in the mission statement on the DfT website which states that: 'Our vision is for a transport system that is an engine for economic growth, but one that is also greener and safer and improves quality of life in our communities'. In this section selected examples are used to illustrate these points.

In 1998 the Labour government's White Paper *A new deal for transport* (DETR, 1998) appeared to embrace the growing environmental movement of the 1990s and to recognise both the negative consequences of transport–related greenhouse gas emissions and the need for change. The White Paper went on to make a clear case for investment in integrated public transport, the improvement of infrastructure for walking and cycling and, crucially, the restriction of car use. For example, it stated that priority would be given to 'the maintenance, and management of existing roads before building new ones' (p 57), and local authorities were required to draw up strategic transport plans that prioritised integrated public transport and regulated car use, including the development of congestion charging, road tolls and workplace parking charges. The document made bold statements about both walking and cycling including a commitment to 'make walking a more viable, attractive and safe option'(p 31), with a requirement placed on local authorities to reallocate road space to pedestrians, improve footpath maintenance and introduce traffic calming among other measures. There was a similar commitment to improve conditions for cyclists, building on the National Cycle Strategy (1996). The document stated 'We want to see better provision for cyclists at their destinations, at interchanges, in the design of junctions and in the way road space is allocated' (p 33), including the improvement of junctions and cycle lanes, the provision of better cycle storage and the reduction of traffic speeds.

While some of the gains outlined above (including investment in Cycling Towns and Cities and the Bikeability and Safe Routes to School schemes) can be seen as evidence that elements of the 1998 'new deal' have come to fruition, with the exception of London there have been minimal restrictions placed on the use of private cars, and thus the problems identified in the 1998 document have continued and, in most cases, multiplied. A shift away from a full commitment to a more sustainable transport policy came as early as 2000 with the publication of the *Transport ten year plan 2000* (DfT, 2000). Although there was a continuing commitment to integrated transport systems, and to increasing walking and cycling, the main thrust of the programme was focused on road and rail. One of the main declared aims of the plan was to modernise the transport network in ways that make it 'bigger, better, safer, cleaner, quicker' (p 4), which hardly sits easily with policies to increase walking and cycling. The major expenditure commitments were to rail (£60 billion) and road (£59 billion) with a commitment to construct 100 new bypasses, undertake 80 major new trunk road schemes and complete 130 additional local road schemes. The dominance of road and rail is emphasised by a simple word search of the document: whereas rail is mentioned 246 times and roads are mentioned 237 times, cycling is referred to on just 19 occasions and walking on 16. There are no references to congestion charging or road pricing. While it can be argued that investment in rail could be seen as a commitment to some aspects of more sustainable mobility, the marginalisation of walking and cycling seems significantly at odds with the 'new deal' policy published (by the same government) only two years previously. A further White Paper, *The future of transport* (DfT, 2004a), confirmed these trends. While a commitment to sustainable transport and traffic management was retained, much greater priority was given to road building.

From the middle of the first decade of the twenty-first century there have been a series of policy documents from, or commissioned by, government that have explored the options for promoting walking and cycling for sustainable urban mobility, have argued the case for investment in 'soft' measures in transport planning, and have highlighted the benefits to be gained from increased levels of 'active travel' in the UK. While all such documents are to be welcomed, it can also be argued that their separation from the mainstream White Papers and plans outlined above is further evidence of the way in which policy on walking and cycling has been placed in a separate compartment of transport planning: something that is worth doing but in a way that should not interfere with the primary aim of improving connectivity by road and rail to promote economic growth. Key documents include the *Walking and cycling action plan* (DfT, 2004b), the consultants' report, *Smarter choices* (Cairns et al, 2004), the *Active travel strategy* (DfT/DoH, 2010), all from effectively the same Labour administration; and the *Creating growth, cutting carbon* White Paper (DfT, 2011b) from the new coalition government elected in May 2010. Collectively the various statements and policies on walking and cycling have aimed to put in place some of the ambitions stated in the 1998 'new deal' but in the context of continuing high levels of investment in road and rail.

All the policy documents emphasise the importance of active travel (walking and cycling) for health, congestion reduction through modal change, and community involvement as walking, in particular, allows more everyday interaction on the street. These objectives were made explicit in the 2004 Action Plan and strategies to achieve these goals were broadly identified as environmental improvements, the provision of improved routes for walking and cycling, programmes to persuade people to change travel behaviour, and provision of cycle training to improve skills and confidence (DfT, 2004b). The potential impact of such 'soft measures' to tackle transport issues was further supported by a more-or-less contemporaneous consultants' report commissioned by the DfT (Cairns et al, 2004). These ideas were piloted between 2004 and 2009 with £10m of government funding to support the development of smarter travel choices in three designated Sustainable Travel Towns: Darlington, Peterborough and Worcester. During this period car trips declined in all three towns and journeys by bike, on foot and by public transport increased (Sloman et al, 2010). The 2010 *Active travel strategy* reflected on achievements so far but was also more ambitious in stating that this was to be the 'Decade of Cycling' in which 'We want cycling to be the preferred mode of local transport in England in the 21st century' (DfT/DoH, 2010, p 9). This was to be achieved through the introduction of 20mph zones in urban residential areas, the expansion of the Bikeability scheme of cycle training, increased engagement with cycle to work schemes and the provision of more secure cycle parking. To promote walking, policies would focus on creation of a safe walking environment and schemes to promote walking for health. The aim was to achieve Dutch levels of walking and cycling, but as much emphasis was placed on the individual health benefits of active travel as on the potential contribution to the reduction of congestion or carbon emissions.

The most recent statement (DfT, 2011b) reflects the Coalition government's policy of shifting responsibility to the local level. The document states that there should be local control of most aspects of transport planning and that a 'one size fits all' approach is not appropriate. Only a small number of areas are reserved for national policies, including the Bikeability schemes, the introduction of smart ticketing on public transport, and the introduction of a national road safety strategy. Local initiatives are to be supported by the Local Sustainable Travel Fund, through which Local Authorities can bid for funds for specific schemes and, although there is extensive reference to active travel (a word search provides a much more equal distribution of references to different modes compared to the ten year plan (DfT, 2000), perhaps indicating that walking and cycling have moved further up the transport policy agenda), the main thrust of the document is on economic development. It is clear that the principal aim of transport policy is to boost economic growth and that other considerations are likely to be secondary. This imperative is clearly seen in the decision in January 2012 to go ahead with the controversial High Speed 2 rail link from London to Birmingham (by 2026) and eventually to Manchester and Leeds by 2033 (DfT website, press release, 10 January 2012; Aizlewood and Wellings, 2011). If the £32.7 billion cost had been committed to more sustainable transport solutions the impact could be considerable. It also makes the £560 million allocated by government to the Local Sustainable Travel Fund look a rather paltry sum and somewhat contradicts policy statements about prioritising active travel.

Academic perspectives

There is an extensive academic literature on transport, travel and mobility, together with an even larger literature on all aspects of sustainability and so-called sustainable development, but such literature does not always connect closely with either the practical problems of mobility faced by individuals and families on a day-to-day basis, or with the development of policies at both national and local levels to deal with such issues. This section does not attempt to review the vast literature that exists, but rather looks selectively at a series of academic approaches to travel and mobility, and relates such studies to the main theme of this book: understanding why much everyday travel behaviour fails to meet basic criteria of sustainability. The discussion covers four main sets of literature, though the division is to some extent arbitrary and there are significant overlaps between them. First, we examine approaches stimulated by the concept of a 'new mobilities paradigm' (Sheller and Urry, 2006), which provide a mainly socio-cultural perspective on the nature and meaning of mobility in the twenty-first century. Second, we focus on research into various aspects of travel behaviour which, though coming from a range of disciplines, draws heavily on theories developed in Social Psychology. Third, we examine literature that is based mainly on issues of environment and sustainability: what are the consequences in terms of (for instance) climate change, pollution and health of not adopting more sustainable modes of travel? Fourth, we look briefly at literature that comes from a traffic engineering perspective: what are the practical problems and solutions to managing traffic and mobility in towns.

The arguments developed by Urry (2000, 2007) and others over the past decade or so have focused on the ways in which the process and experience of mobility has been reconceptualised from the late-twentieth century so that mobility in its own right has become embedded as a key constituent of society, rather than being seen simply as a means to achieve a particular goal (getting to work, for example). This has been termed the 'new mobilities paradigm', and draws on a number of strands of academic research and writing. First, it develops concepts of time–space convergence and time–space compression (Janelle, 1969; Harvey, 1989), which were in turn developed from Hagerstrand's (1970) work on time geographies, to argue that the fact of rapid travel to almost all parts of the world, together with the speeding up of social life (the need to compress as many different activities as possible into available time), has led to new conceptualisations of mobility as something that is a taken-for-granted aspect of modern society: without such high levels of mobility modern society would struggle to function. This is demonstrated by the extent to which what is perceived as 'normal' life is disrupted when mobilities are constrained: for example the impact of the ash cloud from the Icelandic volcano (Eyjafjallajökull) on air travel in 2010 (Birtchnell and Büscher, 2011). Second, this strand of research focuses on the concept of automobility: the way in which motor vehicles – and especially the private car – have become more than a means of transport, but have acquired the status of a path-dependent process that is firmly embedded in social life. The private car provides not only a convenient form of everyday transport, but also confers status, provides privacy and has become a badge of normality within twenty-first century society (Sheller and Urry, 2000; Featherstone et al, 2005; Dennis and Urry, 2009). One consequence of this is that most aspects of urban life and infrastructure are constructed around the assumption that the private car is the normal and expected means of everyday travel, seen most clearly in the ways in which major roads cut through urban areas and in the development of out-of-town retail and leisure facilities with large, free areas of parking. Third, research on mobilities has focused on the development and significance of new forms of mobility, especially virtual mobilities and mobile communication systems. Development of the internet and of mobile communication devices, and their accessibility to a large proportion of the global population, has allowed people to carry on activities, which in the past would have required physical relocation, without moving from their office or armchair. In addition, when corporeal travel is necessary, it is now possible to communicate and work while travelling (especially on public transport). Thus rather than viewing travel time as wasted, it can often be used productively for work or social activities (Laurier, 2004; Lyons and Urry, 2005; Lyons et al, 2007; Watts and Urry, 2008). In a related vein, there has also been a large amount of research on the performance and experience of everyday travel (Jones, 2005; Spinney, 2007, 2009; Bissell, 2009, 2010; Cresswell, 2010; Edensor, 2010). Collectively, it can be argued that these trends – which have developed over a long period and have spread progressively from the rich developed world to most parts of the globe – have transformed not only the way we travel but, what is most important, how we view travel and incorporate it into our lives. Collectively, this literature begins to explain the significance of mobility – in its varied forms – for everyday life and enables the study of sustainable mobilities (walking and cycling) to be situated in their social and cultural contexts.

If the literature discussed above explains how mobility has changed society, research on travel behaviour focuses on why people choose to travel in different ways. Even in the context of a car-dominated society people do have a choice of forms of transport, and many people do prefer not to travel by car for much of their everyday movement. Research on this theme has taken two main approaches. The first, and most straightforward, has carried out social surveys and interviews to try to establish the characteristics of people who use different forms of travel, and to draw generalisations about travel behaviour from these data (Handy, 2005; Salmon et al, 2007; Dawson et al, 2007). Thus, it has been shown (for instance) that buses are (predictably) most likely to be used by the young and the elderly, that women are more likely than men to use public transport, and that active travel may be linked to characteristics of the local environment. Using such data it has then been possible to suggest potential gains to be made by changing such travel behaviours (Mackett, 2001, 2003). A second strand of research takes the study of travel behaviour much further and utilises behavioural theories borrowed from social psychology to attempt to understand mobility decisions and, in some instances, to classify the travelling population into groups according to their attitudes to different forms of transport (Jarvis, 2003; Anable, 2005; Stradling, 2007; Hunecke et al, 2010; Farag and Lyons, 2010). Thus while some people may prefer car use others may have a strong commitment to cycling. Such research has been influential in the development of policy on the assumption that the behaviour that people exhibit is based directly on their attitudes. Thus if people are persuaded to change their attitudes to (for instance) walking or cycling then they would be most likely to also change their behaviour and travel more sustainably (Shove, 2010). This assumption underlies the concept, promoted by the present (2012) UK government, of 'nudging' people into behavioural change (Thaler and Sunstein, 2009; John, 2011). However, such assumptions can be strongly challenged as there is increasing evidence that individual behaviour is not necessarily strongly linked to attitudes and beliefs (House of Lords, 2011). For instance, someone may have a strong belief in the importance of sustainable travel but in practice still use their car for most journeys. This concept has been explored most actively in the literature on theories of practice (Schatzki et al, 2001; Reckwitz, 2002; Warde, 2005; Shove and Walker, 2007; Bräuchler and Postill, 2010) which have been applied to a wide range of different areas of study, but are very relevant to travel behaviour. The current use of practice theory builds on the work of Bourdieu and Giddens (among others) to focus on the social practices that are constituted through the interactions of individual agency and broader social structures. As such, it can begin to explain why what people do is not always closely related to what they believe – a situation that seems to commonly occur in the realm of everyday travel behaviour.

There is a vast literature that focuses on the environmental and social consequences of not changing the ways in which we live and consume resources. This encompasses all aspects of modern life and associated patterns of consumption, but in the context of the development of what Adams (1999, 2005) terms 'hypermobility' the social and environmental implications of everyday travel are substantial. Four key areas can be identified (though there are many interactions between them and other themes could be identified). First, there is a large international literature on the impact of greenhouse gas emissions and the associated carbon footprint from the transport sector (European Conference of Ministers of Transport, 2007; Hensher, 2008; International Transport Forum, 2008; 2011). In the UK transport accounts for some 22% of the nation's greenhouse gas emissions and thus contributes significantly to processes of global climate change. If the UK is to meet its EU commitment to reduce carbon emissions to 21% below the verified 2005 level by 2020 (NAEI website) then a substantial part of that reduction will have to come from the transport sector. This can be achieved by both technological (for instance low–carbon vehicles) and behavioural change, but in practice is likely to require a combination of the two. Second, there has been increasing concern in recent years about the impact of contemporary travel behaviour on human health and levels of obesity (Ogilvie et al, 2004, 2007). While diet is a key component, it is also the case that a combination of sedentary lifestyles and low levels of active travel have created what have been termed obesogenic environments (Hinde and Dixon, 2005; Papas et al, 2007; Lake et al, 2010) that engender unhealthy lifestyles. Active travel, such as walking and cycling, can contribute to both improvements in health and reduction of the carbon footprint (iConnect website). Third, the way in which we travel in cities today generates further negative consequences through congestion and associated pollution. Congestion brings substantial economic costs (Weisbrod et al, 2003; Sankaran et al, 2005) and pollution can further harm human health. It is hard to measure the precise links between different modes of travel and exposure to harmful pollutants, and their impact will vary from one individual to another depending on a wide range of other factors, but it is clear that prolonged exposure to vehicle exhaust fumes in urban areas is potentially harmful, especially to children and the elderly (Briggs et al, 2000, 2008; Mitchell and Maher, 2009). Finally, the consequences of not changing how we travel have been explored in the context of social exclusion. A society that assumes that car travel is the norm automatically begins to exclude those who do not have access to this form of transport (Hine, 2003, 2012; Lucas, 2004, 2006, 2012).

From a practical perspective the main focus has been on managing traffic and travel on urban streets. There is a large literature, from a mainly quantitative and/or engineering background, which studies modal splits between different forms of transport (including walking and cycling); the technical and infrastructural solutions that can be used to encourage people to change travel modes; and the strategies that can be used to enable competing travel forms to perform more effectively and with minimal impact on people and the environment (for instance Choo and Mokhtarian, 2008; Sanni and Albrantes, 2010; Goetzke, 2011; Beck et al, 2011). Such research has informed a large amount of transport planning and, at least until recently, has dominated policy-related thinking at both national and local levels. However, it has two main drawbacks in the context of promoting more sustainable forms of travel such as walking or cycling. First, it uses mainly quantitative approaches to studying travel behaviour and modal choice – based on the development of numerical models of transport systems – and thus fails to take into account the underlying constraints and circumstances that influence day-to-day travel decisions. We argue that these can only be fully appreciated through more qualitative studies that examine the processes of decision making in detail. Second, because this literature comes mainly from an engineering and related background, it focuses on finding technical and infrastructural solutions that are suited to the dominant and most intrusive forms of transport, namely motor vehicles. Thus, most attention is paid to the design and development of more effective road systems to speed the flow of traffic, while low-impact forms of transport have been largely ignored. Intensive lobbying by some cycling pressure groups has led to increased discussion of the design of intersections so that dangers to cyclists are minimised, and to the provision of cycle lanes and paths (for instance Bow roundabout in London (British Cycling website)), but such initiatives remain marginal to the demands of motorised road transport.

Conclusions

This chapter has introduced the key themes to be discussed in this book. It has outlined why more sustainable mobility, and especially walking and cycling in urban areas, are important; it has demonstrated the ways in which both activist groups and government (national and local) policies have responded to these needs; and it has briefly reviewed some of the academic literatures and associated theories that underpin much transport-related research. The remainder of the book does three main things. First, we expand the context within which the research reported in this volume is set by examining the ways in which everyday mobility has changed over time (Chapter Two) and the extent to which the situation in the UK (the main focus of this study) is replicated in other parts of the world (Chapter Three). Second, we provide a detailed account of the research project from which this volume stems, briefly explaining the methods used (Chapter Four) and then exploring the factors that structure everyday decision making about urban travel through analysis of the role of the built environment in decisions to walk or cycle (Chapter Five), examination of what people think about walking and cycling as a means of everyday travel (Chapter Six), and in-depth discussion of the everyday experiences of walking (Chapter Seven) and cycling (Chapter Eight). Third, the final section of the book focuses on the policy solutions that we consider follow from this analysis and suggests some of the implications for the development of long-term sustainable mobility in Britain.

One theme that is important throughout the book, and which is often neglected in both academic work and policy making, is our view that walking and cycling need to be considered as two very different modes of transport that make separate demands both upon the travelling public and on urban infrastructure. All too often in policy documents walking and cycling are linked together as sustainable forms of transport, whereas in reality they are very different and in some cases may be in conflict with each other. Whereas walking is a skill that we almost all acquire when very young, and which requires minimal equipment; cycling is learned later in life and arguably makes additional demands upon both the rider and the existing urban infrastructure. For these reasons at least, and probably also in relation to the ways in which walking and cycling have historically been performed (see Chapter Two), it can be argued that cycling has as much in common with motorised transport as it does with walking. Such tensions are explored in more detail throughout this volume as an unusual mixture of quantitative, qualitative and spatial analytical techniques are combined to understand more about how and why individuals and families engage (or fail to engage) with walking and cycling in their everyday movements around urban areas.

TWO

Where have we come from?
The historical context

How did we travel in the past and what has changed?

Most recent academic writing on mobility in the twenty-first century, and probably most popular opinion, tends to assume that, at least in some respects, levels of mobility and how we travel have changed dramatically over the past two centuries (Cresswell, 2006; Urry, 2007; Adey, 2010; Cresswell and Merriman, 2011; Grieco and Urry, 2012). At one level this is of course the case. Most people on a moderate income, and in many parts of the world, can if they wish fly almost anywhere at short notice should they need to. Most people, in richer parts of the world at least, have access to personal transport that gives them the freedom to travel quickly and conveniently in their everyday lives, and new forms of communication both allow almost instant interaction over long distances and provide access to information about remote places that in the past would have been hard to obtain. In these respects mobility in the twenty-first century is dramatically different from what it was in (for instance) 1800. However, it can also be argued that despite these obvious differences there are also many consistencies and similarities. Even in the richest countries of the world most everyday travel is over short distances and on repeated routes; all the basic technology underpinning the main forms of transport that people use in their everyday lives has existed for at least a century; and the reasons why people travel – and the constraints that they experience – have altered little over time (Pooley et al, 2005a). This chapter explores these issues by focusing on changes in everyday mobility in Britain over about the last 200 years, with particular emphasis on the role of walking and cycling. The following chapter places these changes in a broader context by examining the present-day variability in travel experiences in different parts of the globe.

Three key issues underpin discussion in this chapter. Together, it is argued that they begin to explain the consistency of experience in everyday travel in Britain over the past two centuries. We do not attempt a comprehensive overview of the evolution of urban transport in Britain: excellent reviews are available elsewhere (Dyos and Aldcroft, 1969; Cannadine and Reader, 1982; Freeman and Aldcroft, 1988; Armstrong, 2000). Certainly, there have been key moments of change, and periods in which both walking and cycling have been more or less important, but it is argued that the underlying processes producing such patterns and everyday experiences have been remarkably consistent. First, access to transport has always been, and remains, unequal. Those on the highest incomes, or at least with the greatest disposable income, have always preferred to travel quickly, comfortably and in relative privacy. Those on a limited budget have travelled more slowly, less comfortably and usually in the company of others. Thus, in the early nineteenth century while the rich were transported around the country in a private carriage the poor walked or travelled (often outside) on a mail coach. Today, while a majority of households have access to a private car (providing speed, comfort and privacy), many individuals do not. They rely on often limited forms of public transport. Second, there has always been conflict over road space. Land, especially in urban areas, is a scarce commodity and the amount of space allocated to travel has always been restricted. Those forms of transport that are the most powerful, travel fastest, and command the most status (often seen as the most modern) have tended to dominate road space with slower, older, and cheaper forms of travelling (including walking and cycling) relegated to the margins. In the early nineteenth century a squire's private carriage paid scant attention to the family walking on the road, while in the twenty-first century cars and trucks rarely respect the road space of cyclists. Third, there has always been debate about the extent to which the public highway should be regulated. The specifics have varied from the risks posed by highway robbers in the eighteenth century, through concern about motor cars frightening horses in the late-nineteenth century, to debates about risks to cyclists and the need to restrict car use for environmental reasons in the twenty-first century. What is consistent is the recognition that different forms of travelling have rarely mixed comfortably on the limited road space available and that some form of intervention and regulation is necessary.

Source limitations mean that it is difficult to provide a detailed and fully consistent picture of changes in everyday travel in Britain over the past two centuries. The National Travel Survey began collecting data in 1965/6 and prior to that the only official statistics come from very limited travel to work data in the national censuses of 1921 and from 1951 onwards. During the twentieth century there have been numerous reports, social surveys and planning documents that collectively provide information on such issues as travel behaviour and traffic flows, but these are rarely in a consistent format allowing easy comparison. For the nineteenth century and earlier much less information is available and, for the most part, data on how people travelled has to be culled from a wide range of archival sources including newspapers, reports, surveys and personal accounts. Inevitably, these provide a patchy and partial picture with a tendency to provide most information on the more visible forms of transport, and on travel by the richest and most powerful who were most likely to leave records. The everyday travel behaviour of the poor is often all but invisible. In all time periods the fact that everyday travel is usually seen as routine and is taken for granted, means that it is rarely recorded (even in personal documents such as diaries), unless something notable occurs. Thus we tend to know rather more about rare events (such as travel disruption) than we do about the routine journeys that are undertaken every day. Such problems are normal when studying past societies, and they are certainly not restricted to the analysis of travel trends and behaviours, but they are particularly problematic when trying to reconstruct change over a long period of time (for overviews of problems in the analysis of historical sources see Baker et al, 1970; Butlin, 1993). In this chapter there is no attempt to document all changes in travel and transport but rather, following a brief overview, to focus on key issues and events with particular emphasis on short trips in urban areas and, especially, the changing role of walking and cycling.

In general, the history of everyday travel in Britain has been dominated by the development of new forms of transport that have allowed people to travel faster, more comfortably and in more privacy; together with the gradual democratisation of such forms of travel as they became affordable by a wider cross-section of the population. In the early nineteenth century all but the rich travelled on foot most of the time or, when travelling longer distances with luggage and/ or small children that reduced mobility, on a carrier's cart often together with a range of goods and possibly live animals. From the 1840s the railway opened up longer-distance travel for many, and provided graded classes of travel so that the rich could travel in more privacy and comfort than those of lesser means (Perkin, 1970; Simmons 1986, 1991; Evans and Gough, 2003), but for many of the poorest travel by train remained too expensive and would only rarely be used. As the rail network principally linked major towns and cities, with a denser suburban network only evolving by the late-nineteenth century and then mainly in London and other major conurbations (Kellet, 1969), the railway had minimal impact on the routine everyday journeys of most urban dwellers. For example, even in circa 1900 most working men still walked to work in London, even though the capital had by far the most developed public transport system of any British city (Dyos, 1953). Arguably, for everyday travel in Britain, the development of first the horse-drawn omnibus (from the 1820s) and, second, the tram (horse-drawn from the 1860s, steam from the 1870s, and electric from the 1890s) was of much greater importance (Armstrong, 2000). Electric trams dominated public transport provision in many British towns and cities in the early twentieth century, but were rapidly replaced in the inter-war period by the motor bus which was seen as cheaper, more flexible and more modern (Pooley and Turnbull, 2000). Only London (and to a more limited extent Glasgow) had, and retained, a comprehensive network of suburban rail links (both under and above ground) (Barker and Robbins, 1963–74; Jackson, 1973), and although trams have been gradually re-introduced into many British cities from the late-twentieth century (for instance Manchester, Sheffield, Edinburgh) public transport remains dominated by motor buses in most urban areas.

It can be argued that in all time periods many people have preferred to travel independently rather than to use public transport which requires adherence to a set timetable and route, together with the need to share space with strangers. Walking, in many ways the simplest and most ubiquitous form of urban transport, provides both freedom and independence with a degree of privacy (in that although street space is shared with other pedestrians interaction is not required), but lacks speed (Solnit, 2001; Ingold, 2004; Ingold and Vergunst, 2008). However, for most of the nineteenth century the only alternative private transport was to travel on horseback or in a private carriage: both the preserve of the wealthy. The poor, living in perhaps two rooms in a terraced house, had neither the income nor the space to keep a horse. By the 1880s two more forms of private transport were beginning to appear on British streets (though both had a much longer history of evolution): together the bicycle and the motor car (powered by an internal combustion engine) were to dominate private travel until the present day. From a relatively slow start car use increased steadily to the late-twentieth century, though in Britain car ownership and use has remained relatively stable over the past two decades (Newcomb and Spurr, 1989; Wolf, 1996; O'Connell, 1998; Conley, 2009; DfT, 2011a), but the bicycle has seen much more varied popularity. From a mainly leisure vehicle in the late-nineteenth century, the bicycle became a staple form of transport for working men by the 1930s and 1940s as incomes rose and a large second-hand market in bicycles made them increasingly affordable. However, they declined rapidly in everyday use by the 1960s as car ownership came within the reach of more and more people. For all but a small body of enthusiasts, by the late-twentieth century the bicycle was again mainly seen as a form of leisure transport (Lloyd Jones and Lewis, 2000; Horton et al, 2007). These themes are explored in more detail below.

The changing role of the bicycle in Britain

The bicycle has been strangely neglected in many traditional surveys of transport history: for instance the classic work by Dyos and Aldcroft (1969) on the economic history of British transport since the seventeenth century does not once mention the bicycle. This is probably because non-motorised forms of travel were not considered to have significant economic or infrastructural impacts and thus were of no consequence. This can be disputed. The bicycle industry was an important part of British manufacturing in the first half of the twentieth century and travel by bike enabled many men to travel easily to work, thus making a major contribution to the British economy (Lloyd Jones and Lewis, 2000). However, it is symptomatic of the ways in which histories of everyday travel have focused on the more complex and demanding technologies and have ignored those forms of travel that are simple and relatively non-intrusive. It also reflects the way in which low-impact forms of transport have constantly been marginalised within British transport planning (Horton et al, 2007). The history of cycling in Britain can be told through a variety of lenses. It can be a history of technological change, emphasising that a bicycle is as much a machine as a car or any other vehicle; it can be told from a social and cultural perspective in terms of the ways in which cycling was adopted (who cycled and why?); or it can be told from an infrastructural perspective focusing on the ways in which provision of road space conflicts with the demands of other road users. In this section we focus mainly on the first two approaches.

In common with the motor car, the bicycle was an invention of the nineteenth century and most of the key technological advances were made before 1900. Bicycles have certainly changed in the twentieth century, but mostly through refinements and the use of new materials rather than through radical new developments. The first approximation to a bicycle was invented in Germany in 1817: the wooden 'hobby horse' was a two-wheeled machine with no pedals on which the rider sat and gained propulsion from pushing their feet along the ground. In effect it was assisted walking which gave greater speed with a smaller amount of effort. A cycle with pedals was apparently invented by a Scottish blacksmith in the early 1840s, but the first mass-produced machine that resembled a modern bike was developed in the early 1860s by the Frenchman Pierre Michaux (precise dates for many of these innovations are disputed (Oddy, 2007)). Effectively this 'velocipede' was a hobby horse with pedals fixed to the front wheel which evolved to include the 'penny farthing' or high bike with an enlarged high front wheel. The advantage of a large wheel was that you could travel further with each turn of the pedal, but the height of the bike meant it was hard to ride and cyclists were prone to accidents. By the 1880s the 'safety bicycle' had been developed with a chain and gearing driving the rear wheel, and from 1888 such bicycles were available with pneumatic tyres (Lloyd Jones and Lewis, 2000; Oddy, 2007; Cox and Van de Walle, 2007; Bicycle Association website). From 1886, for example, diamond-framed safety bicycles were being produced at a small workshop in Nottingham and a few years later this became the Raleigh Cycle Company, one of Britain's major cycle manufacturers (Hadland, 2011; Raleigh website). The emergence of the bicycle as an important element of British manufacturing can also be gauged by the formation in 1890 of the 'Cycle and Motorcycle Trades Association' which in 1973 split into two with the Bicycle Association continuing to promote the interests of cycle manufacture and cycling in the UK (Bicycle Association website). In the twentieth century the main developments related to new forms of gearing, the introduction of much lighter and stronger frames (for instance the use of carbon fibre), and the development of specialist machines, for instance for off-road mountain biking, together with the rapid expansion of the industry. By the 1920s the Raleigh factory was capable of producing 100,000 new cycles a year (Lloyd Jones and Lewis, 2000; Hadland, 2011) and this meant that not only was there an abundant supply of new bikes but that there also developed a strong second-hand market which meant that bicycle ownership became increasingly affordable.

If the basic technology behind the bicycle changed relatively little during the twentieth century, the social profile of cyclists has changed markedly since cycling acquired some degree of popularity. In the last quarter of the nineteenth century bicycles were relatively expensive (Lloyd Jones and Lewis, 2000) and they were acquired only by the elite who mostly used bicycles for leisure and pleasure activities. Although some women cycled, the majority of bikes were sold to men, many of whom joined specialist cycle racing and cycle touring associations to pursue their sport and leisure activities (Horton, 2007). Women, and some older men, were more likely to ride a tricycle (available from the 1880s) as it provided a safer and more sedate ride and was more amenable to being used with formal male and female attire. In the 1890s, the clothing that it was thought appropriate for female cyclists to wear caused some controversy. Young women were finding long skirts increasingly cumbersome for cycling and began to wear what they termed 'rational dress', usually either a divided skirt or bloomers (Simpson, 2007; Jungnickel, 2011). However, such more convenient clothing did not become widely accepted for female cyclists until the twentieth century.

Oddy (2007) terms the first quarter of the twentieth century a 'dark age' of cycling on the grounds that it has been relatively neglected by historians of the bicycle and of cycling. He posits that this is due mainly to the technology driven nature of much bicycle history, and that as there were no significant innovations between the safety bicycle of the 1880s and lightweight machines of the interwar period the first two decades of the twentieth century have been neglected. In addition, sociologically –including perspectives from the sociology of science – the early twentieth century has been relatively ignored as it is seen as a lull between the middle-class cycling boom of the 1880s and the age of mass working-class cycling in the mid-twentieth century. Instead, Oddy argues that this was the period of the 'Flâneur on wheels' representing an important transition towards an age of mass consumption that increasingly included the bicycle and a relatively wide social spectrum of the population. Certainly, the evidence suggests that by the 1920s cycling as a means of travelling to and from work – that is, utility rather than leisure travel – had boomed with over a fifth of all such trips undertaken by men being by bicycle.

The peak in cycling in Britain came between 1920 and 1960 when, in many places, the bicycle was the single most important means of transport to and from work for men. Women were also increasingly using the bicycle, both for leisure and utility travel, but cycle use for women remained at about half that of men – rarely exceeding 10% of all journeys to and from work (Pooley et al, 2005a). The key question to be asked of this period is first, why did cycling boom (especially among men) and, second, why did it then decline dramatically. By the 1960s only about 5% of travel to work trips were by bike, though the differential between male and female figures had greatly reduced suggesting that levels of cycling for men declined much more rapidly than for women (in the 1960s male cycling rates were about a quarter of what they had been in the 1940s, but female rates had only fallen to approximately one third of their previous level). Evidence from this period may be of relevance in understanding low levels of cycling in the twenty-first century, and in developing strategies to increase the amount of utility cycling in British towns and cities.

Evidence can be drawn from oral testimonies about everyday travel experiences from the 1930s to the 1960s (Pooley et al, 2005a). Throughout the period reasons given for cycling to and from work (the main form of utility cycling) were remarkably consistent and differed little between men and women. The main advantages of cycling were usually cited as low cost, relative speed (especially for complex cross-town journeys), flexibility, enjoyment and the avoidance of public transport. Those on shift work who had to travel at unsocial hours when public transport was poor or non-existent also often found cycling convenient. Two quotes, one from a male relating to the 1930s and one from a female in the 1950s, summarise many of these themes:

> Well it [cycling] was really the only way. 'Cos there was such a tremendous detour using public transport…well the time factor, it was horrendous. (Manchester, male, 1930s)

> Well I had ridden a bicycle to school and it was just slightly easier. I didn't have the long walk to the bus stop…I didn't have to change buses, it was just easier to go on the bike. (London, female, 1950s)

While cycling was common it was by no means universal, and many respondents gave strong opinions as to why they did not cycle during this period when levels of cycling were high, and thus cycling would be seen as a relatively unremarkable means of transport. Interestingly, too, the reasons given by men and women were somewhat different. Male respondents were most concerned about the lack of a secure place to leave their cycle, inclement weather, the need to wear smart office clothes, together with their own laziness. Female respondents were most likely to cite fear of urban traffic as the main reason for not cycling, together with such factors as the need to undertake complex multi-stage journeys (including collecting children) which could not easily be undertaken by bike, the weather, concern about clothes and the cost of purchasing a bicycle. The critical difference is that while both men and women valued the same positive attributes of cycling (freedom, speed and independence), women were often deterred by urban traffic conditions and other demands on their time whereas men at least did not admit to these being significant factors.

The immediate reason for the decline in cycling from the 1960s is obvious: the increase in car use. Men made the switch to cars as the main and normal means of everyday transport on average about 20 years ahead of women, but by the 1980s the car accounted for some 50% of all travel to work trips by both males and females, and utility bicycle use for travel to and from work had settled at about 7% for men and 5% for women. It is argued that the factors that both attracted travellers to the car from the 1960s to the 1980s, and also those that repelled them, were essentially similar to the reasons people gave for using bicycles in the 1930s and 1940s. The car provided independence, flexibility, privacy (including avoidance of public transport), and comfort. Just as men and women valued most of these characteristics in the bicycle they appreciated them even more in the car. Women, in particular, cited a combination of fear of driving and cost as factors that deterred them from commuting by car in the 1960s and 1970s (when this was already common for men); exactly the same factors that some women gave for not cycling some 30 years earlier. However, as soon as women were able to afford a car most adopted this as their main form of transport. It also became a key asset in completing the complex multi-purpose journeys that made cycling difficult for many women (Dowling, 2000). It can thus be argued that the seeds of the decline of the bicycle for utility travel lay precisely in its success in the inter-war period. In this respect the bicycle and the car can be seen as similar technologies that offer comparable benefits and have similar constraints to use. However, once the motor car became affordable the added benefits of travelling fast while protected from the weather, and with the ability to carry passengers, meant that the bicycle was rapidly eclipsed. It seems unlikely that these common perceived benefits will change in the mind of the travelling public, or that the bicycle will in any way be able to match the greater attraction of the car, and thus if cycling is to be promoted in the twenty-first century then there is need either to promote rather different merits of the bicycle from those that originally attracted both men and women to its use in the 1920s and/or to greatly restrict car use.

Since the car became increasingly dominant from the 1960s, it can be argued that the decline of the bicycle has become cumulative and circular. The fewer cyclists there are on the road the less normal it seems as a means of everyday travel; the more cars there are on the road the greater will be perceived fears about safety; the more that road infrastructure caters mainly for cars the more marginalised cyclists will feel. As outlined in Chapter One, attempts by government and campaigning organisations to increase cycle use have so far had only limited and localised impact, and it can be argued that some of the publicity that particularly links cycling to its health benefits, and which promotes it mainly as a leisure activity, can be almost counterproductive. Most of the gains in cycling that have been made have been in leisure cycling, mostly off road or on quiet lanes designated as part of the national cycle network (Sustrans website). While this does get more people on to bikes, and cycling is beneficial exercise, it can be argued that it also creates an image of the bicycle as a machine that is primarily meant for leisure and pleasure, a toy for children and adults to enjoy, but not a serious means of everyday transport for grown-up people. In this respect, it can be suggested that cycling in the twenty-first century has much more in common with its position in the 1880s than with the 1940s.

The historical dominance and persistence of walking

Walking has always been an important aspect of everyday travel in Britain, but in most academic studies it has remained strangely invisible. It can be argued that this is principally because travelling on foot is so routine and mundane that it is rarely worth recording or studying. It is a taken-for-granted facet of everyday travel that almost disappears from view (de Certeau, 1988). When walking does become the focus of study it is usually to emphasise those aspects of walking that are considered to be unusual, distinctive, particularly visible or unique. Thus Solnit's (2001) book, one of a very small number exclusively on the practice of walking, focuses mainly on the experiential and performative aspects of walking as do many later essays (Ingold, 2004; Ingold and Vergunst, 2008; Wylie, 2005; Lund, 2005; Lorimer, 2011). Although Urry (2007) includes a chapter on walking in his classic work on mobilities most of this section is concerned with issues of spectacle, the flâneur, and outdoor leisure walking, rather than the practice of utility walking to accomplish everyday tasks. In addition, the National Travel Survey accepts that, at least in some years, it has under-recorded short trips on foot (DfT, 2011a). Walking thus also becomes less visible in the statistical record which focuses on more intrusive forms of transport. Middleton (2009a, 2010, 2011a, 2011b) does engage directly with everyday walking in the city, but here again focuses mainly on the experiential aspects with regard to conceptions of time and route rather than on the practical functions of walking as a means of travel to accomplish everyday tasks, though she does also relate her work directly to the promotion of London as a 'walkable city' (Middleton, 2009b). However, in comparison with many other rich countries, it can be argued that Britain is a nation of walkers. According to the comparative figures provided by Pucher and Buehler (2010) levels of walking in the UK are higher than in both North America and most north-west European countries. Although there is clearly scope to increase levels of walking it can be argued that pedestrianism in Britain is a hidden success story in the context of sustainable mobility.

One of the problems encountered in the study of walking is defining exactly what a walking trip is. Almost all journeys involve some walking, even if it is only to walk to a car in the drive or to the nearest bus stop. However, walking as part of a multi-stage journey is rarely explicitly recorded. It can also be suggested that the experience of travelling – to go on a journey – implies something more complex than placing one foot in front of the other. That to travel you must engage with some form of transport which implies use of technology (a bike, bus, train, car, plane) rather than simply walking. After all, walking is something that almost everyone does around the home or office without actually going anywhere. The key question thus becomes what defines walking as a journey or trip that is significant? Does it have to be over a particular distance? Does it have to be to achieve a particular purpose? If we include all forms of walking, from a few steps as part of a multi-stage trip, through short walks to a neighbour's house, to long hikes for leisure or sport, then it can reasonably be argued that even in the twenty-first century walking is by far the most ubiquitous means of travelling in Britain. In the past, when technologies of travel were less well developed and less available, walking was even more common. Indeed, for many, it was the only way in which they could travel for many purposes.

Prior to the twentieth century at least 60% of all travel to work was undertaken on foot, and for most of the nineteenth century this was the normal mode of transport for all but the very rich. The need to be within walking distance of a place of work was a constraint on residential location, and given that the amount of time that people are routinely prepared to commit to travel to work has, over time, remained quite constant at about half an hour (Green, 1988; Pooley and Turnbull, 1999a) this meant that most people lived within about three kilometres of their workplace. Although increased availability of horse-drawn omnibuses from mid-century, and of trams from the later nineteenth century, meant that those on higher and more regular incomes, for example many clerks and other office workers (Anderson, 1976; Crossick, 1978), could commute by public transport and thus live further from their workplace, for the majority of those on lower incomes walking remained the only available means of transport. While travel on foot of perhaps six kilometres a day was normal for most people in the nineteenth century, some workers travelled much further. In rural areas it was not uncommon to have to walk for several hours to reach the nearest market town (perhaps 10–15 km distant) and those trades that were peripatetic required frequent long-distance journeys on foot. Thus, in mid-century, skilled workers would routinely tramp all over the country moving from town to town where work was available, usually staying in lodgings (sometimes arranged through their union) and remitting money back to their family in their home town (Southall, 1991). Despite limited access to mechanised forms of transport many people in the nineteenth century covered long distances on foot, as evidenced by the mobility of vagrants and petty criminals whose activities were traced all over the country (Pooley, 1994). It can reasonably be assumed that most such movement was undertaken on foot.

In the late-twentieth and twenty-first centuries we have adopted almost contradictory attitudes to walking. On the one hand, rising real incomes and increased access to transport technologies have meant that walking has been viewed as a means of transport that is used either as a last resort or by the very poor. For instance, in oral history surveys of travel in the mid-twentieth century, some respondents noted that they walked only when weather or other factors disrupted their normal public transport (Pooley et al, 2005a). Although some respondents in the period 1930–60 said that they enjoyed the walk to work, far more said that they did so out of necessity, most often to save money. On the other hand, particularly in the later-twentieth century, walking as a leisure activity has become increasingly popular. With rising levels of obesity and concerns about health (Ogilvie et al, 2004, 2007) walking has been promoted as an easy and acceptable way to gain exercise. However, such walking is rarely used to undertake everyday activities, though recent health campaigns (for instance from the NHS, Department of Health, Natural England, The Ramblers' Association) have argued for the inclusion of walking in everyday travel routines: for instance getting off the bus a stop early and walking the last part of a journey (NHS website; Natural England website; Ramblers' Association website; Department of Health website). Such messages, to engage in walking for leisure or as part of a healthy everyday lifestyle, are most likely to be heeded by those on higher incomes and with some discretionary time. Thus some aspects of walking have become associated with higher status. Even in the nineteenth century the rich, who would routinely use a private carriage for everyday travel, were aware of the value of walking as a recreational activity (Walton and Walvin, 1983).

Reasons not to walk are easy to find and they have probably remained relatively unchanged over a long period of time. In the past most travellers had fewer options but most would probably have used an alternative, and less energetic, means of transport if they could. Respondents talking about travel in the mid-twentieth century mostly cited time as the main reason why they did not walk to work – it would simply take too long. This view obviously reflects the fact that by that stage many people did have access to alternative means of transport. In the nineteenth century when walking was the only option, home and workplace were much more closely linked and most workers had to live within walking distance of their place of work. By the twentieth century the possibility of exchanging residential migration for commuting became an option for many (Pooley and Turnbull, 1999b). Additional reasons for not walking were similar to those given for not cycling: exposure to the weather, too much effort, too much luggage or ill health/infirmity either of the respondent or of travelling companions. Whereas cyclists cited traffic dangers as a key safety concern, for walkers the main risk was perceived to be from strangers. However, this was rarely cited as a major factor and in periods when walking was more common, and thus more people were on the streets, it is likely that people perceived safety in numbers. Empty streets are likely to be perceived as the most dangerous (Pain, 2006; Pain and Smith, 2008).

If class differences with regard to walking are relatively simple and consistent over time – the poor walk from necessity but the rich walk for pleasure – gender differences are somewhat more complex (Schmucki, 2012). One strand of literature on mobilities has emphasised that in the nineteenth century walking urban streets was a predominantly male activity, and that for women the urban streets were full of risks (Solnit, 2001; Urry, 2007). The implication is that respectable women rarely walked, and if they did would be escorted normally by male companions. Unaccompanied women on the streets could be viewed as prostitutes and would be in both moral and physical danger. It is argued that this is, at best, an oversimplification. There are two main reasons for this line of thinking: first, consideration of the practical realities of everyday life for most women who had access to no other means of transport other than to travel on foot; second, evidence in rare but important diaries and accounts kept by women at the time. The realities of urban life for most women in respectable working-class families was that they had to juggle multiple commitments to childcare, home care, paid employment (often part-time or casual) and social activities (Llewelyn Davies, 1915). These could only be accomplished by frequent independent travel and, of necessity, this meant walking – often alone – to shops, friends, work and elsewhere. Certainly, such journeys would mostly be undertaken along well-known routes in a familiar neighbourhood, but that is true of almost all everyday travel for men and women of all classes. Working-class women rarely left personal records, but diaries of middle- and upper-class women also reveal quite high levels of independent mobility (Gordon and Nair, 2003; Pooley et al, 2010). It was only in the most elite echelons of London society that considerations of class and propriety meant that female mobility was constrained (Dyhouse, 1989). Elsewhere most women had the freedom to travel when and how they liked.

If there is debate about the visibility of women on the street in the nineteenth century, it can be suggested that in the twentieth century the situation has been almost reversed. As men increasingly took to using first bicycles and then cars, women came to dominate slower and more traditional forms of transport that included both public transport and walking. For much of the twentieth century women have been less likely than men to have a driving licence (DfT, 2011a) or, if they could drive, to have access to a car (Deem, 1982; Dobbs, 2005). Due to constraints of childcare and part-time work women also had, on average, a shorter journey to work than men, especially from the 1960s, as men increasingly travelled to work by car. For instance, in the 1970s female travel to work distances were approximately 58% of those undertaken by men (Pooley et al, 2005a). Thus women were much more likely to walk (either for all of a journey or as part of a multi-mode trip). Moreover, it can be suggested that concerns about health, fitness and body shape have been more likely to be adopted by women than by men and, while some of this concern has been reflected in increased indoor exercise in gyms, it has also encouraged more women to take up walking and jogging for fitness. Thus, it can be argued, the street in the twenty-first century has become increasingly feminised.

One way in which walking has both changed over time, and has become differentiated by purpose and status, is in terms of the material possessions that have increasingly become associated with walking as an activity. At its most simple, and for most of the nineteenth century for most people, walking did not require any specialist equipment or preparation. You could travel on foot in everyday clothes and footwear – albeit with the need for warm or protective clothing in inclement weather – and it could be undertaken with little thought or expense. As such, walking was (and still potentially is) the most accessible and democratic form of mobility available. However, there have been a number of trends which, it can be argued, have complicated this picture. First, on some occasions and for some people, walking has always been as much about display as about travelling to a destination. Although most often associated with the late-nineteenth century Parisian male flâneur (Tester, 1994), many ordinary people would also have taken pride in their appearance and wear their best clothes while walking in public, perhaps in the park or on the seaside promenade, on Sundays or public holidays (Walton and Walvin, 1983; Walton, 2000). Thus, on at least some occasions, walking in public meant some expense (or at least effort) to ensure that the right image was projected. In the later twentieth century it can be argued that this trend has been continued through the development of a highly commercial industry that promotes and sells outdoor clothing and equipment (Rose et al, 2007; Rose and Parsons, 2008). Thus to go for a walk today, especially for leisure, increasingly is seen to require specialist and expensive footwear, waterproof clothing, a rucksack and, perhaps, walking poles. While necessary for expeditions to more extreme environments it is very doubtful if such equipment is needed for the relatively short and undemanding leisure walks undertaken by most people. But having the right equipment has become part of the performance of walking (Nelson, 1999; Nash, 2000; Gregson and Rose, 2000; Lorimer and Lund, 2008). It can also be suggested that as walking as a practice has become more associated with specialised leisure or sporting activity that requires particular equipment, this in turn creates a disincentive for utility walking. If there is a belief that walking requires particular clothes and equipment then it becomes much more complex and difficult to achieve. Rather than being viewed as a routine everyday activity that you just have to step outside the door to do, as it almost certainly was in the nineteenth century (and potentially remains today), it becomes something that has to be planned and only done on special occasions in particular environments. Clearly much utility walking does take place, especially in urban environments (see Chapter Eight), but it can also be argued that for many the performance of walking has become more complex.

The final factor to be considered in this brief overview of the history of walking in Britain is the provision of infrastructure. It is usually assumed that walking requires much less infrastructural investment than other forms of transport, and it can be suggested that this is one of the factors that has led to its relative marginalisation in transport planning: if infrastructure is not needed then the activity does not need to be planned for. However, it can be argued that this is a false premise. Three centuries ago specialist infrastructure was indeed limited: few urban streets, and no rural roads, had pavements that separated pedestrians from traffic and few roads had a firm surface. In all but the driest weather walking almost inevitably meant getting muddy feet and clothing. From the eighteenth century onwards roads were increasingly paved and separate pavements for pedestrians provided in urban areas (Dyos and Aldcroft, 1969; Pawson, 1977). This both improved pedestrian safety and reduced exposure to the dirt of the road. During the nineteenth century lighting was introduced to many urban streets (Otter, 2008), but from this point provision of specialist infrastructure for pedestrians has remained almost unchanged to the present day. The main additions have been the introduction of traffic lights and marked pedestrian crossings in the 1930s, the zebra crossing in the 1950s, the development of pedestrian subways and bridges to separate walkers from traffic at busy road crossings (especially pioneered in British post-war new towns), and the introduction of CCTV cameras in city centres to increase security (Tolley, 1990; Fyfe, 1996, 2004; Armstrong, 2000; Webster, 2004). While such innovations may be presented as improving road safety and making pedestrians feel more secure, in practice it can be argued that primarily they act to restrict pedestrian movement as walkers are increasingly channelled into specific routes, often guided by railings at busy junctions, rather than having the freedom to choose their own route (Blomley, 2010). Furthermore, urban pavements have become increasingly dominated by street furniture of various sorts that can impede movement and restrict pedestrian flows, while most rural roads continue to provide no segregated facilities for pedestrians. Thus while in some ways being a pedestrian in Britain has become safer and cleaner, it can also be argued that it has become increasingly constrained as the road space allocated to pedestrians has become progressively defined and restricted to give priority to the demands of the car.

Conclusions: issues of path dependency

This chapter has provided a brief outline of the historic development of some aspects of everyday travel in Britain, with a particular focus on the changing role of walking and cycling in relation to other transport modes. It has argued that for most of the past 200 years road space has been dominated by the largest, fastest and most powerful means of travelling available and that other road users have been marginalised. Moreover, there have been persistent variations in class and gender with rich men in particular increasingly controlling road space. Others have had to develop strategies to negotiate an increasingly hostile travelling environment. What is perhaps surprising about the history of everyday travel in Britain is the way in which, despite substantial technological changes (especially in the nineteenth century), the pattern and process of everyday mobility has been remarkably constant. Most people travel over short distances most of the time, social and gender inequalities persist, and conflicts over road space regularly reoccur with only a slightly varied cast. It can be argued that part of this continuity is due to the path dependency that exists within the British transport system.

Path dependency can be defined as a process whereby a particular technology gains sufficient power and credibility ('lock-in') to influence later developments over a long period of time and in areas only marginally related to its original remit (Arthur, 1994; Magnusson and Ottosson, 1997). It can be argued that the car achieved such dominance in the early twentieth century and that this path dependency has had a negative impact on all other forms of everyday transport ever since (Thrift, 2004; Urry, 2004). This has been demonstrated with regard to the ways in which urban road space has been repeatedly reconfigured to make vehicle movement as easy as possible, usually to the detriment of walkers and cyclists. It has also been seen in the allocation of urban space for purposes such as parking, thus excluding other arguably socially more useful land uses, and through the ways in which car use has been accepted as a normal part of everyday life with, at least until recently, only minimal resistance. The motor car has achieved this dominance by not only being part of a large and increasingly powerful industrial and commercial sector (motor manufacture and the petroleum industry), but also in the eyes of most people it offers an extremely convenient means of everyday travel. We have argued that the priorities that led men and women to use the bicycle in relatively large numbers in the mid-twentieth century can be met even more effectively by the car. Thus the perceived needs and aspirations of the travelling public have changed relatively little, but these goals have been achieved through the use of a different (and more powerful) technology. Arguably, this will only change significantly if a new technology offers the same qualities of travel in a way that is quicker, cheaper or more convenient than the car; if vehicle use is so severely restricted that apparently less attractive means of travel have to be adopted; or if new societal goals and values – perhaps to do with sustainability – come to the fore (Dennis and Urry, 2009).

THREE

The global context: how is Britain different from other places?

Urban travel outside the UK

The significance of everyday travel for individuals, families, economies and societies is clear, but good comparative data on everyday mobility is surprisingly scarce. Moreover, the ability to travel freely, easily and cheaply in order to fulfil essential everyday tasks is rarely taken into account when measures of quality of life or development are constructed. For instance, the United Nations Human Development Reports construct a series of indices, including the Human Development Index (HDI), on which the UK ranked twenty-eighth out of 187 countries in 2011, but in which access to transport and mobility exclusion is not included in any form. The only data on human movement relate to residential migration and then almost exclusively to international migration flows (United Nations, Human Development Reports website). This is, perhaps, surprising as it can be argued that restrictions on everyday mobility because of, for example, poverty, incapacity, lack of transport, fear of violence or political constraints are among the most fundamental of human rights concerns. For instance the Universal Declaration of Human Rights (article 13) states explicitly that 'Everyone has the right to freedom of movement and residence within the borders of each state', while the ability to move freely is an implicit requirement of the ability to carry out many of the other rights stated in the document (United Nations, Universal Declaration of Human Rights website). Where freedom of everyday movement is restricted it is almost always the case that many other human rights are also violated.

The lack of good global comparative data on everyday mobility can be attributed to a number of causes. Because everyday travel is so mundane it is rarely recorded in official documents – indeed attempts to record movement could themselves be construed as restrictions and a breach of human rights – and thus much everyday mobility remains invisible. While many countries, especially in the richer parts of the world, do undertake travel surveys of various sorts, these are rarely constructed in the same way and thus data are not directly comparable (Kunert et al, 2002). In most cases the only data available relate to those aspects of mobility over which (in most cases) governments have some control, such as the provision of infrastructure and the registration of motor vehicles. Thus data remain very partial. In addition, as outlined in Chapter One, travel surveys rarely record all journeys or stages of multi-stage trips and, in particular, the full extent of walking is rarely recorded. A detailed summary and appraisal of existing information on travel and transport across the globe is provided by the Victoria Transport Policy Institute (VTPI), an independent Canadian research organisation that focuses on transportation solutions. Much of the quantitative evidence used in this chapter is drawn from sources provided by this organisation (VTPI website, Transport Statistics). Comparative long-run historical trends are even harder to attain and thus the main focus of this chapter is on recent and current trends in global mobilities.

Even if data are rarely directly comparable, the broad trends of global mobility are reasonably clear. First, there is massive mobility inequality with the richest countries in the world accounting for the greatest proportion of movement, and the resources needed to support this mobility, and with the poorest countries experiencing much lower levels of mobility. Second, changes over the past few decades have begun to show a shift in these trends, with levels of mobility in the poorest countries of the world increasing and rates of mobility in richer countries moving towards stability or, in some instances, a slight decline. Thus poorer countries increasingly account for a higher (though still small) proportion of global mobility. Schafer and Victor (2000) have estimated that in 1960 the richest countries of the world (Western Europe, North America, Australasia and Japan) accounted for 69.6% of total global mobility whereas by 2050 this is predicted to fall to 41.5%. Most of the rest of the world is expected to see increases in mobility with the greatest gains in Asia, the Middle East and North Africa. While the precise methodology underpinning such calculations may be questioned the spread of high levels of mobility to most parts of the world seems inevitable.

The processes that are producing these changes are also easily identifiable (Whitelegg and Haq, 2003; Banister, 2005, 2007). High levels of mobility in the richest countries of the world have been achieved principally by widespread use of fast and expensive forms of transport (private motor vehicles and air travel) with travel by public transport, cycling and walking reduced to a residual position. Such travel practices are a direct result of increased affluence and, unsurprisingly, increasing affluence elsewhere in the world has produced a shift towards car ownership (and use) and air travel, with a shift away from anything that is perceived as a slower or lower status form of transport. According to Schafer (1998) this process began in the last half of the twentieth century with the car accounting for 73.1% of the modal share of motorised mobility (walking and cycling were excluded) in the richest parts of the world (as defined above) in 1960, increasing only marginally to 74.8% by 1990; whereas in what Schafer terms 'developing' regions (Africa, Asia, Latin America) the modal share of motorised transport attributed to cars increased from 18.3% in 1960 to 26.9% in 1990. Although public transport (buses and trains) still accounted for by far the largest component (68.6%) of motorised mobility in the poorest regions of the world Schafer argued that the trend was clear.

However, such statistics paint only a partial picture, and when all travel modes are taken into account mobility disparities between rich and poor countries remain stark. Using data compiled for a selection of Asian and Pacific cities for 2001, whereas in Melbourne (Australia) the car accounted for 55% of all trips (including non-motorised travel) and automobile ownership stood at 341 per thousand population, in Bangalore (India) only 11% of trips were by car and car ownership was 231 per thousand population. Other South Asian cities had similar figures: for instance in Lahore (Pakistan) 18% of trips were by car and in Seoul (South Korea) the figure was 20% with car ownership at 290 per thousand (data from Asian Development Bank via VTPI website, Transport Statistics, 2012). It is also relevant to note that the disparity of car use between Melbourne and the other cities cited is greater than that for car ownership, thus suggesting that there are significant differences in travel behaviour between the countries as well as in the ability to purchase a motor vehicle. Such differences are also reflected in energy consumption and greenhouse gas emissions. As shown in Chapter One, transport is a major component of global greenhouse gas emissions and the contrast between rich and poor countries in terms of total emissions is clear. While in 2008 Australia produced 19 tonnes of carbon dioxide per capita, in India the figure was 1.5 tonnes and in Pakistan 0.9 tonnes per capita (United Nations website, Human Development Reports).

Although the general picture over the past few decades has been for high car use in rich countries and increasing car use in poorer countries, there are significant variations that buck these trends. It is usually assumed that increasing affluence necessarily leads to higher car use, but this is not always the case (Kenworthy and Laube, 1999). One example of an affluent city with low car use is Hong Kong. In 2001 just 8% of all recorded trips were by car with 87% by public transport, though short walking and cycling trips are almost certainly under-recorded. Car ownership was recorded as just 47 per 1,000 inhabitants (Asian Development Bank via VTPI website, Transport Statistics). Hong Kong (China) ranks thirteenth on the UN HDI with a gross national income (GNI) of over $44,000 per person. This compares to an Australian GNI of some $34,000 and a HDI rank of two (behind Norway). The most obvious explanation for the very low car ownership and usage rates in Hong Kong is the high urban density and compact urban form of the city, making car use unnecessary. However, it can also be argued that low car use is also a result of positive measures to shape travel behaviour, including investment in good public transport and the high cost of car ownership (Cullinane, 2003; Tang and Hong, 2008).

Hong Kong provides an instructive comparison with some Western European cities that can claim to have sustainable urban transport systems. Although rates of cycling in particular are high in many north-west European countries this is mostly at the expense of public transport, and levels of car use remain high. Thus in The Netherlands, despite 47% of all journeys being by bike or on foot, 48% are by car and just 5% on public transport. Car use is higher than this in almost all other comparable countries with public transport use mostly below 12%: for instance in Belgium just 6% of trips are by public transport with some 70% by car (Bassett et al, 2008). Even in a city such as Groningen (The Netherlands), which with 58% of journeys on bike or by foot claims to have some of the highest levels of sustainable transport in the developed world, only 6% of journeys are on public transport and 36% are by car. Thus in terms of sustainable mobility (including public transport) Groningen remains some way behind Hong Kong, and the figures suggest that although by European standards car use is low, much of the modal transfer has been from public transport to bikes rather than from cars. Some of the lowest levels of car use in Europe are in Spain where both public transport use and non-motorised trips are high. Thus in Barcelona car use is 29% and in Vitoria just 17%. This contrasts markedly with a city such as Ghent (Belgium) which, despite having relatively high levels of walking and cycling (34%), also has very high levels of car use at 56% of all recorded trips (1998 data from ADONIS report via VTPI website, Transport Statistics). In most such cities there are also large differences between the central areas, with low car use and high levels of walking and cycling, and suburban areas where the car remains dominant.

This brief review has shown that a full comparison of travel behaviour across a wide range of countries is difficult. Truly comparable statistics, for similar time periods, are rarely available. However, it can be argued that although the mobility goals that people have seem to be broadly consistent, and that access to adequate mobility is thus an essential component of everyday life, there are considerable differences in how people travel. Moreover, these not only vary across nations that are very different, but also between countries with similar economies and cultures. While the main differentiating factors are economic, with poor countries aspiring to become more like rich countries with high levels of car ownership and use, not all richer nations are equally car dependent. Factors that influence these differences are various, but most crucially include policies to restrict car use and to provide fast, efficient and low-cost alternatives; together with cultural considerations that construct particular images of what forms of everyday travel are normal and expected. These may, in turn, be quite deeply embedded in the historical make-up of a country. Although other considerations such as topography, climate, urban density and structure undoubtedly also play a role, they seem to be subsidiary to the common goals of why people travel and the common constraints (or influences) of economy and culture.

Everyday travel in Britain is broadly similar to that of many other rich (OECD) nations, situated somewhere between the extremes of, on the one hand, Australia and the USA (with very high car dependence and low levels of walking and cycling) and on the other hand Switzerland, or the Netherlands (which have relatively lower car use and a higher dependence on a combination of public transport, cycling or walking). Thus in both the USA (78%) and Australia (76%) more than three-quarters of all trips are by car whereas in The Netherlands (48%) and Switzerland (38%) fewer than half of all trips are by this mode. In the UK the car accounts for some 65% of all journeys (Bassett et al, 2008). These differences in travel behaviour have some significant social and economic consequences. Road traffic fatalities are broadly (though not perfectly) correlated with car use with the USA recording 14.5 deaths per 100,000 population, Australia 8.6, the UK 5.7 and The Netherlands 4.9. Exceptions include Spain which has low car use but a high casualty rate of 11.5 fatalities per 100,000 population, which presumably reflects both road conditions and driving habits. High car use is also related to levels of obesity with the highest rates again in the USA (34.3%) and the lowest in Switzerland (8%). In the UK some 24% of the population is obese. Transport-related energy use is also highest in the USA (2.18 per capita tonnes petrol equivalent) with Australia consuming 1.47 tonnes and most of Western Europe around 0.9 tonnes per capita and, not surprisingly given the size of the country and levels of car dependence, motorists in the USA drive each year approximately double the distance that motorists in Europe travel. The high economic and cultural dependence on the car in the USA has also worked to keep the price of fuel low, with petrol/gasoline prices in Europe 2.5 to 3 times their level in the USA (2006 data from OECD via VTPI website).

It is clear that no countries in the rich parts of the world achieve the highest levels of sustainable travel. While some are more car dependent than others, even those with high levels of walking or cycling often also have significant car use. Globally, poverty produces relatively higher levels of sustainable mobility with very high dependence on public transport and on walking for short trips. However these forms of transport are rarely used by choice, and as countries get richer then levels of sustainability mostly, though not inevitably, fall. The UK inhabits a middle position in the overall global sustainability rankings with 8.5 per capita tonnes of carbon dioxide (CO_2) emissions in 2008 compared to 53.5 tonnes in Qatar (the highest), and practically zero in the Democratic Republic of Congo, Chad, Mali and a number of other very poor countries (United Nations, Human Development Reports website). Given that the transport sector, and car use in particular, constitutes a significant proportion of CO_2 emissions there remains considerable room for change in the way in which we travel. It is these issues that are explored in the detailed case studies presented in Chapters Four to Eight.

Places where walking is normal

In this book we are developing an argument that current strategies to increase levels of walking and cycling for short trips in English urban areas are unlikely to be successful unless these modes of travel are normalised within British economy and society. One good starting point for this analysis is to examine those situations and places where walking or cycling are seen as (relatively) normal ways to travel, to assess the factors that have produced this situation, and to evaluate the potential for harnessing such factors to make more sustainable urban travel easy and commonplace in the UK. In this section we focus on walking and in the following section on cycling. We identify four broad situations where walking (including by those that use mobility aids) is likely to be the normal and expected means of travel.

First, in all parts of the world, walking is the taken-for-granted means of moving around indoors: in the home, the office or in public spaces such as shopping malls. In very large public spaces, such as airports, transport may be provided for those with restricted mobility, and for heavy luggage, but most people will walk relatively long distances, albeit often with the assistance of moving walkways. Issues of space, infrastructure and the sheer density of people obviously prevent use of all but the occasional official vehicle even in large indoor spaces, but the crucial factor is that it is accepted by most people that walking is how you travel in indoor spaces. It is very likely that some people will walk further indoors in an airport than they would ever consider walking out of doors (for instance it is over 800 m by pedestrian walkway from the railway terminus to departure gates in Manchester airport). Second, walking is normal in those situations where very slow progress and frequent stops are part of the experience. The most obvious example would be shopping. Although most people may drive or use public transport to get to a city centre or out-of-town retail park, once there travel on foot becomes the expected and most convenient option. Again, the distances travelled on foot while shopping in a city centre are likely to be much greater than many people would consider walking for other purposes (for instance it is easy to wander several kilometres when shopping in a large city centre, and the distance from one end of the (indoor) Trafford Centre in Manchester to the other is approximately 800 m). Third, walking is perceived by many people (especially in the richer parts of the world) to be a normal leisure activity, undertaken for pleasure or health, but not something that is done for utility travel. Thus, the phrase 'going for a walk' conveys meanings of pleasure and leisure and is not normally associated with mundane, everyday travel (Ingold and Vergunst, 2008). However, it can be suggested that many people need a reason to take a recreational walk: they have a dog to walk, they feel a small child needs amusing or would benefit from fresh air, or their doctor has told them to exercise more. This implies that walking for pleasure is only normal for at least some people when there is a specific reason. How many dog owners would walk regularly if they did not own a dog? Finally, walking is normal in many very poor countries, for instance in much of sub-Saharan Africa (Tolley and Whitelegg, 2001; Porter, 2002a). In much of rural Africa or Asia, where there are no alternatives, walking to the well, to the market, or to the field is the normal and expected means of transport. This is walking from necessity. The implications of this brief discussion are that, while some people do walk substantial distances for pleasure (Lorimer and Lund, 2008; Lorimer 2011), for many people walking is an activity only undertaken in situations where it is necessary, prescribed, or perceived to be the only socially acceptable means of travel. This implies that if we are to persuade more people to walk for everyday trips in urban areas (as opposed to walking for leisure and pleasure) then it needs to be either legally or socially expected with, presumably, the second option more acceptable to most people than the first.

Although, as outlined above, access to motorised transport is increasing in many poorer regions of the world, walking remains the normal means of travel for many, especially in rural areas. Lack of access to adequate infrastructure and motorised transport remains a significant development issue (Porter, 2002a, 2002b, 2007; Bryceson and Bradbury, 2008). Reliable statistics on levels of walking in the poorest countries of the world are scarce, and most surveys either under-record or fail to record walking trips. For instance, data from the Asian Development Bank (2001, via VTPI website) give modal splits for walking for a selection of Asian cities that vary from 60% in Dhaka (Bangladesh) to zero in a number of cities including Colombo (Sri Lanka) and Phnom Penh (Cambodia). It is inconceivable that no trips in these cities were undertaken on foot, but both cities also show a high dependence on various low-cost forms of motorised transport: 75% of trips in Colombo were recorded as being by public transport and 60% of trips in Phnom Penh by motor cycle or three-wheel vehicle. Thus, it can be argued, that even taking into account the undoubted deficiency of official statistics, in cities where alternatives to walking are available people will routinely use them. The motor bike, or other low-cost powered vehicles, can be seen as one stage in the transition to high car use. In most instances walking will also take place as part of a multi-stage journey, though this is rarely recorded in surveys, but it is much more important in cities with high public transport use than in those where the private car (parked close to the home) is routinely used. Thus, data which show a low modal split for walking in, for instance, Asian cities should not be interpreted as implying that the streets are empty of pedestrians. The degree to which people depend on walking for everyday travel in remote rural areas varies with both the quality of the road infrastructure and the ability to afford motorised transport. In a study of six rural field sites across three countries in Africa and Asia, Bryceson and Bradbury (2008) concluded that investment in road infrastructure alone is not sufficient to improve accessibility as it has also to be linked to programmes of poverty reduction to enable people to access motorised transport. Moreover, they also identified significant variations in mobility behaviour between study sites with, for instance, normal walking distances in Ethiopia much greater than those in their field site in Vietnam. In summary, although walking in both rural and urban areas in many of the poorest parts of the world remains normal and commonplace, where there are alternatives these are almost universally preferred.

In rich countries although there remain substantial inequalities in wealth and access to transport (explored briefly below), most travellers do have alternatives to walking. Relatively few people walk from necessity. There are, however, substantial variations in the proportion of trips undertaken on foot in (for instance) OECD countries and, although data from travel surveys are not totally comparable (and official bodies such as Eurostat only record data on motorised travel), the evidence is likely to be more consistent than for the poorest nations in the world. According to data compiled by Bassett et al (2008) the modal split for walking in a selection of rich countries ranges from 45% in Switzerland and 35% in Spain to 5% in Australia, 7% in Canada and 9% in the USA. Even allowing for variations in recording travel mode and trips, these differences are significant. In the UK some 24% of all trips are on foot: a figure that is similar to many other north-west European countries, including The Netherlands, Sweden, Finland, Norway and Germany, but higher than in Ireland, Belgium or Denmark. Bassett et al (2008) state that utility walking tends to be more common in Europe than in North

America, where most recorded walking trips are for leisure purposes, though active utility travel is more common in older US cities with mixed land use.

It can be thus be suggested that in countries where most people have an option about how they travel, and have ready access to some form of motorised transport, the choice to walk depends on a combination of local environmental factors (urban structure and access to services), personal preference, and attitudes to exercise as a leisure or utility activity. Many studies have argued that urban structure is an important determinant of active travel, though the nature and extent of such influence is debated (Ewing and Cervero, 2001, 2010; McMillan, 2007): our study of walking and cycling in four English towns (Chapters Four to Eight) includes an evaluation of such factors in the context of a much wider range of personal and household determinants of everyday travel. An assessment of 'walking needs' in relation to the physical environment across a range of European countries can be found in Methorst et al, (2010). Reasons for the particularly high levels of walking in Switzerland and Spain can only be speculated on, but are likely to relate to the relative high urban density of at least some towns (a characteristic of many European urban areas compared to those in North America or Australia), together with either an outdoor environment or climate that favours walking for both leisure and utility purposes. For instance, a study by Kasanko et al (2006) has shown that although most European cities have become more decentralised over the past half century, those in southern Europe remain relatively compact. It can be suggested that this creates an environment in which walking is viewed as a practical and easy way in which to complete at least some utility travel. Leisure walking is strongly correlated with levels of income and development: in a study of over 19,000 university students in 23 countries Haase et al (2004) found that leisure-time inactivity levels were lowest in Western Europe and North America (23% of time), and highest in poorer developing nations (44%). This emphasises the importance of leisure rather than utility walking in most rich countries of the world, with studies showing similar levels of all types of physical activity across most European countries (Vaz de Almeida et al, 1999; Bassett et al, 2008), and probably also reflects the much greater levels of physical activity undertaken by those in poor countries during non-leisure time.

Not only are there spatial variations in levels of walking, but also there are differences in who walks. The main variations are by social class (the rich walk for pleasure, the poor walk from necessity); by age (children, with access to fewer alternative forms of transport, are much more likely to walk than most adults); and by gender (women are more likely to walk than men). These differences tend to be quite consistent across most parts of the globe and can have significant implications in terms of mobility-related social exclusion from employment, education and social activities (Hine, 2003, 2012; Lucas, 2004, 2012; Porter, 2007, 2010; Keeling, 2009). For instance, in large parts of the Middle East women face constraints on their ability to travel independently – far greater than any restrictions that may have been placed on women in Victorian Britain (Chapter Two) – and in much of sub-Saharan Africa the patriarchal nature of society, especially in rural areas, means that the burdens of work, childcare and home-keeping severely restrict both the time that women have available to travel and the income they have to spend on motorised transport (Njoh, 1999; Porter, 2008; Grieco et al, 2009; Grieco and Crowther, 2011; Grieco and McQuaid 2012). In many parts of sub-Saharan Africa the carriage of heavy loads on the head or back is a normal task for women (for example, water from a well or crops from the fields), and this can have significant health impacts (Lloyd et al, 2010a, 2010b). Although gender-related mobility inequalities are less obvious in most rich countries, none-the-less they have long historical antecedents and still persist today (Law, 1999; Uteng and Cresswell, 2008; Walsh, 2010; Schmucki, 2012), with many women who have family and home-care responsibilities being more restricted than men by lack of time, money or access to a car. Women are also much more likely to walk with children. In Britain and many other European countries walking is the single most important means by which primary school children travel by school, and most of them will be accompanied by a parent, other relative or childminder who is most likely to be female (Bianchi, 2000; Pooley et al, 2005b; Walker et al, 2009). For all these reasons in both rich and poor countries women are more visible walking the streets than are men.

The safety of children, and the degree to which they should be allowed independent mobility, is a concern in all parts of the world. However, such concerns are often constructed through rather different lenses depending on the economic and social situation. In much of the rich world where children are in education and dependent on parents at least until late teenage, there have been increasing concerns about the safety of young children, sometimes construed as 'paranoid parenting', which collectively have constrained children's independent mobility and reduced their ability to walk alone and their visibility on the streets (Hillman et al, 1990; Furedi, 2001; Pain, 2001, 2006; Shaw et al, 2013). However, in many poorer parts of the world notions of childhood and adolescence are constructed rather differently. Pressures to earn an income, care for a sick relative and to take on other family responsibilities, combined with the cost of education, mean that many young people have to take on what the West views as adult roles at a young age. Inevitably this has an impact on their mobility: both increasing their need to travel for essential activities but reducing their free time for leisure travel and play. Given that most such children have limited access to motorised transport then young children frequently have to travel long distances on foot and alone. This is not without risk, but a necessary part of their everyday life (Robson, 2004; Ansell, 2005; Porter, 2010; Ansell et al 2011). It can be suggested that fears associated with walking are constructed in the context of the society in which they are placed. Where we have the option of avoiding walking (by access to a car or reliable and safe public transport) the risks associated with walking are emphasised. However, where most people walk from necessity the risks are rationalised and although real rarely prevent mobility.

Places where cycling is normal

The bicycle sits uneasily between walking and motorised forms of transport. As argued in Chapter Two, in Britain in the 1940s and 1950s for many (especially men) the bicycle was an intermediate step between walking or public transport and the freedom to travel provided by the car. Once people could afford to buy and run a car they mostly abandoned the bike for a faster, more comfortable and less energetic machine. Like a car, a bicycle is a machine (albeit a relatively simple one) that needs to be maintained and repaired: for the technologically averse this can present problems, but for those who embrace technology the car is likely to prove much more attractive. Thus, it can be argued that the bicycle is often seen as an intermediate stage in what could be termed the transport development cycle as countries progress from low to high car ownership and eventually back to low impact travel (MacKinnon et al, 2008). Concerns about sustainability, pollution and resource use in the twenty-first century have placed the focus firmly on low-impact forms of transport, while concerns about ill-health and obesity have led to the promotion of active travel. In this context the bicycle can be viewed as an ideal intermediate technology that offers active travel on a relatively low-cost and low maintenance machine, and which has minimal direct environmental impact. It can be argued that the most recent phase in this hypothesised transport development cycle is away from car dependency toward more sustainable travel. Some rich countries in north-west Europe (for instance the Netherlands, Denmark, Germany, Sweden) are beginning to come full circle with levels of cycling by choice approaching (or in some cases exceeding) those that were achieved from necessity over half a century ago. In other rich countries (Britain, the USA, Australia) the car remains dominant and, despite the sorts of promotional activities outlined in Chapter One, there is little evidence of a significant upward shift in bicycle use. In many poorer countries where bicycle use, together with other low impact forms of transport including walking and buses, has traditionally been high, most people aspire to car ownership. As incomes rise in such countries so bicycle use is declining and motorised transport (including electric bikes and motorbikes but especially the car) increasingly dominates urban areas, often using a transport infrastructure that has failed to keep pace with the demands placed upon it. Such countries are at an early stage of the transport development cycle and, if global sustainability of transport is to be achieved, then it can be suggested that it is necessary to interrupt this process and retain high levels of low-impact travel, but from choice rather than from necessity (Parkin, 2012). However, such an approach would sit very uneasily with traditional development discourses, and could easily be accused of promoting neo-colonial views, with the West being perceived as preventing other nations from achieving something they already have, and are often reluctant to give up (Tomlinson, 1991).

India and China are, perhaps, the countries currently undergoing the most fundamental changes in economy and society, including in their transport infrastructure. In both cases they are nations in which the bicycle has played, and to a large degree still does play, an important part in the provision of urban transport, but where the transition to motorised urban transport, and especially the private car, is occurring rapidly (Pucher et al, 2007; Tiwari, 2011; Haixiao, 2011, 2012; Brussel and Zuidgeest, 2012). In both India and China walking was traditionally the main form of everyday travel over short distances, with public transport used for longer trips. In India the bicycle was introduced quite early in the twentieth century by colonial British rulers, but although the total number of bikes in India in the 1940s was high they accounted for a small share of all travel. Certainly much lower than in most Western European countries at that time (Arnold and DeWald, 2011). However, with increasing affluence many urban dwellers acquired bicycles, or other non-motorised vehicles such as the bicycle rickshaw, and both became a common sight in many Asian cities (Whitelegg and Williams, 2000). By the end of the twentieth century cycling accounted for 40% or more of all trips in many Indian and Chinese cities (de Boom et al, 2001; Hathaway, 1996; Tiwari, 2001). In both India and China there is evidence that cycle use was highest, and has persisted longer, in small cities: in 2007 cycling accounted for approximately 20% of all trips in Indian cities with a population of 500,000 to one million, but only 11% of journeys in cities of over four million people. Cycling rates were also low in settlements with fewer than 500,000 inhabitants, where walking remains the dominant form of everyday transport (data from Smith (2008) via VTPA website; see also Pucher et al, 2007 and Tiwari and Jain, 2008). The fall in bicycle use has also been greatest in large cities with cycling in Delhi falling from 36% of all trips in 1957 to 7% in 1994 (Tiwari and Jain, 2008), and in Beijing from 30% in 2005 to 18% in 2009 (Haixiao, 2011). Although much of this transfer has been to private motor vehicles, with consequent implications for both pollution and road safety (Tiwari, 2011), in both India and China there has also been a recent increase in the use of electric bicycles which are becoming an attractive low-cost alternative to pedalling. It is estimated that there will be some one million electric bikes sold in China in 2011, that in China there are currently four times as many electric bikes as there are cars (McKenzie, 2011), and it is estimated that in Shanghai some 70% of traffic in bicycle lanes is accounted for by e-bikes (Haixiao, 2011). The big unknown in this trend is the extent to which this will become an established and long-term trend, or part of a transition from non-motorised to motorised travel which will rapidly lead to electric bikes being replaced by the car. The history of everyday travel in Britain the 1950s and 1960s suggests that the latter is most likely.

As outlined above, much of Western Europe has levels of cycle use well above that found in Britain, and in some cities (for instance, Amsterdam, Copenhagen, Groningen) levels of cycling equal or exceed those recorded in medium-sized cities in India or China. For instance in The Netherlands as a whole 25% of all trips are by bike (Bassett et al, 2008) with almost all residents of a city such as Amsterdam owning and regularly using a bicycle (Buehler and Pucher, 2009). Groningen claims to be the 'world's cycling city' with some 57% of residents travelling regularly by bike on the city's 46 dedicated cycling routes (Carbusters website), and in Copenhagen some 55% of all trips within the city are by bike with over 1,000 km of dedicated bike lanes (Copenhagenize website; City of Copenhagen website). Such high levels of cycling have not always been achieved and, as in Britain, most continental European cities saw a decline in cycling from the 1950s. For instance whereas in Germany in the 1930s cycling accounted for 15–40% of all journeys in German cities, rising to 60% in Berlin, by the late-1960s bikes provided only 5% of all urban trips (Maddox, 2001; Ebert, 2004). However, there was a 50% increase in cycling in Germany from the 1970s to the 1990s, so that by 2008 9% of all travel in Germany was by bike (Pucher and Dijkstra, 2003; Pucher and Buehler, 2008; Bassett et al 2008; Ebert and Carstensen, 2012). There are a number of reasons for the relative success of cycling in at least some European cities, but crucial to all are the provision of dedicated and fully segregated cycle lanes and the imposition of restrictions on motor vehicles. When combined with the promotion of cycling as a clean, environmentally friendly and efficient way to complete short journeys in urban areas, this has been sufficient to create an environment in which cycling has become the obvious choice of transport for many people (Pucher and Dijkstra, 2003; Pucher and Buehler, 2008; Horton et al 2007; Parkin, 2012). Unlike cities in India and China where, at least until recently, cycling has been mainly through necessity rather than choice, in cities such as Amsterdam and Copenhagen cycling has for many become the normally selected means of travel. However, in order to facilitate such choices the provision of an extensive network of dedicated cycle paths has been essential. Pucher and Buehler (2008) analyse the rise of cycling in Germany, Denmark and The Netherlands, and identify seven key policy areas which they argue have, collectively, been responsible for securing relatively high levels of cycling in these countries. These can be summarised as the provision of high quality separate cycle lanes; the modification of intersections and the timing of traffic lights to prioritise cyclists; traffic calming; extensive and safe bicycle parking facilities; co-ordination of cycling with public transport, especially through provision of cycle hire and storage; good cycling education and training; and enforced traffic laws that protect cyclists. Moreover, such policies have achieved high levels of cycling in countries that also continue to have relatively high levels of car ownership. In Germany, The Netherlands and Denmark car ownership is very similar to that found in Britain (where cycling rates are very low) with all four countries recording rates of between 520 and 550 vehicles per 1,000 inhabitants (Eurostat, 2010). The difference is that whereas in Britain car use is seen as normal in almost all situations, in countries such as The Netherlands motor vehicles are used for longer trips or those few shorter journeys that cannot be easily completed on foot, by bike or on public transport.

Travel surveys that examine journey purpose usually show that cycling tends to be undertaken either for simple solo utility trips, such as travel to work, or as a leisure activity. Journeys that require multiple stages, that are accompanied by other family members, or that require the carriage of heavy loads are more difficult – though not impossible – to achieve by bike (Pucher and Buehler,

2010). Following from this, it can be suggested that people who cycle regularly can be broadly classified as falling into one of three different cycling identities. First, there are those people who enjoy cycling, and who cycle regularly, but who mostly do so for leisure purposes, usually off-road or on quiet lanes, and rarely use their bikes for utility travel. They are keen cyclists but see cycling principally as exercise and pleasure rather than as a means of transport. They probably own a car and use it for most everyday journeys, including in some cases transporting bikes to scenic areas for off-road leisure cycling (Goeft and Alder, 2001; Needham et al, 2004). Second, there are those people whose primary identity is as a cyclist, in that they see this as their main form of transport, they probably do not own a car and certainly use a car rarely, and they organise their lives (and the lives of other family members) in such a way that most activities can be undertaken by bike. This group forms the core membership of most cycling organisations and pressure groups and is at the forefront of promoting cycle-friendly cities. It is also the group that forms the focus of most studies of cycling identities (Spinney, 2006; Fincham, 2007; Aldred, 2010; Steinbach et al, 2011). Third, and from a global perspective, by far the largest group of cyclists is likely to be composed of people who cycle regularly for at least some utility trips (to work, to shops, to school), and probably gain enjoyment from doing so, but their primary reason for using this form of transport is that they perceive it as the most accessible and efficient. Thus they may be cycling mainly from economic necessity, as is the case in many of the poorest countries of the world, or they may be cycling because it is the quickest and easiest way to travel around (as is arguably the case in cities such as Amsterdam or Copenhagen), but they do not necessarily have strong identities as cyclists. They could easily change their mode of transport if either they were more affluent, or if the urban infrastructure became less conducive to cycling. In this context the contrast with walking can again be emphasised. Whereas almost everyone walks sometimes, and walking is considered a normal thing to do on at least some occasions and in some contexts, for many people cycling is perceived as an abnormal activity and those who do cycle regularly are likely to do so for a variety of different reasons. Looked at from this perspective it can be argued that, compared to walking, levels of cycling in urban areas around the globe are very likely to be subject to substantial fluctuations as standards of living and urban infrastructure change. Places with high rates of cycling today may not necessarily sustain these far into the future if conditions were to alter.

Conclusions: Britain in a global context

The aim of this chapter has been to provide a global context within which discussion of detailed research on walking and cycling in England (Chapters Four to Eight) can sit. The review presented here has necessarily been brief and has focused on highlighting broad trends rather than presenting detailed evidence. This can be followed up in the references provided. We have demonstrated that there are persistent inequalities in the ways in which people travel, replicated at a variety of spatial scales around the globe, and that these inequalities are likely to be exacerbated by some of the trends currently seen in global societies and economies. We have argued that at a global level while some people choose walking or cycling as their primary means of travel around urban areas, for the majority of people who walk or cycle they do so out of necessity. Once they can gain access to faster and more comfortable forms of transport they are likely to do so, driven by the embedded nature of 'automobility' within global economic, social and political systems, even though cycling or walking may be as quick as car use in congested urban cities. This has potentially serious implications for global sustainability. We have shown that in global terms levels of walking and cycling in Britain fall within the mid-range of developed countries (substantially more than in North America or Australia but far less than in much of continental Europe), but that in common with all rich nations travel in Britain is currently much less sustainable than in most poorer countries in the world. It is often assumed that increasing affluence automatically brings greater car dependence and less sustainable travel, but there is some evidence that these trends, certainly common to the history of many countries, are not inevitable (Cox, 2010). Where a combination of compact urban form, restrictions on car use, and excellent infrastructure for non-motorised travel and public transport exist, then it is possible for cities in rich countries to move towards a post-car mobility system that avoids the apocalyptic scenarios provided by Dennis and Urry (2009). Cities such as Copenhagen, Amsterdam and Hong Kong are by no means perfect, but they do provide models of more sustainable urban transport to which other places can aspire.

At various points in this discussion we have emphasised local and regional variability. Although transport and travel statistics are often only available at a national level, there are frequently significant variations between localities within one country, and between different groups of people within the same location. Any discussion of large scale global or even national trends must thus be interpreted with caution. Even within the UK there are important differences in the ways in which transport policies are developed, with the devolved governments or assemblies of Scotland, Wales and Northern Ireland having control over some of their own transport policies (Shaw et al 2009; Butcher et al, 2010). Reserved matters, those retained in Westminster, mostly relate to those aspects where coordinated policy within the UK is deemed to be essential. Within England primary responsibility for transport planning in London has been devolved to the Mayor of London via Transport for London, and there are plans to give English regions and local communities more control over major transport projects rather than them being decided in Westminster (DfT website, Devolution of local transport). There is thus considerable scope for transport policies and practices to vary considerably across the UK and if, for instance, Scotland were to gain complete independence (a key aim of the Scottish National Party which currently has a majority in the Scottish Parliament (SNP website)), then it would be possible to see each part of the British Isles pursuing a very different mobility future.

The remainder of this book focuses on detailed research on walking and cycling carried out in four English towns. It explains how the research was carried out (Chapter Four), and then presents the key results and their implications. The focus throughout is on understanding and explaining how everyday travel decisions are made, and the implications that this has for sustainable and active travel modes such as walking and cycling. The final chapters of the book provide a series of policy proposals that we believe would enable more sustainable travel to become embedded within British towns and cities. Although the case study towns are all drawn from England, we believe that the broad results and conclusions from the study potentially have much wider relevance. There is certainly no reason why they should not apply to the whole of the UK and, with appropriate adjustments for cultural and economic differences, many of the broader implications could have relevance globally. After all, in most parts of the world individuals and families have to make similar decisions about how they live their lives and, increasingly, they are faced with a similar range of transport choices. However, while a global perspective is important, our research in four English communities has also emphasised the significance of local variations. Understanding how and why people make everyday travel decisions, how these become embedded into everyday lives, and the implications that this has for sustainable mobility requires consideration of individual, household and community concerns. It is at this level that most of the remainder of the book is focused.

Section II

THE RESEARCH

FOUR

Researching walking and cycling

The UWAC approach: introduction to the data

It is important that policy making in any area is evidence based, and that it is clear how exactly this evidence was derived. In this chapter we outline the research methods that were used to produce results discussed in Chapters Five to Eight, and from which we derive the policies proposed in Chapters Nine and Ten. A reader eager to get to the results could skip this chapter, but would have to take the evidence presented at face value without fully understanding how it was collected or why we adopted the approach that we did. Research reported in this volume has not developed any new methods, but is unusual and distinctive in the way in which it utilises and combines different elements of a wide range of research methods. We believe that a multi-method approach in which the varying strengths and weaknesses of quantitative and qualitative research are fully recognized, and through which different methods are used to reinforce and strengthen each other, can produce much more insightful and robust research findings than can be generated from studies that utilise only a single approach. Multi-method research is not new, but it is often deployed in limited ways and has rarely been applied in the study of travel behaviour. Most commonly, different methods are utilised in a linear way: for instance, a quantitative questionnaire may be used to provide an overview prior to in-depth interviews with a selection of respondents; or focus groups may be used to identify key themes that are then followed up through a questionnaire. However, in such cases although more than one method is deployed they tend to be interpreted independently, and the different techniques rarely talk directly to each other. This is not surprising as true integration of different approaches is hard to achieve (Castro et al, 2010). However, the Understanding Walking and Cycling (UWAC) research reported in this volume was designed as an integrated package of quantitative, qualitative and spatial research methods and, although we do not avoid all the pitfalls of multi-method research, we have attempted to utilise a wide range of approaches and data to produce a fuller and more integrated interpretation of everyday travel behaviour than is usually the case. Although each of the individual chapters (Five to Eight) do focus largely on a specific set of methods, each is informed by the other, and the discussion and policy recommendations in Chapters Nine and Ten seek to integrate this material into a coherent whole.

The UWAC research project utilised four principal research methods: a structured mainly quantitative questionnaire survey probing attitudes to and experiences of walking and cycling; detailed analysis of the built environment including assessment of connectivity and land use characteristics and their influence on travel behaviour; in-depth interviews to explore the process of decision making and experiences of everyday travel carried out both in the home and while travelling; and the application of a range of ethnographic methods in selected communities to analyse in more depth the everyday household and family factors that influenced travel decisions. These methods were deployed across four English towns (Leeds, Leicester, Worcester and Lancaster) with the main period of data collection lasting from January 2009 to April 2011. In this section we provide details of the precise research methodology used while additional information about the four study areas, including our reasons for selecting them, is given in the following section.

Two separate questionnaire schedules were prepared, one focusing on walking and one on cycling. Questions were designed to collect data on the experience of and attitudes towards either walking or cycling and were constructed to be analysed within the context of the theory of planned behaviour (Ajzen, 1991; Bamberg et al, 2003). This assumes, in the context of everyday travel, that how someone travels is determined by a person's intention to travel in a particular way, and that these intentions are structured by series of attitudes and subjective norms towards different forms of mobility. Thus the questionnaires were designed to elicit information not only on how people travel, but also on their attitudes to different forms of transport, the degree to which these were affected by significant others, their past experiences of everyday travel, and their future intentions. Respondents were asked to focus only on short journeys in urban areas (when answering the questionnaire respondents were asked to think about a local journey which they made regularly that was under four miles (6.4 km) long), and to answer all questions regardless of whether they ever walked or cycled for everyday journeys. It was important for the research that we gained the views of a wide cross-section of the population and not only those who were dedicated cyclists or pedestrians.

Walking or cycling questionnaires were sent to a sample of households evenly split across all four study areas and stratified using location and the index of multiple deprivation (IMD) measured at the lower super output area (LSOA) level to produce a cross-section of the population. The IMD is derived from 37 indicators that are grouped into seven domains: income; employment; health and disability; education, skills and training; barriers to housing and services; living environment; and crime. The LSOA provides a spatial framework of small areal units each with a maximum of 1,000 people or 400 households. These were analysed for the built-up area of each of the four study sites using the 2004 rural and urban classification to exclude LSOAs within each district that did not fall within the urban area. It was felt that this provided a good basis on which to construct a representative sample and a spatial framework that would allow detailed subsequent analysis, including the linkage of questionnaire data with that collected for the built environment and from qualitative research. In total 15,000 postal questionnaires were distributed across the four areas with a response rate of almost 10% giving 1,417 usable returns (798 walking and 619 cycling). Response rates varied little between the study areas but with a slightly lower return in

Leicester than in other areas. Although low, these response rates are in line with similar surveys elsewhere (Fink, 2009; Marsden and Wright, 2010). The sample of respondents was broadly representative of the total population but with some over-representation of females (especially for the walking questionnaire), older age groups, car owners and those with a degree level qualification (especially for the cycling questionnaire). Bearing in mind the inevitable limitations of survey instruments of this sort, we consider that the questionnaire provided robust base-line data on travel attitudes and behaviours in the four study areas. Results from this analysis are presented principally in Chapter Six.

Spatial analysis of the four case study towns consisted of detailed land-use mapping and identification of the network of all routes that could be used for walking and cycling (which can differ significantly from the road network). This was achieved through the careful analysis of both cartographic and field evidence. Multiple centrality assessment (MCA) was then used to assess connectivity within the city. MCA is a technique that computes various measures of connectivity and centrality for a network of routes (Porta et al, 2008; 2012). Its application is based on the assumption, substantiated in a considerable volume of research, that travel behaviour is directly influenced by the form of the built environment and by the ease with which it is possible to connect one location with another (Saelens et al, 2003; Dill, 2004; Naess, 2006; Leslie et al, 2007; Van Dyck et al, 2009). Three measures of centrality were computed using MCA (defined precisely in Chapter Five). These statistics were calculated and mapped at both global (entire town) and local (neighbourhood) levels for the total route network (road, cycle path and footpath) for the four case study towns. In addition, detailed land-use maps were constructed from map and field evidence. While maps of connectivity and land use provide useful background information about the four communities, the real value of these data is when they are linked to other information. Using the home address of all questionnaire respondents in each town, the MCA data were used to examine the degree to which built environment and land use characteristics influenced recorded travel behaviour. Indices of connectivity and land use were correlated with self-reported data on levels of walking and cycling provided by the questionnaire survey to assess the extent to which land use and connectivity influence levels of walking and cycling. Results from this analysis are reported in Chapter Five which also provides more detailed information on the technique and its limitations.

Eighty semi-structured interviews were undertaken with people selected (mainly) from their questionnaire responses to be broadly representative of the demographic structure and travelling characteristics of the population of each of the four towns. Respondents were drawn from across the built-up area of the four communities so that a good cross-section of the population was included. Forty interviews were undertaken in households (often including group interviews with several household members) probing attitudes to walking and cycling and the reasons why people chose particular modes of travel, and 40 interviews were conducted as either walking or cycling 'go-alongs'. Respondents were accompanied on a 'usual' journey and the interview focused on the motivations for travelling on foot or by bike, on route selection, and on the experience of the journey. Half of the mobile interviews were on foot and half were undertaken while cycling, and a small number of the cycle journeys were also recorded visually with a head cam. While the household interviews were relatively unproblematic, mobile interviews proved much more challenging (Kusenbach, 2003; Ricketts et al, 2008; Carpiano, 2009). Key issues included the need to negotiate access to a convenient journey where being accompanied did not interfere too much with the respondent's normal routine; ensuring enough time at the start and end of the journey to collect necessary additional data and review the interview; the practical constraints of speaking and recording a conversation while travelling; and issues of safety both for the respondent and interviewer.

The walking interviews proved relatively straightforward when the pace was slow and it was possible to walk side by side or pause and talk, but some interviews were carried out at a fast pace through congested pavements where communication was more difficult. In general, the cycling interviews were much more challenging. In many cases constraints of traffic or the road lay out meant that it was not possible (or at least not safe) to ride side-by-side and carry on a conversation, and thus the interviewer cycled behind the respondent observing their behaviour and recording this into a microphone as they travelled. If possible, either during or at the end of a journey, time was then found to review the sections where conversation was not possible and to fill in details. Whereas walking interviews were almost always leisurely, some cycling respondents seemed to view the interview as a challenge and took the opportunity to demonstrate how fast they could ride in heavy traffic. In some instances this meant that the interviewer lost contact with the respondent for short periods. In addition to the journey itself we were also interested in the change-over period as people completed their trip and moved into their daily routine. Again, with walking trips this was relatively unproblematic, but with cycling go-alongs we had to negotiate access into (for instance) the home or work place to see where the bike was stored and if there were shower and changing facilities for the cyclist. Despite such issues the mobile interviews yielded high-quality data which allows us to understand much better the experience of different everyday journeys (Fincham et al, 2009; Middleton, 2011b).

In addition to the methods outlined above we also wanted to probe in much more detail the ways in which everyday travel decisions are made in particular households. To achieve this, ethnographies were undertaken with 20 households (five in each town). In each urban area one neighbourhood was selected – designed to reflect particular demographic and spatial characteristics – and all respondents were recruited from that location. This allowed the researchers to immerse themselves in the local community and begin to understand the ways in which people moved around. The purpose of the ethnographic research was to observe and understand the nature of everyday journeys within a community, and this was done using a combination of research tools including interviews, go-alongs, mobility inventories, observations, mapping exercises and community participation (Wallman, 1984; Silverstone et al, 1991; Descartes et al, 2007). A typical strategy was for the researchers to start by familiarising themselves with the locality, observing the nature of local travel movements, and identifying key neighbourhood characteristics. In some areas we had been given initial contacts and these people provided access to respondent households, but more often households were recruited though a combination of snowballing from an initial contact and informal contact in the community. As the researchers became visible in the community then more contacts could be generated.

Ideally we would work with a family for a period of several weeks, probably starting with an interview in the home and then arranging accompanied journeys and, if possible, periods of observation in the home. Subsequent interventions included the collection of data on what items the household had for everyday travel (bikes, outdoor clothes, boots, umbrellas, etc.) and where they were stored in the home; the compilation of travel diaries over a period of several days; and the analysis of mental maps of the routes that people routinely used. In practice, the precise nature of the ethnographic research varied across the four districts in recognition of the need to engage different communities and individuals in particular ways. While some communities and individuals responded positively to the ethnographic approach and were prepared to invite researchers into their home and commit time to the project, in other locations potential respondents were much more wary and alternative approaches had to be adopted such as group interviews in community centres or access through particular neighbourhood groups that met regularly in a neutral setting. Although these differences obviously complicate direct comparisons, we argue that such flexibility in the face of local variability is one of the strengths of employing a multi-sited ethnographic method. Without such flexibility we would simply not have been able to collect the rich data that inform the discussion in Chapters Seven and Eight. Approximately three months were spent in each community and in total the interviews and ethnographies generated 262 separate transcripts and produced over 1.5 million words of text. All names cited in the text are pseudonyms.

Analysis of qualitative data is complex because observations, encounters and experiences cannot be readily reduced to a set of data that can be easily analysed using standard computer packages (as is the case with most quantitative data). Most interventions did produce a written record, and we adopted a number of approaches to the analysis of these textual data. First, all interviews, observations and other interventions were fully transcribed. Second these data were coded and prepared for the text analysis programme, ATLAS.ti, using a relatively simple and flat coding scheme so as to retain the structure of the interviews and not break them down into too many component parts (Muhr, 1991; Barry, 1998). Atlas could then be used to retrieve data on a range of topics identified through the coding scheme. Third, all members of the research team read the entire transcripts and identified a series of extracts which they considered reflected key characteristics of the database. These were then grouped into themes: in total 1,008 separate statements were identified and were grouped into 14 themes. This database has been used to generate representative quotes from the mass of original data.

Analysis of qualitative data inevitably requires a degree of subjectivity in deciding how to identify key themes and which quotes to select. To introduce additional rigour into this process Q methodology was also used to identify the key themes that emerged from the textual data. Q methodology is a technique, originally used in Psychology, to analyse subjectivity: that is the viewpoints that people hold (Amin, 2000; Watts and Stenner, 2005; Eden et al, 2005). It can be equally easily applied to a range of fields including issues of transport, environment and sustainability (Steg et al, 2001; Van Exel et al, 2005; Ellis et al, 2007; Raje, 2007). It involves subjecting a concourse of representative statements to a process of sorting by respondents and then analysis using principal components analysis to identify the key factors or themes that emerge and account for the variance in the data set. In this project the research team first selected from our database of over 1,000 quotes from respondents, 50 statements that we agreed reflected a range of views. The statements were further grouped into five themes: walking and cycling practices, performance, identity, conflicts, and visions for the future. These were then taken back to a sample of 25 original respondents from the four case-study towns, chosen to reflect a range of travel characteristics and attitudes, who were asked to indicate their level of agreement or disagreement with each statement. This Q sort was constrained so that each statement had to have a separate position on a predetermined matrix. These Q sorts were then analysed using principal components analysis to produce a series of components that reflect the key elements of variation in the data set (Jones et al, 2012). The application of such quantitative techniques to textual data is debated by researchers, and it can be argued that it contradicts the whole purpose of a qualitative research methodology (Ellis et al, 2007). In this project we used Q methodology as one of a number of approaches to interpret the textual data and to provide additional rigour to our subjective interpretation of the key themes emerging from the analysis.

The case study communities

The four English cities (we use the terms town and city interchangeably) chosen as case study sites (Leeds, Leicester, Worcester, Lancaster) were selected to be broadly representative of a range of communities within the country. London was deliberately excluded on the grounds that travel and transport characteristics in London are very different from those in the rest of the country, and because the capital has been the subject of more extensive research and monitoring than most other places. In this section we briefly explain the main characteristics of the four communities: their location is shown in Map 4.1. Data are drawn from field research, local planning reports and national statistics. Most simply, the four case study towns differ in terms of their size and location. Leeds is a large city of over 700,000 people situated in northern England; Leicester is a medium-sized city (over a quarter of a million population) in the East Midlands; Worcester is a

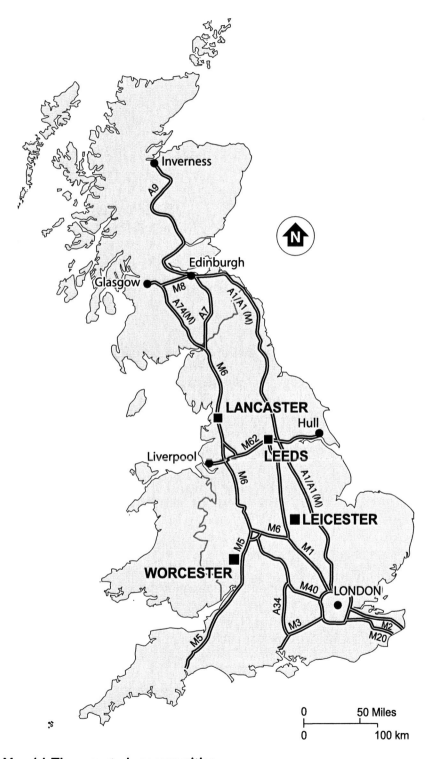

Map 4.1: The case study communities

small city (under 100,000 population) in the south-west Midlands; and Lancaster is of a similar size but in north-west England. Each city is well-connected into the national transport network with good road and rail communications. There are some significant differences in the everyday travel characteristics as revealed by 2001 census data (the data used to select the communities). Worcester and Lancaster have the highest rates of car ownership with only 22.6% of households in Worcester not having a car, and 28.1% in Lancaster. In contrast in Leeds over one third (34.5%) of households do not have a car, rising to 38.3% in Leicester. However, there is not a close correlation between car ownership and levels of cycling and walking. Using data on usual mode of travel to work from the 2001 census Worcester, Leicester and Lancaster all have relatively high levels of both cycling and walking but Leeds (with low car ownership) also has the lowest rates of walking and, especially, cycling. For instance whereas in Worcester 4.7% of journeys to work are by bike, in Leeds the figure is just 1.3%, though bus use in the city is high. These data suggest that levels of walking and cycling are largely independent of car ownership, but rather reflect different decisions about car use and attitudes to public transport which will be influenced both by the characteristics of the individual and the local environment.

The communities also differ in terms of their social, economic and cultural characteristics. Using the 2007 index of multiple deprivation (the IMD data on which case study selection was based) which summarise a range of social and economic variables, Leicester has by far the greatest levels of deprivation with a rank of 23 (out of 354) local authorities in Britain (where a rank of one indicates most deprivation). The other three communities are more similar with Leeds ranked 114, Lancaster 135 and Worcester 185. These rankings broadly correspond with levels of unemployment: in 2001 (when unemployment nationally was relatively low) Leicester recording the highest unemployment levels (4.9%) and Worcester the lowest (2.8%). This is confirmed by more recent data which is contemporaneous with survey and ethnographic material collected in the four towns. For instance, in August 2010 whereas 14% of the working age population was claiming benefits of some kind in Leeds, Lancaster and Worcester (slightly below the national mean of 15%), in Leicester 20% of the working-age population were benefits claimants. There are also marked differences in the cultural make-up of the communities. Leicester is one of the most multi-cultural communities in Britain with 39% of its population recorded as of 'non-white' ethnicity according to the 2001 census definition. This is more than three times higher than the level recorded in Leeds (11%) and approximately six times that in Lancaster (5%) and Worcester (6%). In contrast, differences in the age structure of the population are small with Lancaster recording the highest mean age (39.2 years) and Leicester the lowest (35.5 years). Collectively the communities reflect the varied social, economic and cultural characteristics of contemporary Britain (all data from National Statistics).

It can be suggested that levels of walking and cycling are affected by local environmental conditions including weather, topography and the structure of the built environment. Britain is a relatively small country so variations in weather conditions are limited, however on average the south and east of the country has drier and warmer weather than the north and west. None of the settlements studied present extremes in terms of local topography. Lancaster and Leeds both have localities that are hilly, but for most journeys it is also possible to avoid the worst hills and many routes are relatively flat. In Leicester and Worcester topography is muted and there are only gentle slopes that are unlikely to cause most people difficulty when travelling on foot or by bike.

The cities do vary in their lay-out and compactness. Worcester is relatively compact and few places are more than about three kilometres from the city centre. Although Lancaster District is only slightly larger than Worcester in terms of population, it is a much more dispersed urban area consisting of the historic town of Lancaster, the seaside resort of Morecambe and the port of Heysham. Although Lancaster itself is compact, it is about 12 km from Lancaster city centre to the port of Heysham, so it is possible to undertake quite long journeys within the urban area. For a medium-sized city Leicester is also relatively compact with most suburbs no more than six kilometres from the city centre, a distance that many people could cycle; and even in the large city of Leeds most suburbs are within ten kilometres of the city centre. What this suggests is that everyday travel distances within one built-up area depend much more on urban structure than they do on city size. Potentially people in Lancaster have to travel further to carry out everyday activities within the urban areas of Lancaster District than do residents of Leeds, a city some seven times the size. This is borne out by mean travel to work distances (from the 2001 census) where the longest mean distances (15.3 km) are in Lancaster compared to mean distances of only 8.9 km in Leicester and 11.6 km in Leeds. The other key factor influencing such data is the size and nature of the urban labour market. In small towns such as Lancaster and Worcester it is more likely that workers travel to other towns in the region for employment, thus inflating travel to work distances, whereas in larger settlements such as Leeds or Leicester it is more likely that employment is available locally. This could explain the relatively high mean travel to work distances in Worcester (12.6 km) despite the fact that the Worcester urban area is relatively compact.

There are also differences in the urban infrastructure and consequent 'feel' of the four towns, which influence the degree to which they seem amenable to activities such as walking and cycling rather than being dominated by the car. Leeds is probably the city where at first sight walking and cycling is most challenging. Urban redevelopment in the 1960s included the construction of a series of urban freeways that cut through parts of the inner city, providing rapid access routes for cars but often impeding the flow of pedestrians and cyclists. The urban structure of Leicester was also affected by post-war redevelopment, including a ring road that cuts through part of the city, but Leicester seems less dominated by the car than Leeds and has the benefit of a major pedestrian greenway (New Walk) originally developed in the eighteenth century that runs from close to the city centre some 1.1 km to Victoria Park, and with links to both Leicester University and some residential areas to the south of the city. Worcester and Lancaster have several similarities in terms of the way in which their urban structure and development affects everyday travel. Both have historic city centres with restricted road systems that become clogged with traffic, both have river crossings that cause a bottle neck, and both have arterial roads or inner ring roads that carry high volumes of traffic, though in Lancaster there is an on-going and long-running debate about the development of additional road links. All four cities have some central areas that are at least nominally car free, probably developed most fully in Leicester, but in all four towns the impact of the car is immediately visible to any pedestrian or cyclist (data from field observations and planning documents). The road network of each town is shown in Maps 5.2–5.5 in the following chapter.

All urban areas have undertaken a number of interventions to seek to manage the impact of motor vehicles in urban areas and to promote more sustainable and active travel. The four case study towns are no exception, but the impact of such schemes varies considerably. Lancaster and Worcester have both been part of national schemes to promote active travel, with Worcester designated a Sustainable Travel Town in 2004 and Lancaster a Cycling Demonstration town in 2005. In theory such schemes should have had significant impacts on the way people travelled in these two communities during the UWAC fieldwork. It would also be anticipated that Lancaster and Worcester might demonstrate conditions for everyday travel by bike or on foot that were rather different from those in Leeds and Leicester that did not have such designations and associated funding. Two of the four communities have seen major infrastructural initiatives: the Millennium Bridge in Lancaster, part-funded by a National Lottery grant, was opened to pedestrians and cyclists in 2001 and provides a car-free link across the River Lune connected to some of the 80 km of mainly off-road cycle routes in and around the district; and in Worcester the Diglis Bridge (opened in July 2010 as part of the Sustrans Connect2 programme) provides a car-free crossing of the River Severn. The Diglis Bridge was opened just after our main period of fieldwork in Worcester, but any impact from the Lune Millennium Bridge should have been visible in Lancaster. In addition, and without any special designation, Leicester City Council has invested in a major 'streets and spaces' regeneration scheme that includes a large car-free area in the city centre with improved pedestrian routes elsewhere and some 100 km of signposted cycle ways, and also has a Connect2 scheme to the north of the city where new infrastructure in Watermead park provides access for leisure and commuting (Leicester City Council, 2011). This scheme was only partially implemented during the fieldwork and is less relevant for short trips within the urban area.

All four towns have also implemented a range of soft measure to promote more active and sustainable travel. Thus Worcester has introduced individualised travel marketing (Choose How You Move) to make people aware of different travel options, and has worked with employers to develop work-place travel schemes. In Lancaster Travel Smart and cycle training and promotion schemes have been in place, and in Leeds lottery funding was secured for the U Travel Active programme (2008–12) designed to promote walking and cycling within the city. This was centred mainly on the two universities and has seen both the provision of additional cycle routes and cycle parking spaces, and the active promotion of walking and cycling. A Core Cycle Network Scheme is also planned for the period 2012–17, and in 2010 a cycle point offering bike parking, cycle hire, repair and information was established opposite Leeds central station. The city of Leicester has also been very proactive in promoting more active travel and has been particularly visible in the promotion of cycling with a range of facilities including regular cycle workshops, a Bikeability programme and the Leicester Sky Ride. Thus, although only two of the four case study towns were included in particular national schemes, all have been proactive in working with national funding and campaigning bodies to invest in and promote both walking and cycling (all data from fieldwork and planning documents).

Within each of the case study towns one community was selected for more detailed research using the ethnographic methods outlined above. These were chosen using a number of criteria: they should be relatively clearly physically bounded with similar infrastructure and urban environmental characteristics throughout; they should represent distinctly different sorts of communities as defined in social, economic, cultural or physical forms; and they must be within circa five kilometres of the city centre and major facilities so that walking or cycling for at least some everyday needs would be realistic. Within this broad framework the areas were selected on the basis of local fieldwork, cartographic and statistical evidence, and expert advice from informed locals. In Lancaster the chosen community lies close to the city centre and railway station (nowhere is more than two kilometres from the town centre and many dwellings are only a few minutes' walk from most central urban facilities), and consists of a mixture of terrace housing and more modern detached and semi-detached dwellings. There are pavements on all roads (though some are narrow and uneven) but no segregated cycle routes linking most of the area with the town centre (though there are links to the city's off-road routes). In the area of terrace housing there is almost no off-road parking and thus on-road parking is common, sometimes on quite narrow streets. There are relatively few local facilities but proximity to the town centre means that there is easy access to a range of shops. Close to the town the topography is relatively flat but there is a significant hill between the town and the more modern housing area. The area contains a mixture of social groups and lies within an electoral ward with strong Green credentials that is just in the top (that is worst) 30% of most deprived wards in the country. However, the area chosen was predominantly middle class and recruitment of families into the study was relatively unproblematic. Potential respondents understood what the research was about and were prepared to allow researchers into their home for interviews and observations.

The area selected for detailed study in Worcester has some similarities to that in Lancaster but is slightly further from the city centre (approximately 3.5 km), is more homogeneous, and is separated from the centre by the River Severn.

Since completing fieldwork the Diglis Bridge provides an alternative (though slightly longer) pedestrian and cycle route to the centre, but during the study all travellers had to use the single bridge linking this area to the city centre. The area was developed as middle-class suburban housing in the 1960s and remains an attractive location to live. Most houses have gardens and drives so off-road parking is available. There is a small row of shops, a primary school, but few other services locally. The ward in which the district falls is mostly affluent, ranked in the bottom (that is best) 25% of wards nationally according to the Index of Multiple Deprivation. Crime levels are low and mean incomes are slightly above the Worcestershire average. As in Lancaster this was a relatively easy area in which to do fieldwork, although in contrast to Lancaster the field researchers had no prior knowledge of the area and thus there was a period of familiarisation prior to the main phase of research. The ethnographic methods included intensive observations and interviews and, once initial contacts were established, we were able to identify families who were prepared to participate fully in the research programme. There was a general understanding of what the research was about and there were no major difficulties encountered during field research.

The city of Leicester has a multi-cultural population and the area used for ethnographic study was chosen to reflect this fact. Situated about three kilometres from the city centre this community is quite tightly bounded by major roads and consists mainly of streets of late-Victorian and Edwardian terraced housing, with commercial premises along the major roads. There is a reasonable range of local facilities, including supermarkets, and access to open space in a local park. The population is mostly of South Asian origin (many of East African Asian heritage). The largest single group are Hindu but the area contains a broad mix of other religions and cultures. The overall feel of the area is busy and vibrant. The ward in which the area is situated is among the 10% most deprived in the country according to the Index of Multiple Deprivation and at the 2001 census some 44% of the population had been born outside of the EU, with 63% of respondents declaring themselves to be of British Asian Indian ethnicity. Leicester city centre is relatively near but access entails using busy main roads that are not necessarily conducive to walking or cycling. It was much harder to undertake ethnographic fieldwork in this area than in either Worcester or Lancaster. The researchers (both white European) stood out as different from the majority population in the area and it was initially difficult to establish contacts. However, through a combination of gradual familiarisation with the locality, use of key informants, and contact with neighbourhood community organisations it was possible to gain the trust of some members of the community. This included gaining access to homes, extended interviews, and observations with some respondents. None-the-less, many people remained wary of involvement or simply puzzled as to why an activity so mundane as walking, or as rarely practised as cycling, should be of interest to researchers from a distant university.

In Leeds the ethnographic research focused on a small area of high-rise social housing, almost immediately adjacent to the city centre but cut through by major urban roads which limit routes from the estate to the main retail area of the city. Developed in the 1960s the area has been repeatedly refurbished but still shows many marks of acute poverty and deprivation. There are some local facilities (a row of shops, two pubs and a community centre) but most shopping is likely to take place in the nearby, low-cost, shopping mall in central Leeds. The population of the area is very mixed including some long-term white British residents, a small group of younger people who have recently chosen to live here because of a commitment to city centre living, and recent immigrants from many parts of the world that have mostly arrived as refugees or asylum seekers and have limited housing choices. The area lies within a heterogeneous central ward, which includes the commercial core of Leeds, and thus ward statistics are not really representative of the area. Undertaking ethnographic research in this area was difficult. Outsiders were often viewed with suspicion and most people were reluctant to engage in conversation or invite researchers into their home. By late afternoon as it was getting dark (the research was undertaken in winter and early spring) there were few people on the streets and personal safety became an issue. By working with key contacts in Leeds we were able to establish links with the local community centre and much of the research was undertaken in this environment, though the main motivation for participating in the research often appeared to be the £10 voucher that we gave to respondents following an interview. For most people issues of sustainable mobility were totally irrelevant as they struggled to survive in a hostile urban environment.

One theme that has emerged throughout the research is that of local variability. Although the brief descriptions of the case study towns and ethnographic research areas provide an accurate summary of key characteristics, it also became apparent that even within the small areas chosen for ethnographic research there was much variability. It was frequently the case that when conducting research two respondents in adjacent streets would give very different accounts of their everyday mobility and travel decisions. Even within families there were differences of opinion and experience, sometimes structured by age or gender, but sometimes just reflecting different personalities or preferences. Although, inevitably, we do make generalisations from the research undertaken, underlying such statements there is a recognition that travel behaviour remains highly varied and personal and cannot be separated from the social, economic and cultural reality of the everyday lives that people live. While this was most obvious in the more deprived ethnographic field areas in Leeds and Leicester, it was true for all the locations studied.

The limitations: what the research cannot be used to show

All research has limitations and it is important to identify the things that this research did not address and cannot be used to show. As outlined above, the focus of the research was on understanding everyday travel behaviour, especially with regard to walking and cycling, and on relating this to the household and community situations in which people lived their lives. Most crucially, we wanted to talk to a range of people about how and why they travelled around the town in which they lived. The mixed method approach, combining a questionnaire survey, analysis of the built environment, interviews and ethnographies yielded a mass of data; but there are many questions that the research cannot answer. First, we focus only on four case study communities and, given especially that we emphasise variability, great care must be taken when generalising from these data. Although the four cities studied do represent a range of English urban areas, and the ethnographic communities were selected to reflect a range of characteristics, we have not studied the full extent of urban experience in Britain. In particular, and as stated earlier, travel patterns and experiences in London are rather different from those in most other parts of the country and thus relating the research findings to the metropolis should be done with caution.

Second, we have deliberately focused only on certain types of travel: short trips within urban areas that could reasonably be undertaken by many people on foot or by bike. Such journeys do form the majority of all trips that we undertake (according to the 2010 National Travel Survey (NTS) 37.6% of all journeys in Britain are under two miles and 66.3% are under five miles (DfT, 2011a)). However, we recognize that there will always be some journeys that are much longer than this and these vary both by location and by journey purpose. For instance, according to the NTS people in London and other large metropolitan centres travel on average only approximately half as far each year as those living in rural areas in Britain, and journeys for commuting and business are on average longer than those for education, shopping or social activities. Thus, according to the NTS mean travel distance for business travel was 20.7 miles (33.3 km) in 2010 and for travel to work nine miles (14.5 km), but for education 3.4 miles (5.5 km) and for escorting children to school just 2.4 miles (3.9 km). However, it also needs to be remembered that such averages may be inflated by a few very long trips and that for many people travel to work distances are also short. For example, in the large city of Leeds 17.6% of travel to work journeys recorded in the 2001 census were under two kilometres and 42% were less than five kilometres. These are distances that might reasonably be walked or cycled by many people if other factors did not intervene.

Third, our research focuses on how and why people travel in particular ways and for specific purposes, and how this relates to the rhythm and pattern of their everyday life. We deliberately did not ask respondents to tell us how they would like to see transport systems in British towns changed (though some volunteered this information). Thus we provide a detailed analysis of the experience of everyday travel in British towns, we relate this to the social, economic, cultural and built environment in which these people live, and we provide explanations for people's behaviour. All this is based on data culled directly from respondents in the ways outlined above. The policy recommendations that we make in Section III represent our interpretation of what we believe needs to change if a significant proportion of our respondents are to switch at least some of their everyday travel to walking or cycling. Fourth, and related to the above point, we did not set out to evaluate the success or acceptability to the travelling public of different existing schemes to improve conditions for walking and cycling in cities. Thus we did not directly ask respondents if they wanted fully segregated cycle routes or wider pavements, and we did not systematically ask about the success or otherwise of particular schemes in our case study towns. Inevitably, opinions on existing schemes were voiced during the interviews, but the purpose of the research was not to evaluate recent interventions to promote sustainable transport but rather to understand how and why people travel in particular ways and, especially, the barriers they face to walking and cycling.

Finally, and echoing the point made above about variability, readers must be cautious in drawing generalisations from the research. Throughout the succeeding chapters we have tried to identify those findings that we consider to be capable of generalisation, and to distinguish those we consider to be specific to particular contexts. In general, we argue that the insights that the research provides to the ways in which people make everyday travel decisions; the constraints that they experience based on familial, economic, social and cultural conditions; and their experience of the built environment and travel conditions common to most British towns and cities can be extended to most, if not all, urban communities in Britain. However, the ways in which such issues might be tackled, and more sustainable travel encouraged, are likely to vary considerably depending on local circumstances. This is why policy recommendations in Section III are stated at a broad level with the recognition that they could be implemented in a variety of different ways across the country.

FIVE

How the built environment influences walking and cycling

Context: the built environment and sustainable travel

This chapter considers the built environment and the potential impact of its configuration on walking and cycling. First we examine key facets of the built environment and how it has been conceptualised. Second, we consider how the built environment might shape travel behaviour and the policy response. Third, we briefly highlight previous research that has attempted to investigate the link between built form and travel behaviour. Finally we present the results of our spatial analysis and demonstrate their significance within the broader context of understanding factors that affect household decision making in relation to journeys on foot or by bicycle. The built environment is generally defined as that part of the physical environment created by human activity, including land use patterns and distribution of activities across space; buildings; transportation systems and their infrastructure such as roads, rails, pavements and cycle lanes; and the arrangement and appearance of those physical elements through urban design (Saelens and Handy, 2008). Urban form is a broad term used to describe the physical characteristics and arrangement of the built environment in relation to its size, shape, land-use pattern and street configuration. Dempsey et al (2010), for example, categorise urban form into five broad inter-related elements: density, housing/building type, layout, land use, transport infrastructure. The morphological attributes of urban form can be described from the city scale right down to the spatial arrangement and layout of a single housing development (Williams et al, 2000). It is these concepts that we address in this chapter.

There is considerable interest in, and debate about, how urban form affects sustainable practice, particularly in relation to travel behaviour. One concept that has gained currency is that of the 'compact city' (Jenks et al, 1996; Jenks and Dempsey, 2005) which advocates a halt to decentralisation and urban sprawl through a process of urban containment and the development of higher density housing in proximity to a mix of everyday activities on existing land in urban areas. It is argued that this approach reduces travel distances and promotes a shift to sustainable methods of travel such as walking and cycling, leading to an overall reduction in transport energy consumption and related emissions (Hillman, 1996). Since the early 1990s, the European Commission has been an influential advocate of compact urban form (Commission of the European Communities, 1990). This approach to urban development is also reflected in the UK Urban Policy White Paper of 1999 which sets out a framework for urban renaissance (DETR, 1999).

The White Paper makes explicit that lower density development consumes larger amounts of land and increases journey distance between activities, thereby inducing excessive car use and making it difficult to justify public transport provision. The document highlights the benefits to quality of life gained through the promotion of dense, mixed-use developments within existing urban areas:

> One of the main attractions of city living is proximity to work, shops and basic social, educational and leisure uses…good urban design should encourage more people to live near to those service which they require on a daily basis…[and even in more suburban locations]… well-located shops, community facilities, and a more flexible approach to live–work units can be encouraged. (DETR, 1999, pp 64–5)

While the compact city concept has gained currency, and now appears to be the default setting in terms of policy thinking, it has not gone unchallenged. Breheny (1996), for example, has argued that the concept is naïve and too simplistic on a number of fronts. First, curtailment of urban decentralisation is unrealistic given that the major post-war geographical trend in the UK has been towards counter–urbanisation. Second, the attractions of city living and quality of life promised by more compact urban living undermine the very British ideal of lower density suburban living. Finally, even with compaction policies, development of some green-field land is inevitable given housing demand. Breheny proposes an alternative 'Social City Region' model to suit differing conditions (across six UK settlement types) but which in sum total for a region as a whole could contribute to sustainable objectives including more sustainable travel (Breheny and Rookwood, 1993).

The connectivity of the street network and access to facilities

An important component of urban form is the street network which Marshall (2005, p 13) describes as the, 'fundamental building block of urban structure… "movement space" constituted by streets forms the essential connective tissue of public urban space'. The configuration of the street network in terms of its connectivity (or permeability) is thought to have an important influence on walking and cycling (Gehl and Gemzøe, 2004). The Victoria Transport Policy Institute (2012) provides a useful definition of connectivity and an explanation of its importance for walking and cycling:

> *Connectivity* refers to the density of connections in path or road network and the directness of links. A well-connected road or path network has many short links, numerous intersections, and minimal dead-ends (cul-de-sacs). As connectivity increases, travel distances decrease and route options increase, allowing more direct travel between destinations, creating a more accessible and resilient system (VTPI, 2012).

In the 1950s, when planners started to grapple with the increasing demands of motor traffic, moves were made to provide a distinction between types of highway to accommodate different road users and to reduce conflict with pedestrians. A hierarchy was developed where distributor roads were designed for movement of motor traffic (from which pedestrians were largely excluded or deterred from using); and access roads to serve buildings were designed to make the pedestrian environment more amenable (Buchanan, 1964). This approach of segregating uses created layouts where buildings were set away from streets rather than on them, typically linked by alleyways, subways and raised decks. Essentially this created development patterns across most UK suburbs typified by housing located along culs-de-sac linked to circuitous distributor roads with few access points and reduced levels of connectivity for walking and cycling. While designed to segregate 'incompatible' uses and limit the movement of through traffic, this type of layout typically caused problems with congestion where the principal access road within the housing development met the main distributor road. For pedestrians and cyclists lengthier journeys were created along circuitous routes, or through alleyways and green space that were often perceived as unsafe for walking because they were remote or not overlooked (and which, in any case, often prohibited cycling). This layout was also less appealing to public transport operators who were reluctant to run buses along circuitous routes through estates because of increased journey times and lost revenue. The legacy of this phase of urban design can be seen in most British towns and cities.

In recent years there has been a move away from this type of 'modern' urban layout characterised by circular routes and culs-de-sac towards more 'traditional' patterned layouts with 'grid-like' street patterns. These are designed to increase route choice and encourage walking and cycling over car use. Map 5.1 provides an illustration of the better connected 'traditional' layout (a) compared to the 'modern' disconnected layout (b) based on the actual street layout in one of our case study towns. Current design guidance now reinforces the importance of ensuring that

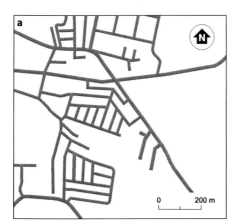
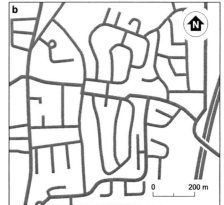

Map 5.1: Types of urban design (a) 'traditional' grid layout (b) 'modern' curved layout. Based on two neighbourhoods in Lancaster.

the layout of street networks maximises permeability: street networks should, in general, be connected as permeable networks encourage walking and cycling, and make places easier to navigate through. They also lead to a more even spread of motor traffic throughout the area and so avoid the need for distributor roads with no frontage development (DCLG, 2007, p 41).

Walking and cycling are obviously more sensitive to distance than more 'passive' forms of mobility such as driving because they rely on higher levels of personal energy expenditure. Providing a mix of activities along a highly connected street network within a densely populated area (as opposed to mono-functional, segregated and more sparsely populated areas) could, therefore, theoretically increase the possibility of more people making a greater number of journeys to access everyday facilities on foot and by cycle. Taking the home as an important starting point for everyday journeys, it follows, that those households located in the most highly connected (or 'plugged-in') areas along the street network, and that have good access to everyday activities in terms of number and diversity, are more likely to walk and cycle. The next section considers existing evidence on the links between urban form and travel behaviour before explaining in more detail how the Understanding Walking and Cycling study investigated this relationship and the results that were generated.

Spatial analysis of travel and transport: principles and problems

There has been a considerable amount of research investigating the relationship between urban form and travel behaviour. This has typically been focused at the city or regional level, and on density or settlement size and travel behaviour. For example, a study by Newman and Kenworthy (1989, 1999) investigated the relationship between per capita petroleum consumption and population density across 84 cities and revealed a strong inverse correlation between density and energy consumption. Similar research (mainly focused on US cities) has also established relationships between population density and total vehicle miles (Holtzclaw, 1994; Ewing, 1997; Ewing and Cervero, 2001). In the UK research by the consultancy firm ECOTEC (1993) showed that larger settlements have lower travel distances and less travel by car, while Dargay and Hanly (2004) analysed the British National Travel Survey (NTS) and measures of land use to demonstrate that such factors play a significant role in car ownership and use, with density having a greater impact than settlement size. Despite a growing body of evidence, investigating the relationship between land use and travel behaviour at the regional and city scale is complex and the evidence is often contradictory. As Hickman and Banister (2005, p 117) point out, in their review of knowledge gaps on the link between land use and travel behaviour, 'the world is a complicated place, and any attempt to simplify the land use and transport relationship into a series of statistical relationships is, to some extent, an exercise in aporia, that is, an unpassable path or a "route to nowhere"'.

While studies in the field of urban planning and transport have traditionally focused on the relationship between land use and levels of motor vehicle travel at the macro-scale, there is a growing body of research (particularly in public health) concerned with non-motorised travel and how configuration of the built environment at the local scale can affect levels of walking and cycling (Handy, 2005). Research strategies include selecting so-called 'walkable' and 'cyclable' neighbourhoods and then conducting social surveys with residents within those neighbourhoods to correlate levels of walking and cycling with measures of connectivity (Van Dyck et al, 2009; Giles-Corti et al, 2011) and facility provision close to home (Hillman et al, 1976; Farthing et al, 1996). Evidence tends to support the hypothesis that built form has an effect on levels of walking and cycling (Saelens et al, 2003), and that mixed land use is the most important characteristic of the built environment in encouraging walking and cycling (so-called 'active travel') because of the increased opportunities and convenience of accessing destinations (Badland and Schofield, 2005). However, the evidence for walking is more compelling than for cycling. For example, an overview of original studies and reviews published between 2002 and 2006 on the relationship between the built environment and transportation and recreational walking reveals a consistent set of conclusions on the significance of proximity, mixed land use and density in promoting walking (Saelens and Handy, 2008), but there is less convincing evidence for cycling.

While it seems intuitive that the connectivity (or permeability) of the street network (as opposed to land use) is also a key influence on walking and cycling, surprisingly there is little empirical research supporting this hypothesis. Moreover, there is also ambiguity and inconsistency in how to actually measure connectivity or what level of connectivity is desirable for walking and cycling to flourish. The general inconsistency in methods of measuring the built environment and levels of 'walkability' or 'cyclability' makes it difficult for reliable and valid comparison to be made across separate studies or geographical areas (Moudon and Lee, 2003), and studies to date typically focus on the North American and Australian context with few examining the different spatial contexts across Europe.

Reliable and consistent measures of connectivity could certainly help in researching the link between walking and cycling and urban form. Dill (2004) has considered how connectivity can be more accurately measured and calls for the advancement of techniques for measuring built environment factors such as connectivity and land use mix to enable more robust conclusions to be made about their apparent influence on walking and cycling. The UWAC study developed an original approach to measure the connectivity of the street network and levels of access to everyday activities, and to test the relationship with self-reported frequency of walking and cycling within the English urban context. If connectivity and access to activities are significant determining factors of walking and cycling then one would expect to see higher recorded levels of walking and cycling in those locations with good connectivity together with high levels of access to a mix of activities.

Evaluating associations between street network connectivity, access to everyday activities and walking and cycling

As outlined in Chapter Four, the mixed-method approach adopted in this study provided an opportunity to combine data from the social survey of households across the four cities with spatial analyses. Self-reported travel behaviour from the survey was established by asking respondents to write in the frequency and mode of travel for five non-work related journey purposes during a typical week. These five purposes were: visiting nearby friends and relatives; leisure journeys; personal business; grocery shopping; and other shopping. Around 1,400 responses were received. These were spread evenly throughout each of the four cities providing adequate variability in spatial attributes to test associations with travel behaviour. For the spatial analysis, first Ordnance Survey Integrated Transport Network (OS ITN) layers were imported into GIS software and used as a basis to construct the series of 'nodes' (intersections) and 'edges' (links) that make up the entire street network for each city. Special attention was given to representing accurately the actual walking and cycling network to ensure that no crucial links were missed and that those not obviously amenable to walking and cycling were omitted, for example, motorways and some parts of the trunk road network. In any large scale spatial analysis it is difficult to include all potential short cuts, desire lines and alleyways without a level of on the ground field analysis that was beyond the scope of this research. As a compromise, local transport authority walking and cycling maps were used to identify gaps in the network and to ensure that public rights of way and purpose-built walk/cycle paths that inadvertently might not have appeared on the ITN layer were included. It should also be noted that the final network represents opportunities to move through space unencumbered by any regulatory systems and therefore is likely to over-represent the reality on the ground.

After creating street networks for each city respondents' addresses were plotted on a map layer and then line-based network buffers were created around each respondent's home. The line-based approach was used in preference to Euclidian 'crow-flies' circular buffers because of greater accuracy in representing what is actually accessible within a given space (Oliver et al, 2007). A network buffer of 800 metres was used for walking and 2,400 metres for cycling (in all available directions) based on the assumption that, on average, this is roughly the distance travelled by each method over an 'acceptable' uninterrupted travel time of 10–15 minutes. The National Travel Survey (DfT, 2011a) reports that the average walking trip is 1.1 km and the average distance cycled is 4.7 km, so the distances used for this analysis are fairly conservative. A series of 'local' and 'global' network connectivity measures were then generated from within each 800 m and 2,400 m buffer for each respondent and included as additional variables in the social survey dataset. The local measures aimed to assess connectivity within the immediate environment of each individual respondent's home while the global measures provided an indication of connectivity of the home within the entire street network of the city. It was hypothesised that this may be particularly important for cycling given its extended range compared to walking. Three measures were used to evaluate the connectivity of the street network at the local level. First, street density measured the total length of street available within each network buffer (and therefore the total amount of path that is potentially navigable); second, node density measured the total number of intersections within the network buffer (providing an indication of the number of potential changes in path deviation); and third, average node degree gave an indication of route options by way of the average number of streets branching off each node. By way of illustration, Table 5.1 shows the number of intersections (nodes), number of streets (edges), average node degree and average street length for the entire urban area of each case study city. The hypothesis to be tested was that there is a positive relationship between each of the local spatial measures (street density, node density and average node degree) and the frequency of walking and cycling.

As well as these local spatial measures, an assessment was also made of the prevalence and diversity of local everyday activities within each buffer. Using Ordnance Survey Base Function categories from OS MasterMap Address Layer 2 data (Ordnance Survey, 2011) ten typologies representing common activities were identified (finance, post office, non-food retail, food retail, catering, informal recreation (e.g. parks), formal recreation (e.g. sports centres), health, education and general commercial). Using GIS software, these were overlain on two maps containing separate buffers for walking (800 m) and cycling (2,400 m). As well as an absolute count of activities, an entropy index was applied to provide a measure of diversity and evenness of activities within each buffer. In this case the hypothesis to be tested was that there is a positive relationship between the number and diversity of local activities and the frequency of walking and cycling.

The 'global' measures used to indicate the level of connectivity of respondents' home locations in relation to the entire city street network were derived using a technique called Multiple Centrality Assessment (MCA) (Porta et al, 2006, 2008, 2012). MCA generates a set of measures based on topographical properties (the relationship of each intersection, or 'node', to every other intersection) and spatial properties (the distance along streets, or 'edges', between intersections) and is therefore useful for investigating walking and cycling given their sensitivity to journey distance (Scheurer and Porta, 2006). Centrality measures for a city street

Table 5.1: An illustration of the characteristics of the street network in each of the case study areas

Street network	Lancaster & Morecambe	Leeds	Leicester	Worcester
Total number of streets (edges)	15,567	44,577	8,896	5,538
Average street length (metres)	96.8	82.3	98.5	94.8
Number of intersections (nodes)	5,913	38,068	7,186	4,685
Average node degree (no. of edges linked to node)	2.5	2.3	2.5	2.4

network can be visualised with darker lines indicating areas of high centrality (or connectedness), and lighter lines showing areas of low centrality across the entire network (as shown for betweeness centrality in Maps 5.2–5.5). In total, three centrality measures were used: betweeness, closeness and straightness. Each of the measures captures a different aspect of a specific location's significance in terms of 'being central' in relation to all other points in the network. Originating from quantitative sociology (Freeman, 1977; Sabidussi, 1966), betweeness centrality indicates the level of strategic importance of a location within the network. Those nodes with higher strategic importance are those that are traversed by many of the shortest paths connecting pairs of nodes. Closeness centrality indicates the extent to which a node is near to all other nodes along the shortest paths. Finally, straightness centrality indicates the extent to which the connecting route between nodes deviates from the virtual straight route or, to put it another way, the level of directness between two nodes. Measures were generated by taking both the average and sum of values within each network buffer around each respondent's home. The hypothesis to be tested was that there is a positive relationship between

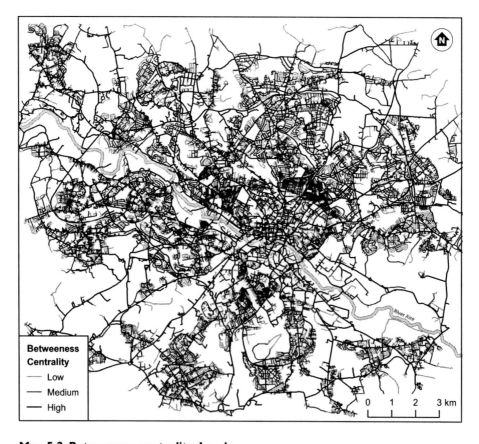

Map 5.2: Betweeness centrality: Leeds

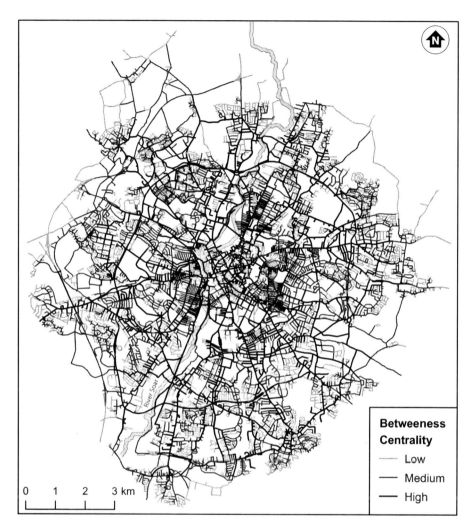

Map 5.3: Betweeness centrality: Leicester

centrality (betweeness, closeness and straightness) and frequency of walking and cycling. In other words, those households located along streets that are more 'plugged-in' to the city street network are more likely to walk and cycle more frequently.

It should be noted that the 'global' centrality measures are specific to each case study city street network and meaningful comparisons cannot be made between cities because the data are not normalised. However, it is reasonable to assume that if results for each measure within each individual city point in the same direction, then they corroborate each other and firm conclusions can be made about the strength and direction of the relationship between connectivity and walking and cycling behaviour (and similarly for 'local' measures). A summary

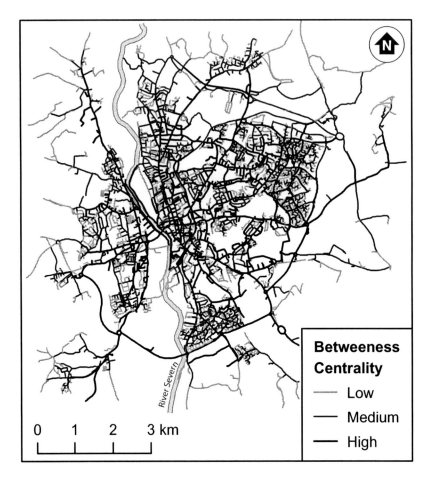

Map 5.4: Betweeness centrality: Worcester

of each of the variables included in the analysis and their definition is shown in Table 5.2. A total of 1,266 cases provided both travel and spatial data (Lancaster n=403; Leeds n=273; Leicester n=287; and Worcester n=303) and were included in the analysis to test associations between spatial measures and self-reported walking and cycling behaviour.

As we would anticipate, walking was more prevalent than cycling among the survey respondents. Around one half of the sample reported walking to undertake a specific non-work related journey during a typical week compared to approximately one quarter for cycling. Table 5.3 shows the mean frequency of non-work related walking and cycling journeys during a typical week that were reported across the entire sample. The overall mean number of reported journeys on foot was 2.7 compared to 0.9 by bike suggesting that walking is more prevalent than cycling by an order of three to one, but in Leeds the ratio was much higher with walking outnumbering cycling by approximately eight to one. The main purposes of non-work related walking trips across the cities

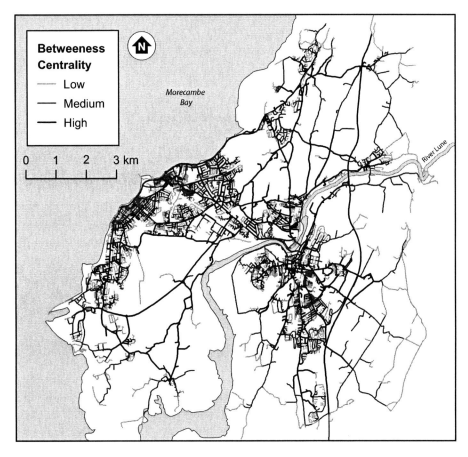

Map 5.5: Betweeness centrality: Lancaster

Table 5.2: Summary of variables measured within each buffer

Global measures of connectivity	
Closeness centrality (C^C_{GLOB})	Defined as the extent to which a node is near to all the other nodes along the shortest paths, or to put it another way, the shortest path length between two nodes throughout all possible paths.
Betweeness centrality (C^B_{GLOB})	Represents the average proportion of paths between two nodes that traverse the node in question. A node is central if it lies between many other nodes in the sense that it is traversed by many of the shortest paths connecting couples of nodes.
Straightness centrality (C^S_{GLOB})	Represents efficiency in communication between two nodes and is equal to the inverse of the shortest path length. Captures the extent to which the connecting route between nodes deviates from the virtual straight route.

(continued)

Table 5.2: Summary of variables measured within each buffer (continued)

Local measures of connectivity	
Street density	Total length of streets (edges) within the network buffer.
Street length (average)	The average length of street (edges) between two nodes within the network buffer.
Street density	Total length of streets (edges) within the network buffer.
Node density	The total number of intersections (nodes) within the network buffer.
Node degree (average)	The average number of streets (edges) per intersection (node) within the network buffer.

Local measures of land-use activity	
Land-use categories	Aggregated from Ordnance Survey Base Function categories in Address Layer 2 data. Ten classifications were derived: 1 Finance 2 Post office 3 Non-food retail 4 Food retail 5 Catering 6 Informal recreation 7 Formal recreation 8 Health 9 Education 10 General commercial
Activity number	The total number of land-use activities (indicated using the ten land-use activity categories) within the network buffer.
Activity diversity	The diversity of land-use activities (using the frequency of each of the ten land-use categories) within the network buffer and derived from the Shannon Entropy Index $H = \sum p_i \, log_2 \, (p_i)$ where p_i is the probability of the ith event

were: other shopping; visiting nearby friends and relatives; and personal business. For cycling the main purpose was visiting nearby friends or relatives (Table 5.4).

Maps 5.2 to 5.5 show betweeness centrality maps for Leeds, Leicester, Worcester and Lancaster District. It is noticeable that on each of the network maps arterial routes that are aligned like spokes in a wheel are mostly dark and are therefore among the most significant links in the network. This is because nodes along these routes are typically located between many other nodes, meaning that intersections along these links are more likely to be crossed when travelling between points across the entire city network. Conversely, those links in a lighter shade are less likely to be crossed when moving between points across the network. These are typically housing areas with fewer access points epitomised by circuitous layouts and culs-de-sac so common in 1960s/1970s suburban developments. Further analysis of the average street length (or 'block' being the distance between nodes or intersections) provides a very good descriptive indicator of street connectivity. Shorter street lengths between intersections generally provide a greater array of

Table 5.3: Reported mean number of non-work related walking and cycling journeys in a typical week

	N	Walking Mean (SD)	Cycling Mean (SD)
All	1266	2.7 (4.4)	0.9 (2.3)
Lancaster	403	2.5 (3.7)	0.8 (1.9)
Leeds	273	2.5 (4.1)	0.3 (1.5)
Leicester	287	2.6 (4.4)	1.0 (2.9)
Worcester	303	2.8 (5.2)	1.2 (2.4)

Note: National Travel Survey 2010 reports on average that a person makes four trips per week on foot and 0.4 trips per week by cycle for all journey purposes.

Table 5.4: Proportion of respondents who reported making at least one journey on foot or by bike across different journey purposes during a typical week

		Proportion (%) who reported walking for				
	n=	visiting nearby friends/relatives	leisure journeys	personal business	grocery shopping	other shopping
All	1266	39	32	39	33	41
Lancaster	403	36	38	45	31	46
Leeds	273	42	21	34	33	32
Leicester	287	39	28	37	31	45
Worcester	303	40	40	38	40	41
		Proportion (%) who reported cycling for				
	n=	visiting nearby friends/relatives	leisure journeys	personal business	grocery shopping	other shopping
All	1266	24	9	9	7	10
Lancaster	403	29	9	10	7	9
Leeds	273	5	4	3	3	3
Leicester	287	26	9	9	8	12
Worcester	303	34	12	11	10	14

route options. For Lancaster, the average street length on the north side of the river covering Morecambe and Heysham (93 m) is shorter than the south side (103 m). For Leicester, the average street length in the inner area is shorter (100 m) than the outer zone beyond the ring-road (108 m). For Worcester, street segments on the east side of the river are significantly shorter (average 90 m) compared to the west side (average 113 m). Leeds provides a more complex picture given the size of the conurbation and the less easily decipherable spatial configuration and therefore average street length has not been included here. In general, short streets in a grid layout have higher betweeness. Such streets can be clearly seen with darker shading on Maps 5.2–5.5, especially in areas of central Leeds and Leicester.

The core part of this analysis is our evaluation of the relationship between the measures of connectivity and land use and reported levels of walking and cycling. These are summarised in Tables 5.5–5.10. Although a great deal of work went into the calculation of these data, results can be reported quite briefly. Correlation analysis between local spatial indices estimated within an 800 m network buffer and reported frequency of walking trips for non-work related journeys shows that there is a positive correlation between local spatial measures and walking frequency for non-work related journeys, but that this relationship is weak (in the tables statistically significant associations are shown in bold). The prevalence of a range of potential activities and the actual street density within the 800 m network buffer are particularly associated with a higher frequency of walking, while the diversity of activities, node degree and node density provide a less conclusive relationship because there are not clear associations across all four cities (Table 5.5). Further analysis of the association between local land use activity and specific non-work related walking trip purposes again shows generally positive but weak correlations. The strongest association is between prevalence of activities in the local area and frequency of walking for personal business. Associations between street connectivity measures and walking for non-work related journey purposes are again weak (or there are no correlations) with the strongest association being street density (Table 5.6). Further analysis of the correlation between global spatial indices estimated within an 800 m network buffer and reported frequency of walking for non-work related purposes also indicates a positive but weak correlation between the majority of global spatial indices and frequency of non-work related walking for all of the cities apart from Leeds where no relationship was found between any of the measures (Table 5.7). In summary our analysis of walking shows that correlations between the frequency with which walking was recorded by respondents and the characteristics that we measured were positive but generally weak. This suggests that, at the local neighbourhood level, street density (the number of possible paths close to home) together with the number and diversity of local land uses, particularly those that can accommodate journeys for personal business, are most likely to encourage travel on foot. At the global (city) level those living nearest to the city centre are most likely to walk (as measured by the index of closeness).

Table 5.5: Association between local measures (800 metre network buffer) and reported walking trip frequency

| | Land-use activity | | Street connectivity | | | |
	Activity diversity	Activity number	Node density	Node degree (ave. metres)	Street density	Street length (ave. metres)
All	**0.10****	**0.19****	**0.09****	**0.07***	**0.14****	−0.05
Lancaster	0.02	**0.19****	0.09	**0.12***	**0.13***	−0.08
Leeds	0.03	**0.18****	0.09	**0.14***	**0.12***	−0.04
Leicester	**0.15***	**0.21****	**0.19****	0.06	**0.21****	−0.10
Worcester	**0.14***	**0.18****	0.07	0.05	**0.14***	0.04

Note: Significance level: *=p<.01; **=p<.001

Table 5.6: Association between reported frequency of walking by purpose and local spatial measures within 800 metre network buffer

	Land-use activity		Street connectivity			
	Activity diversity	**Activity number**	**Node density**	**Node degree (ave. metres)**	**Street density**	**Street length (ave. metres)**
Visiting friends and relatives	**0.08****	**0.06***	0.02	–0.02	0.03	–0.01
Leisure journeys	**0.06****	**0.11****	0.05	**0.08****	**0.09****	–0.02
Personal business	**0.07***	**0.21****	**0.18****	**0.12****	**0.20****	**–0.08****
Grocery shopping	**0.06****	**0.13****	0.05	0.01	**0.07****	–0.04
Other shopping	0.04	**0.13****	**0.06***	**0.10****	**0.11****	–0.18

Note: Significance level: *=p<.01; **=p<.001

Table 5.7: Association between global measures (within 800 metre network buffer) and reported walking trip frequency

	Sum betweeness	**Average betweeness**	**Sum closeness**	**Average closeness**	**Sum straight-ness**	**Average straight-ness**
Lancaster	**0.11***	0.03	**0.15****	**0.11***	**0.12***	**0.15****
Leeds	0.13	0.02	0.16	0.10	0.16	0.08
Leicester	**0.23****	**0.19****	**0.22****	**0.24****	**0.19****	0.04
Worcester	**0.15****	**0.11***	**0.12***	**0.13***	0.09	0.09

Note: Significance level: *=p<.01; **=p<.001

The procedure outlined above was also carried out to examine the association between spatial and land use measures and reported levels of cycling. Whereas for walking there were some statistically significant (but weak) associations, for cycling significant correlations were mostly absent. Analysis of the association between local spatial indices estimated within a 2,400 m network buffer and reported frequency of cycling for non-work related journeys shows that there is no correlation between any of the local spatial measures and cycling (Table 5.8). Further analysis of the association between land use activity and non-work related cycling for specific purposes again highlights that there are no significant correlations (other than between the number of activities present and personal business and grocery shopping, but these positive correlations are very weak), and this is also generally the case for street connectivity measures (Table 5.9). The

Table 5.8: Association between local measures (2,400 metre network buffer) and reported cycling trip frequency

	Land-use activity		Street connectivity			
	Activity diversity	**Activity number**	**Node density**	**Node degree (ave. metres)**	**Street density**	**Street length (ave. metres)**
All	0.01	0.03	−0.02	0.04	0.00	0.05
Lancaster	−0.08	0.08	0.05	−0.00	0.07	0.04
Leeds	0.01	0.08	0.04	0.01	0.03	−0.01
Leicester	0.05	−0.05	0.02	0.03	0.03	−0.04
Worcester	0.01	0.05	0.02	−0.01	0.02	−0.01

Note: Significance level: *=p<.01; **=p<.001

Table 5.9: Association between reported frequency of cycling by purpose and local spatial measures within 2,400 metre network buffer

	Land-use activity		Street connectivity			
	Activity diversity	**Activity number**	**Node density**	**Node degree (ave. metres)**	**Street density**	**Street length (ave. metres)**
Visiting friends and relatives	0.04	−0.03	−0.01	0.02	0.004	0.02
Leisure journeys	0.01	0.03	−0.01	0.01	0.01	0.04
Personal business	−0.02	**0.06***	−0.004	0.05	0.01	0.02
Grocery shopping	−0.04	**0.08****	0.004	0.02	0.01	0.01
Other shopping	−0.05	0.04	−0.05	0.03	−0.03	**0.08****

Note: Significance level: *=p<.01; **=p<.001

result of correlation analysis between global spatial indices estimated within a 2,400 m network buffer and reported frequency of cycling for non-work related journeys again shows that there is no correlation between any of the global spatial measures and cycling (Table 5.10). In summary our analysis of cycling shows that there is no evidence for any association between the frequency with which cycling journeys were recorded by respondents and the spatial characteristics that we measured. This suggests that factors over and above land use and built environment measures principally influence levels of cycling in the cities studied. Negative conclusions are always disappointing, but they need to be explained as much as positive results do. This is done in the following chapters using detailed qualitative evidence.

Table 5.10: Association between global measures (2,400 metre network buffer) and reported cycle trip frequency

	Sum betweeness	Average betweeness	Sum closeness	Average closeness	Sum straight-ness	Average straight-ness
Lancaster	0.08	0.06	0.06	0.06	0.03	−0.05
Leeds	0.03	−0.01	0.04	0.03	0.03	0.05
Leicester	0.03	0.02	0.03	0.03	0.03	0.06
Worcester	0.05	0.05	0.01	−0.04	0.02	−0.04

Note: Significance level: *=p<.01; **=p<.001

Conclusions and evaluation

Planners and researchers of the built environment place considerable emphasis on the contribution that urban form might make to influencing travel behaviour. This chapter has discussed conceptualisations of urban form and the move by policy makers in Europe towards policies that attempt to contain urban decentralisation and sprawl by channelling development to brown-field sites within existing urban areas. This 'new urbanist' approach aims to encourage people to live near to everyday services on the basis that it provides opportunities to replace car based travel with walking and cycling given that these methods are more sensitive to journey distance. As well as proximity to everyday activities the connectivity between homes and those activities is considered vitally important if walking and cycling are to be encouraged. Highly connected networks are assumed to have an important influence on walking and cycling because more permeable street patterns increase route options, reduce inconvenient deviations and facilitate more direct travel between destinations. Despite the assumptions made about the importance of connectivity and access to a range of activities, the paucity of research in this area was noted as well as the inconsistencies in measurement. However, the growing interest among public health researchers in the link between the built environment and physical activity (including so-called 'active travel') has increased the focus of investigation at the neighbourhood level. As a result, new methods of measuring aspects of urban form such as connectivity are emerging (Higgs et al, 2012; Chin et al, 2008; Dill, 2004). Still, challenges remain not only in measuring attributes of urban form, but also in attempting to link these measures to travel behaviour. Further studies are required that consider the European context because most studies to date have focused on new world examples.

The approach adopted in this study was novel in that it used multiple indicators at both the 'local' (neighbourhood) and 'global' (city) levels, and clearly defined line-based network buffers to test associations with self-reported walking and cycling behaviour. The results show that for all bar one (Leeds) of the case study cities included in the research there was a significant positive correlation between local and global spatial measures and walking but that this was generally weak. For cycling, no correlation was found between any of the local or global spatial measures. The findings from this element of the UWAC research suggest that the connectivity of the street network and the availability of everyday activities within walking and cycling distance of the home may have some influence on levels of active travel, but are insufficient on their own to encourage walking and particularly cycling. However, this does not suggest that they are of no consequence, but rather that they are not the dominant factors shaping everyday travel decisions at least within the case study areas investigated. The configuration of the built environment provides the foundations for walking and cycling to flourish, but as we reveal in subsequent chapters, other factors militate against their use for everyday travel.

It should be noted that there are compromises and limitations with any approach that seeks to measure accurately the urban environment: the UWAC study was not immune from these. For example, it was noted earlier that, despite best efforts, it was simply impractical to obtain the 'real' walking and cycling network which includes all informal links. Furthermore, the 'regulatory network' was not taken into account, such as one-way systems that prohibit vehicular movement and again affect the 'true' network, particularly for cycling. Finally, no account was taken of household transport availability or transport system characteristics, for example the level or quality of dedicated walking and cycling provision or the speed and volume of traffic on neighbouring roads. In summary, and contrary to some of the established literature, analysis of the built environment on its own is not a good indicator of levels of walking and cycling. In particular, it tells us very little about the process of everyday movement: how and why people make decisions about their travel in the context of real household and community constraints. The quantitative assessment of the walking and cycling network in each city did, however, form the basis for exploring and explaining travel characteristics using the qualitative techniques outlined in subsequent chapters. The power of this mixed-method approach is that it helps us to better understand why walking and (particularly) cycling fail to dominate, even in those areas that are better connected and have access to a range of everyday facilities.

SIX

What do people think about everyday travel in urban areas?

Introduction

Having examined the ways in which aspects of the built environment and land use influence everyday travel, especially the propensity to walk or cycle, we now explore in more detail the views that people have about walking and cycling for short trips in urban areas. The chapter draws, first, on the questionnaire data collected in a large sample survey from the case study towns and, second, from statistical analysis of the mass of qualitative evidence collected through interviews, go-alongs and ethnographic study. Details of how these data were collected, and some of their limitations, were given in Chapter Four and are not repeated here. Responses to both questionnaires and interviews about how people travel, and how they would like to travel, must be interpreted with caution. Some respondents may feel constrained to give answers that they feel are expected, or which show them in a good light, while others may simply feel that a question is irrelevant to them. However, responses gained from both the questionnaire and interview data collected in the UWAC project are broadly in line with other similar research data (for instance Mackett, 2003) and with results from the National Travel Survey (DfT, 2011a) thus increasing confidence in their credibility. In this short chapter the views of residents in our four case study towns are summarised to provide context for the detailed appraisal of experiences of walking and cycling provided in Chapters Seven and Eight.

What do people say about how they travel?

The questionnaires asked a wide range of questions about how people travel, the reasons why they do certain things, and their aspirations and thoughts for the future. Our survey shows that walking is an important mode of transport in all four case study communities. Because results are broadly similar in all locations studied data are presented only at an aggregate level for the whole sample. Of the respondents, 38% made journeys on foot on a daily basis and almost 90% at least once a week, though, what is important is that respondents reported an overall decline in their walking compared to the (unspecified) past (46% reported previously making daily journeys on foot and more than 90% at least once a week). Walking was a particularly important mode for social and leisure trips, personal business and local shopping, but rather less so for commuting (though perhaps this is not too surprising given the average commute distance of the sample is around

10 miles). Overall cycling was rather less important as a mode of transport: 6.8% said they made daily journeys on a bicycle, though 24.6% did so at least once per week. This is higher than usually found in similar surveys elsewhere and may suggest that our survey generated a stronger response from those that participated in cycling more often than is the norm in England (though we stressed that the survey was relevant to all regardless of whether they walked or cycled). Of the trip purposes asked about, cycling is least important for school trips, business and escorting family members.

Generally, most respondents found walking easy (72%), though rather fewer felt the same way about cycling (38.8%). Table 6.1 summarises some of the main reasons why people walked. As can be seen, health and fitness were consistently the most important reasons why people walked, though practicality, ease of access, environmental and financial reasons were also important. When asked why they cycled (Table 6.2), health and fitness was the key reason, though saving money also appeared important (and more so than for walking). Simply preferring walking or cycling compared to other methods of travel was important. The proportion of respondents stating that this was higher for cycling than for walking, suggests that those who do cycle have a very strong commitment to, and identity with, this mode of transport. Overall, however, the kinds of responses cited for using these two modes, and their relative importance, seemed remarkably similar. We also asked why people did not choose to walk or cycle (Tables 6.3 and 6.4). The weather appears to be the most important deterrent to walking for a lot of people, though other important reasons given were health, time constraints, distance and personal security. Some of these reasons may only relate to specific journeys rather than to all journeys on foot, for example rain may only be a deterrent when it is important that one arrives at a destination looking smart and ready for work.

Table 6.1: Reasons for walking (for those who offered one)*

First reason: top 5 (n=693)	Second reason: top 5 (n=643)	Third reason: top 5 (n=515)
Health, fitness (including children's) and wellbeing – 59.5%	Health, etc. – 27%	Health, etc. – 14%
Access local amenities/make short trips (including 'to reach a specified destination/for a specified journey') – 7%	Save money – 16%	Save money – 14%
Save money – 5.5%	Enjoyment/relaxation + Scenic/enjoy outdoors (rural/urban)/fresh air –11%	Enjoyment/relaxation + Scenic/enjoy outdoors (rural/urban)/fresh air – 15%
Enjoyment/relaxation + Scenic/enjoy outdoors (rural/urban)/fresh air – 5%	Environment – 9%	Environment – 10%
No perceived alternative – 4%	Access local amenities – 7%	Access local amenities – 8.5%

Note: *Respondents were asked to rank their reasons for walking for short everyday travel.

Table 6.2: Reasons for cycling (for those who offered one)*

First reason: top 5 (n=365)	Second reason: top 5 (n=343)	Third reason: top 5 (n=281)
Health, fitness (including children's) and wellbeing – 55.1%	Health, etc. – 27.7%	Health, etc. – 19.2%
Save money – 11.5%	Save money – 22.7%	Save money – 15.7%
Prefer the mode – 10.1%	Environment – 12.5%	Enjoyment/relaxation + Scenic/enjoy outdoors (rural/urban)/fresh air – 15.3%
Environment – 7.4%	Prefer the mode – 11.4%	Environment – 14.9%
Enjoyment/relaxation + Scenic/enjoy outdoors (rural/urban)/fresh air – 3.3%	Enjoyment/relaxation + Scenic/enjoy outdoors (rural/urban)/fresh air – 5.8%	Prefer the mode – 12.8%

Note: *Respondents were asked to rank their reasons for cycling for short everyday travel.

Table 6.3: Reasons for not walking (for those who offered one)*

First reason: top 5 (n=377)	Second reason: top 5 (n=263)	Third reason: top 5 (n=163)
(Bad) weather – 25%	(Bad) weather – 21%	Time constraints – 23%
Health & disability – 14%	Time constraints – 19%	(Bad) weather – 15%
Time constraints – 13%	Personal security concerns – 10%	Personal security concerns – 10%
Distance – 11%	Distance – 8%	Other alternative – 10%
Shopping to carry – 8.5%	Shopping to carry – 8%	Distance – 8%

Note: *Respondents were asked to rank their reasons for not walking for short everyday travel

Table 6.4: Reasons for not cycling (for those who offered one)*

First reason: top 5 (n=427)	Second reason: top 5 (n=332)	Third reason: top 5 (n=246)
Not safe – 28.6%	Not Safe – 20.8%	Not safe – 17.9%
No bicycle – 12.9%	Health and disability – 9.6%	(Bad) weather – 13.0%
(Bad) weather – 11.5%	(Bad) weather – 9.6%	No bicycle – 7.3%
Too old – 10.1%	Other alternative – 6.9%	Concerns over security of bicycle – 6.5%
Health and disability – 7.0%	Poor cycling infrastructure – 5.1%	Prefer alternative – 6.1%

Note: *Respondents were asked to rank their reasons for not cycling for short everyday travel.

Although bad weather was an important deterrent to cycling, the most important reason for not cycling was that people felt it was not safe to do so. This is not something that was highlighted to the same extent with respect to walking. There also appears to be a sense for some people that you reach an age where you are too old for cycling, which is also not apparent for walking.

There is evidence from the data that at least sometimes people are influenced in their mode choice by others with whom they travel and by the views of those who are significant to them (Table 6.5). For both walking and cycling, needing to give a lift to, or otherwise to care for older people, children or others can be a reason for not walking or cycling because this adds to the complexity or difficulty of the journey. However, needing to care or provide for another person does not necessarily prevent walking. For children there was evidence that, provided the distances are not too great for the child to walk, this is still possible: indeed, in many cases the child can provide the stimulus for the walk in the first place in that it provides an opportunity to play out of doors (83% indicated that they sometimes make a journey on foot specifically to take a child for a walk).

We examined correlations between a number of key descriptors of walking and the background variables of gender, age and car ownership. Table 6.6 shows the cases where a statistically significant relationship (at the 0.1 level of confidence) was apparent for at least one variable. There is no significant relationship between current and past walking behaviour and either gender or age, though perhaps not surprisingly past walking behaviour is highly positively correlated with current walking behaviour. Car/van ownership is correlated with lower levels of walking (past and current) – as car ownership increases levels of walking decline. Females are significantly less associated with trips by bicycle than males, both for past and current trips. Older age groups make fewer current bicycle trips, though no such relationship is apparent for past bicycle trips, and having made lots of trips by bicycle in the past is significantly positively correlated with current bicycle trips.

In terms of the influence of others on making walking and cycling trips, for both modes females are more likely to be influenced by perceived fear of attack. Perhaps surprisingly there is no link for either mode between gender and risk of a road accident. Age is positively linked to the perceived risk of attack for both modes, and for cycling with the risk of a road accident. Higher car ownership is linked to others influencing trips on foot due to the perceived risk of attack. There was also a strong correlation between influence on trips due to risk of a

Table 6.5: Effect of significant others on journey patterns on foot and by bicycle

Those reporting that they are often or sometimes unable to make journeys because....	Walking (%)	Cycling (%)
they need to give a lift to an older person	29	38
they need to give a lift to a child	41	53
they need to give a lift to someone else they care for	36	49

Table 6.6: Correlations between various travel characteristics and gender, age and car/van ownership

	Gender	Age	Car/van ownership
Journeys			
Walk in the past	Not sig	Not sig	Fewer cars more likely
Bicycle in the past	Females less likely	Not sig	Not sig
Walk now	Not sig	Not sig	Fewer cars more likely
Bicycle now	Females less likely	Young more likely	Not sig
Influence of significant others restricts modal choice			
Due to perceived risk of road accident on foot	Not sig	Not sig	Not sig
Due to perceived risk of road accident cycling	Not sig	Older more likely	Not sig
Due to perceived risk of attack on foot	Females more likely	Older more likely	More cars more likely
Due to perceived risk of attack cycling	Females more likely	Older more likely	Not sig
Views on walking and cycling			
Walking is important	Not sig	Not sig	Fewer cars more important
Confident I can make walk journeys	Males more confident	Young more confident	Not sig
Up to me if I make walk journeys	Not sig	Not sig	Not sig
Cycling is easy	Males find easier	Young find easier	Not sig
Hilliness where I live	Not sig	Older more of an issue	More cars more of an issue

road accident and risk of an attack. There is a significant and slightly negative correlation between the perceived importance of walking and car ownership; however there are significant positive correlations between perceived importance of walking and confidence in making journeys on foot, and with autonomy in making journeys on foot. Confidence in making journeys on foot is more apparent in males and negatively correlated with age. Confidence in making journeys on foot is positively correlated with autonomy in making journeys on foot. For cycling, females found it less easy than males to make bicycle trips and as age increased people found it more difficult to make journeys by bicycle. Households with more cars tended to think it was hillier where they live as do people who think it is more difficult to make journeys by bicycle. All this suggests that views on walking and cycling are formed quite early in life; that they vary with gender, age, household structure and car ownership; and that they can be strongly influenced by the views of significant others.

What do people say about how they would like to travel?

We asked people a series of questions about how they might feel about undertaking walking and cycling journeys at some point in the future. For walking there was generally a strong sense that such travel is enjoyable (85% agree or strongly agree) and it makes people feel good about themselves (81%). There was almost no sense that others would feel sorry for them for making such choices (5.5%) and no sense that walking was low status (4.5%). Most notably very large proportions of people agreed that walking would provide time and space to think (82%) and would be beneficial to health (96%). There was also a sense that walking provided some sense of control in terms of travel: it was relatively easy to judge how long a trip might take, there was a high degree of reliability in the estimates, and one had choice of when to travel. There were, however, some worries about risk of accidents at night (17.4% agreeing or strongly agreeing that this was an issue), though very little concern during daylight hours (4.5%). On the positive side people generally felt that there would be environmental benefits from choosing to walk, both in terms of climate change (75%) and in terms of local air pollution (81%).

Cycling also scored relatively highly in terms of enjoyment (65.8% agreeing). It also made people feel good about themselves (73.9%) and provided a sense of freedom (62.0%). Again there was no sense that others would think badly of a person for cycling. Like walking, health reasons scored very highly (89.9%), though space to think was less important. Not surprisingly there were fears about risk of accidents (39.8% agreeing or strongly agreeing it was an issue in daylight and 57.7% in darkness) and that wearing a helmet (73.5%) and safety related clothing was important (75.3%). As was the case for walking, there was the sense that cycling potentially contributes to environmental improvements (75.4% felt it would reduce their impact on climate change and 83.7% felt it would reduce their impact on local air pollution). There was also a sense that it provided a degree of control over journeys in terms of reliability (43.2%). On the negative side carrying things is perceived to be problematic (71.8%) and relatively large numbers feel that they will face bad experiences using cycling infrastructure (32.7%) and roads (58.0%).

We also examined intentions for the future among our respondents. Future intentions to undertake local walking are high for almost all our respondents: only around 5% envisaged that they would not and almost 80% thought that they would walk frequently in the future. Specifically, 88% intended to make at least one walking journey a week in the future. For cycling the picture is somewhat different: 46.2% intended to make a journey by bike in the future, while 37.6% felt that they might do this at least once per week. We undertook a range of correlation analyses between some of these features of future walking and the background variables of gender, age and car/van ownership. Key findings (significant at the 0.01 level of confidence) are shown in Tables 6.7 and 6.8 for walking and cycling respectively. Many of the relationships found in these tables are, perhaps, to be expected. There is clearly a strong association between danger

Table 6.7: Relationships between likelihood of walking and gender, age and car/van ownership

If I make or were to make journeys on foot ...	Gender	Age	Car ownership
I would find walking enjoyable	Not sig	Older more likely	Not sig
(When it is daylight) I would be afraid of being attacked	Female more likely	Not sig	More cars more likely
(When it is dark) I would be afraid of being attacked	Female more likely	Not sig	More cars more likely
(When it is daylight) I would be afraid of being involved in an accident	Not sig	Not sig	More cars more likely
(When it is dark) I would be afraid of being involved in an accident	Female more likely	Not sig	More cars more likely
It would provide me with space and time to think	Female more likely	Young more likely	Not sig
Benefit my health	Female more likely	Young more likely	Not sig
Be too far to walk to the places I usually travel to	Not sig	Not sig	More cars more likely
Save me money	Not sig	Older more likely	Not sig
Be a bad experience using the existing footpaths	Female more likely	Not sig	More cars more likely
Mean I contribute less to climate change	Not sig	Young more likely	Not sig
Be too much physical effort	Not sig	Older more likely	Not sig
More than likely expose me to wet or windy weather	Female more likely	Young more likely	Not sig
Increase my exposure to air pollution	Female more likely	Not sig	Not sig
Allow me to choose when I travel	Not sig	Not sig	More cars less likely
Give me a number of choices over which routes I take	Not sig	Not sig	More cars less likely
Mean I contribute less to local air pollution	Not sig	Young more likely	Not sig
Take me too long to get to the places I usually travel to	Not sig	Not sig	More cars more likely
Be difficult to carry the things I often have to carry	Females more likely	Not sig	Not sig
Be convenient for me	Not sig	Not sig	More cars less likely
Be safe when crossing the road	Not sig	Young more likely	Not sig

Table 6.8: Relationships between likelihood of cycling and gender, age and car/van ownership

If I make or were to make journeys on bicycle ...	Gender	Age	Car ownership
I would find cycling enjoyable	Not sig	Older more likely	Not sig
(When it is daylight) I would be afraid of being attacked	Female more likely	Not sig	Not sig
(When it is dark) I would be afraid of being attacked	Female more likely	Not sig	Not sig
(When it is daylight) I would be afraid of being involved in an accident	Female more likely	Not sig	Not sig
(When it is dark) I would be afraid of being involved in an accident	Female more likely	Not sig	Not sig
It would provide me with space and time to think	Not sig	Older more likely	Not sig
Other people would think I am poor	Not sig	Older more likely	Not sig
I would feel part of my community	Not sig	Young more likely	Not sig
Wearing a helmet would be important from a safety perspective	Female more likely	Not sig	Not sig
Wearing a helmet would make me feel silly	Not sig	Older more likely	Not sig
Wearing a helmet would mean I have a bad hair day	Female more likely	Older more likely	Not sig
Wearing high visibility clothing for safety is important	Not sig	Young more likely	Not sig
Wearing high visibility clothing make me feel silly	Not sig	Older more likely	Not sig
Benefit my health	Not sig	Older more likely	Not sig
Save money	Not sig	Older more likely	Not sig
Be too much physical effort	Not sig	Young more likely	Not sig
Increase my exposure to air pollution	Not sig	Young more likely	Not sig
Be a sociable means of getting around	Not sig	Young more likely	Not sig

in its various guises, and gender, and to some extent an association of feeling that walking is not practicable or is less controllable with car ownership. The young appear more aware or worried about environment and health from a walking perspective, though actually (as Table 6.8 shows) less so from a cycling perspective. The older seem more aware of their physical limitations. For cycling, many of the relationships show a similarity to walking, for example in terms of the link between risk and gender, but some things are different: the older participants seem more aware of image while car ownership seems to have very little influence on the findings.

How do people feel and relate to travel?

The analysis using Q methodology took a pool of statements representing different opinions about walking and cycling generated from the interviews and applied statistical analysis (briefly outlined in Chapter Four) to summarise respondents' views of walking and cycling. These data add depth to the findings outlined above. Three distinct discourses on walking and cycling in English cities were identified and labelled 'cycling sanctifiers'; 'pedestrian prioritisers'; and 'automobile adherents'. Together, these summarised 42% of variance in the data set. Key characteristics are given below and full details can be found in Jones et al (2012).

Cycling sanctifiers (17% of total variance)

This discourse represents a strong moral pro-cycling stance. Cycling is seen as providing ultimate freedom and more convenient door-to-door access to activities than by car when moving around the city. That the car provides the best option for moving around the city compared to other alternatives is not accepted. Cycling is routinely practiced and is preferable to walking because of the extended distance it can cover over the same journey time. It is not regarded as a particularly stressful way of moving around the city despite the interactions with motor traffic. In fact, in comparison with driving, cycling (and even walking and public transport) is valued precisely because of the opportunities it provides for interaction with the environment. People who subscribe to this discourse are confident riders and tend not to be self-conscious or too concerned over public opinion about the image of cycling and the more negative connotations often associated with its practice. Interacting with and overtaking other cyclists when driving a car is not regarded as problematic, and there is the view that cyclists should not necessarily have to move out of the way of cars and stick to cycle lanes if they are available. Cyclists are regarded as legitimate roads users who have a fundamental right to use the road. The proposition that they should be removed and put on separate cycle tracks is strongly rejected.

Pedestrian prioritisers (16% of total variance)

This discourse reflects the very positive and 'normal' image assigned to walking as a means of travel to get from place to place, and the desire to see more priority given to people moving on foot in cities as opposed to travelling by car. Walking is regarded as an important practice for accomplishing everyday activities, including food shopping. Travelling by car to bulk buy goods at supermarkets is not regarded as an absolute necessity and there is little support for stores that purposely locate to the edge of town in order to provide easier access by car. Walking (and, in some cases, cycling) is the default option for short journeys and is preferred to going by car even if weather conditions are poor. Government investment targeted at non-car modes is regarded as fundamental in getting more people to reduce their car use and to walk and cycle more. However, there is also a desire to see more restrictions placed on driving in the city, including speed reduction to improve safety and conditions for walking and cycling. This does not necessarily mean that pedestrian prioritisers are car averse: this discourse arises from people who are mostly car owners themselves. Rather, there is a view that the car is problematic in terms of what it has come to symbolise and the corrupting influence on its users, as reflected in driver aggression and impatient behaviour when moving by car through city streets. One example of this is annoyance with people who park their cars on pavements obstructing passage by pedestrians. There is scepticism over the proposition that people have choice of how to travel around, and this is perhaps reflected in the strong view that cyclists should be provided with separated cycle tracks. This may not necessarily mean that there is a personal desire to cycle (or cycle more) were separated tracks to be put in place, but may be related to the perception that both cyclists and pedestrians would fare better in less stressful environments away from cars and each other. Moreover, while pavement cycling appears to be tolerated rather than condoned, separated cycle tracks are perhaps seen as one way of creating an environment where cyclists would not feel the need to utilise the pavement, thus improving the quality of the walking environment.

Automobile adherents (9% of total variance)

The key feature of this discourse is support for the status quo and the present car system in facilitating everyday activities. The discourse is underpinned by the belief that people have a choice of how to travel around and it is up to them to exercise this choice. The car is seen in a positive light and the negative symbolism within the pedestrian prioritiser discourse is strongly repudiated. The car is regarded as a necessary tool for activities such as food shopping. Car-based bulk buying at supermarkets is agreeable and the location of supermarkets in out-of-town centres is appreciated and supported for the perceived ease and convenience that they provide for car users. Driving in the city is regarded as a positive experience and certainly preferable to being out walking or cycling, particularly if it is raining. Using the car for short journeys is seen as justifiable and there is no feeling of guilt or regret when choosing to use the car instead of other means of travel. Such are the demands of modern life that conducting daily activities on foot or by cycle is simply regarded as not an option. Walking is seen largely as a pleasurable recreational activity, and certainly not as a means of conducting day-to-day personal business; while cycling is viewed as fashionable because of environmental issues and practised by committed environmentalists or enthusiasts. There appears to be no potential for cycling to play a personal role as a means of everyday transport because of concerns about public opinion and some of the negative identities associated with its practice. Moreover, cycling is perceived to lack the freedom offered by moving around the city by car. There is strong disagreement with the proposition that traffic should be slowed right down to improve safety and conditions for pedestrians and cyclists. Furthermore, there is little sympathy for those who cycle on the pavement even if they do so for their own safety, or indeed for the proposition that pedestrians should be given priority over cars in towns and cities.

Conclusions

The data from the questionnaire surveys provide a wealth of information about walking and cycling, motivations for travel and the extent to which people are willing and able to make shifts in their travel behaviour. Due to limitations of space, the results presented here touch on only a small part of the data available. However, it is clear from the data that most respondents are likely to undertake more journeys on foot than by bicycle, and that motivations for more sustainable travel are more likely to be linked to concerns about personal health and wellbeing than consideration of global environmental issues. There is a strong relationship between past behaviours in relation to both walking and cycling and current likelihood of selecting those modes or looking positively on them. There are important variations between different age groups and between men and women in the ways that travel on foot or by bike is perceived, the levels of confidence that individuals feel for the modes and the perceived constraints placed upon them by the views of significant other people in their lives. There is a strong negative correlation between car ownership (and presumably regular use) and the likelihood of walking and cycling. For cycling, experience of what cycling is really like and the reality of hills and other perceived barriers tends to increase the likelihood of use. The views on walking as a future mode (and to a lesser extent cycling) are generally positive, and the results give some clues as to how use (and enjoyment of) these modes might be increased. Perhaps the strongest of these is the importance of creating a safe environment for cycling before significant numbers of people will consider venturing onto the roads.

Q methodology was useful in unearthing the discourses within a large source of qualitative data. The three discourses that emerged might suggest that participants simply align around favoured modes of urban travel, but on closer inspection the picture is actually more complex. The analysis suggests that it is not just a question of individual traits that determine membership of a particular discourse, as each cut across gender, age, car ownership, and home location. Although pedestrian prioritisers have some problems with car use and how cars are symbolised, what is interesting is that participants who contributed to this discourse are largely car owners themselves. Pedestrian prioritisers were more inclined to desire change to the current transport system relative to cycling sanctifiers and automobile adherents who would appear, to a greater or lesser degree, more satisfied with the status quo. Both of the latter two discourses seek to maintain their right to perform their mobility under current circumstances and are not seeking changes to how their mobility is currently practiced. Pedestrian prioritisers, on the other hand, clearly desire change in the form of restrictions on motoring and a different approach to catering for cycling on the highway. It is also significant that 58% of variance in the dataset remains unexplained. This suggests that many people are not highly committed to any one form of everyday transport and that the picture is somewhat more complex. The factors influencing such views are explored in more detail in Chapters Seven and Eight using a wide range of qualitative evidence.

SEVEN

The place of walking in the urban environment

Why people walk

As shown in Chapter Six, respondents to the questionnaire survey tend to associate walking with enjoyment and this is a view replicated in many of the interviews undertaken during the qualitative phase of the research. However, although respondents frequently expressed positive views about walking, implying that they walk because they like to do so, in most cases walking is conditional. It occurs at certain times, in particular places and for specific reasons. Clearly walking is only practicable for relatively short trips, but even the most enthusiastic pedestrians set limits that are not purely related to the distance travelled. In this section we explore the reasons that respondents give for walking and the situations in which they find it a positive experience. The times and places where people do not commonly walk are then examined in later sections of the chapter. Most frequently walking is associated with general feelings of wellbeing: it gives time and space to think, to clear the head, and to relax after a day's work (Box 7.1). These views were expressed by respondents in all four towns. Some respondents compared walking to driving, which they found less relaxing and more stressful, and several respondents placed particular emphasis on engagement with the environment; for example Holly who deliberately extends her walk because of enjoyment of the experience. One factor that is implicit in many statements, and is made explicit by Molly, is the issue of control: she feels that walking provides her with independence and freedom. The concept of 'locus of control' is central to much research in social psychology and related areas (Lefcourt, 1976; Ajzen, 2002; Chen and Wang, 2007), arguing that people establish stronger feelings of wellbeing and satisfaction when they perceive themselves to be in control of a situation. This is most often applied in contexts such as the workplace or healthcare, but is just as relevant to everyday travel. As argued in Chapter Two, the ability to take control of one's everyday mobility was an important component of the popularity of the bicycle in the 1940s and 1950s, and also of the motor car from the 1960s. When walking is perceived as offering the same advantages it can become a powerful reason for using this means of travelling.

Enjoyment of walking is also enhanced for many respondents by their ability to engage directly with what they view as an interesting and stimulating environment (Box 7.2). For instance, Rebecca and Max explained how during their journeys they might take the opportunity to explore parts of the city of Leicester with which they were not familiar, thus enhancing their enjoyment of the walk. While

Box 7.1: The enjoyment of walking*

I think the walking beats everything. And actually if I ever do get a little bit of time I really enjoy walking. (Percy, Worcester, go-along)

I enjoy walking, I do enjoy getting out in the fresh air and to get some exercise after I have been inside at work all day. It's a long time to be indoors. (Steve, Leeds, ethno)

To go into town I take the bus and I usually walk back. 'Cause when I go to town I have a purpose, but I walk back, 'cause it's nice to have that stroll just walking back home and you know once you get home you are just going to sit down and relax. (Anju and Pooja, Leicester, ethno)

I like to walk a lot, so I have a car but I very rarely use it…Car is not my first choice, I would sooner walk or else get the bus, but sometimes I can't be bothered to wait five or ten minutes for the bus so I'll walk. (Bill and Dee, Lancaster, interview)

Walking through an area gives you a better insight than driving. I quite like walking, particularly going through town there are places you see that you don't on a normal drive. It's more interesting walking than driving. (Vince, Leeds, interview)

I just like the scenery and walking, it just relaxes me, it gives me time to think and I'm getting exercise at the same time. (Dan and Catrina, Lancaster, interview)

Sometimes I will elongate my walking route just for the pleasure of it…I find walking more enjoyable than driving, I enjoy walking. (Holly, Lancaster, interview)

I feel better when I've had a walk…People who walk consistently start to feel deprived if they can't walk. (Moses and Lisa, Worcester, interview)

I'd much rather walk anywhere than getting in the car. (Matt, Leicester, interview)

Walking is calming, it allows you to think through problems, clear your mind. (Pierce, Leicester, interview)

Walking gives me full control over movements. In a way I can control everything. You don't rely on anybody, you only rely on yourself…I like to think through the day, talking to myself and planning for the next day, it's a thinking and planning activity. Very relaxing, wind away all the stress and pressures of the day. (Molly, Leicester, interview)

Note: *In all text boxes names are pseudonyms and locational details have been removed to preserve anonymity; 'interview' refers to a static interview (usually in the home but sometimes in a public space) with an individual or group; 'go-along' refers to an interview carried out while travelling with the respondent(s); 'ethno' refers to material recorded during an intervention made during the in-depth ethnographic study. Interviews and go-alongs are recorded for people who live anywhere in the built-up area of the four towns studied but ethnographic data relates only to the specific locality studied in depth (described in Chapter 4).

such enjoyment may be stimulated or increased by a particularly 'imageable' urban environment (one that creates a particularly strong image for the observer (Lynch, 1960; Appleyard et al, 1981)), the implication is that any environment will provide opportunities for stimulation and exploration. However, leisurely walking with time to explore and enjoy the environment is not something that can easily be built into the busy everyday routines of most people (though some do manage to do so), and thus walking is often seen as an activity that is enjoyable but is practised at weekends, on holiday and in other situations when time is not pressing (Box 7.3). This can lead to apparently contradictory views, as expressed by Matt who states that he would rather walk than drive (Box 7.1), but then also says that if he goes for a walk this generally first entails a drive into the countryside (Box 7.3). In such situations, where the enjoyment of walking is linked to specific environments that are perceived to be more attractive than those in which one lives, motivations for walking can also lead to increased levels of driving.

Box 7.2: Exploring the environment through walking

If there is anything potentially interesting to have a look at, that gives me a target for a walk. (Oscar, Leicester, interview)

I really like this bit of my walk, by the river, hearing the birds. (Harriet, Lancaster, ethno)

I tend to vary my walking route, I like to go a different way each time, sometimes I'll go a heck of a way round, just because it's a nice day and I've got the time. (Kirsty, Lancaster, interview)

If you were walking you can stop and have a look at something nice and interesting, like if you saw a nice flower you could just smell it, but in the car you just drive past, you don't even get a good look at it. (Liam and family, Worcester, interview)

If you walk or take a bus or train or tram you can actually see more of your environment, so it makes it more interesting…you look at buildings and see things about the history of a place which you can't do if you are driving…I like exploring as well so for instance if I walk by the street and I happen to spot an interesting looking alleyway and I've got time I just think, 'Oh, I'll just go and see where that leads' and then find an alternative way round to get to the destination [meeting]…We all feel quite resentful about going to work and try and make it a bit better if we can so that's one way of making it a bit better. (Rebecca and Max, Leicester, interview)

Box 7.3: Walking for leisure

I like walking out in the Dales and on the moors and out in the fresh air in general. (Jan, Leeds, interview)

I like going for walks, at weekends I do longer walks...I love walking around here, two minutes and I'm in the countryside and I like rolling hills. (Nancy, Leeds, interview)

On my holidays I quite enjoy doing a bit of walking. (Oscar, Leicester, interview)

I would build walking into a holiday. (Katie, Leeds, interview)

We tend to do a lot of our walking when we're away on holiday. (Jack and Deidre, Leeds, interview)

I don't seem to be able to marry walking and business, I just want to walk for pleasure. I don't want to walk when I have to do something when I get there. (Deborah, Lancaster, ethno)

We own a car because there are certain things you can only do in a car, to go walking in the countryside, our weekly shopping trip, to take my mother out. (Audrey, Lancaster, interview)

Generally, if we go for a walk, it's a drive first and then a walk from there. (Matt, Leicester, interview)

Although many respondents did express their enjoyment of walking, for some this was combined with issues of necessity and convenience. A common theme was that, given the alternatives available, walking was the only sensible way of undertaking a particular journey. This could be due to financial constraints (walking is cheap), the lack of an alternative, or to high levels of congestion that made travel by car or bus slow and inconvenient. In some cases such journeys were also associated with enjoyment (though the extent to which this a rationalisation of an unavoidable situation is hard to assess), but in others there is evidence that given different conditions then an alternative form of transport would be chosen (Boxes 7.4 and 7.5). Relatively few respondents seemed totally constrained by finances, but many chose to save money by walking to allow them to spend on other things. It is also likely that respondents were unwilling to admit to poverty and thus found other ways (such as convenience) to explain their dependence on walking. Lack of income as a constraint was most obvious in the ethnographic study area in Leeds, where many of the people we spoke to were struggling to survive on very little. However, this housing estate was situated so close to most services in central Leeds that it was just as logical to cite convenience as a reason for walking.

Box 7.4: Walking for financial reasons

We've always had a walk, walk always in our lives. Not much money when we were young, periods without a car. (Wanda, Lancaster, interview)

If I need to go to town, to avoid parking charges, I usually park in residential streets/ free car parking and walk in. (Jen, Worcester, interview)

We're pretty environmentally friendly, I suppose it's the price of petrol. (Andy, Worcester, go-along)

I still keep walking just because, well, to get the bus it's, like, £1.90...I can't afford it. (Steve, Leeds, ethno)

I try and walk wherever I go and I think that's more of a monetary thing, trying to save on the expenditure of getting a taxi or whatever it might be...I save a lot of money by walking places and plus it's an exercise thing really. (Tim, Leicester, go-along)

If it's going to cost you at least £1.10 each time it's [catching the bus] a bit silly when you can go direct on foot. (Oscar, Leicester, interview)

I'd rather walk than spend money on the bus. (Ben, Worcester, interview)

Box 7.5: Walking for convenience

I walk to work and back. I don't own a car and I don't have a bike, wouldn't be worth it for the distance. I might get one, but with the flat it would need to be a folding bike. Did have a bike, but it got nicked, I would need to keep it inside. (Oscar, Leicester, interview)

The shopping centre is just a five minute walk so you may as well walk and there's no stress with the parking. (Jackie, Leicester, interview)

There are a lot of journeys that are just not worth getting the bike out for 'cause by the time you've got the bike out you'd have walked it. (Liam and family, Worcester, interview)

It just seemed ridiculous getting the car out just to go a mile and a half/two miles down the road. (Sally, Worcester, interview)

By the time you go into town in the car, got there, parked the car, paid to park it or whatever, you pretty much could have walked it into town. (Moses and Lisa, Worcester, interview)

These days because if we go to town we would either walk, depending on time or we would drive part way, park and then walk in. (Bea, Worcester, interview)

I prefer to walk, from work to home rather than home to work. (Kapil, Leicester, go-along)

Walking is convenient because the buses don't always run on time. (Raj, Leicester, ethno)

When the bus is completely packed, I'll walk. (Anju and Pooja, Leicester, ethno)

I would always choose to walk simply because I would spend that amount of time in traffic so I might as well be out making the journey and feeling like I'm accomplishing something rather than sitting there getting wound up in a car. (Tim, Leicester, go-along)

If I took the bus it's 20 minutes and if I walk it will be 20 minutes. They're about the same because if I took a bus you have to wait for the bus and if you're just walking, just continue walking without any stopping. (Kev, Leeds, ethno)

If financial constraints were a secondary factor for most people, many more chose walking for at least some short journeys because it was the obvious way to travel (Box 7.5). Any other means of travel was perceived as less convenient. Key factors were distance, speed and comfort. Many people who lived close to their place of work, or near to services that they used regularly, saw no point in using the car. The combination of getting a car out of the garage, driving and parking would both take longer than walking and be substantially more expensive. If public transport was perceived to be slow, crowded or unreliable it was also sometimes shunned in favour of walking. These views were expressed most commonly by respondents in Worcester. This probably reflects both a relatively compact urban area and high levels of traffic congestion, especially across the main river crossing, but similar views were expressed to some degree in all four cities. The convenience of walking also becomes entwined with other factors that operate both as attractions and constraints. For instance, Kapil makes a distinction between the journey to and from work. While he finds walking home when he has more time and can relax when he gets home attractive, he prefers not to walk on the journey to work which is constrained by the need to arrive on time and in a state to immediately start work. Other research has shown similar distinctions in children's journeys to and from school (Walker et al, 2009), and emphasises the degree to which the enjoyment and convenience of walking may be contingent on other factors. Oscar, in Leicester, highlights another issue. He favours walking over cycling in part because he has no space in his flat to store a bike. He gives the impression that the greater speed that a bike provides could be attractive (and he used to have one but it was stolen) but at present the problems of storage and security mean that for him walking is the more attractive and convenient option. Tim also gives another example of the importance of being in control of a journey: instead of being stuck in a traffic jam he would rather be walking because it gives him a sense of accomplishing something.

Thus in many of these instances while respondents did express some enjoyment of, and satisfaction with, walking as a form of transport for short trips in urban areas, they did so in the context of a number of constraining factors (finance, convenience, lack of alternatives) that made walking the obvious choice at that point in time. However, one implication is that if circumstances were different then routines might change and car use could increase. This was, perhaps, expressed most strongly (and almost paradoxically) by Jim in Lancaster who while on the one hand espousing environmental values, claiming to be a 'deep ecologist and environmentalist,' also admitted that he did at times find not owning a car inconvenient (especially for access to the countryside) and that if he had more money he would probably own a car (though not necessarily use it for short trips in urban areas):

> I don't have a car. Which is partly on grounds of not really wanting to pollute the environment but also probably quite largely because I don't have the money to run one. If I was earning £100,000 a year I'd probably have a car. I'm not priding myself on it, I have a 50/50 on it. So I walk; nearly always I walk and I don't go very far. I have a sort of radius of about a mile and I virtually never go past the roundabout to the university and I virtually never go over the river…The thing where I really miss having a car is there is such beautiful countryside around here, and the best thing about living in Lancaster is the countryside, but to get out there, to start on a walk, it takes a while to get there when you don't have a car. (Jim, Lancaster, interview)

This suggests that while walking is attractive to many people, it is often only the case under certain circumstances, and that the flexibility offered by the car is more appealing when this becomes either affordable or more convenient and apparently sensible to use.

As well as certain environments being attractive for walking and others repelling (see below), some people choose to create their own environments. In other words they make lifestyle choices that reflect their views on environmental or social issues and, in doing so, have been able to and have deliberately made sustainable forms of travel easy. Our sample of respondents included some who had indeed adopted this approach to urban living. Their choice of where to live had been determined largely by access to a combination of their place of work and the services or facilities they used regularly in such a way that they could dispense with a car for most, if not all, purposes. They depended on walking (or cycling) for everyday travel and used public transport for longer journeys (Box 7.6). Interestingly, such views were most often expressed by respondents in Worcester and Lancaster who had chosen to live within walking distance of the historic town centres, though people with such views were a small minority in all cities studied.

However, for respondents such as Polly or Liam (and family) accommodation close to the centre of town offered an attractive option and they deliberately rejected suburban living which was the norm for most Worcester residents (including those in the locality selected for ethnographic study). As demonstrated from the questionnaire survey (Chapter Six) environmental considerations were not a high priority for most respondents when it came to considering travelling on foot (or by bike), and when environmental considerations were identified they mostly related to the local neighbourhood rather than to more global issues.

Box 7.6: Choosing a walking lifestyle

I don't want to pollute the environment any more than I absolutely have to. (Kapil, Leicester, go-along)

I walk everywhere 'cause I live in the city centre and everything is very central so all the shops, the restaurants, shopping – everything is walking. I don't have to rely on public transport or cars or anything…Every time I've looked for work I made sure I wouldn't have to rely on transport too much. (Anju and Pooja, Leicester, interview)

If it is a two-mile radius I'll pretty well walk everywhere. I walk to all the shops. (Bob, Leeds, interview)

Home location choice is crucial with respect to walking. (Abigail, Lancaster, go-along)

We just sort of decided that to be in a city, 'cause one of the things we wanted to do was to reduce our car use and being in the city was the logical extension of that actually…We were very definite we didn't want to move to a suburb of Worcester because we wanted to reduce our car use and we also wanted to be within walking distance of my work. (Liam and family, Worcester, interview)

We took all that [ease of getting to local shops and the town centre] into consideration, before we actually accepted the flat and did our own researches to what was in the area and whether we'd be accepted at the local surgery and dentist…Everything's within walking distance which is brilliant. (Polly, Worcester, go-along)

We chose to live in this area because it is within walking distance into town, but far enough out not to be bothered by, you know, the busyness of town itself. (Don, Worcester, interview)

One of the reasons we came here was specifically looking towards our old age. And knowing that everything that we would ever be likely to need is on the doorstep. (Moses and Lisa, Worcester, interview)

Building walking and other forms of active travel into everyday life was also done for health reasons, with personal health and sustainable living often being seen as twin goals of urban living. While some respondents took pride in their fitness and their ability to walk quite long distances, others were restricted by their lack of fitness but often recognised that more active travel would be good for them (Box 7.7). There is ample research evidence to demonstrate that building walking into everyday routines can have a major impact on personal health (Ogilvie et al, 2004; 2007): many of our respondents recognised this, though they did not always find it easy to achieve. Whereas some people, such as Bill and Andy, were obviously physically fit and considered walking unproblematic, others walked despite mentioning that their fitness could be much better (Bea, Jackie). At the other extreme from Andy (a regular runner) was Kay, a grandmother in Leeds, who still walked when she could despite considerable health problems. Most respondents stressed that exercise did make them feel better: it lifted their mood and gave them energy. A combination of lifestyle, health, enjoyment and environmental factors all contributed towards the reasons why those people who walked regularly did so, despite the fact that they often faced difficulties in achieving this goal. The barriers to walking that people experienced are discussed in the third section of this chapter.

Box 7.7: Walking for health and fitness

Walking used to be part of my job when I worked for Royal Mail and so I am physically fit. (Bill, Lancaster, interview)

I try to walk for environmental purposes as well and health...I've recently changed the child care arrangements, so don't walk there now – have put on a stone since then. (Bea, Worcester, interview)

It's like almost if you go for a run, once you get past that first, say, four weeks of running then it never becomes an issue again, you can run for the rest of your life. (Andy, Worcester, go-along)

It's not the distance [that makes it a big journey] it's the fact that because I'm not very fit I'm just going to be exhausted. That's what puts me off...Sometimes it's good to take a walk just to clear your head and to have a bit of a think. Obviously you can't do that when driving. (Jackie, Leicester, interview)

The supermarket is about a 45–50 min walk and up a big hill, but I don't mind because I think it keeps me fit. (Lara, Leeds, interview)

I'll walk because it's nice to have the exercise. (Jen, Worcester, interview)

> If I walk anywhere, I have to take a stick because I have rheumatoid arthritis and spinal stenosis so I have problems walking. (Kay, Leeds, ethno)
>
> Because it is good for health and definitely fresh air we can get, so definitely walking is good exercise. (Rose, Leicester, ethno)
>
> I think walking gives you more energy. (Molly, Leicester, interview)
>
> I like to build a walk in to whatever I do because it makes me feel physically better. (Deidre, Lancaster, interview)

One characteristic of walking that we noticed through field observations and ethnographic study is the relative invisibility of walking in many communities. Although it takes place it is barely acknowledged as a form of transport or even as an activity that is worthy of note. The extent to which this was the case varied according to the type of walking – with recreational walking appearing to be much more visible to (and so commented on by) people than everyday, utility walking. It seemed also to vary according to the degree to which people seemed literate in recent policy discourses that construct walking as 'a good thing'. In Lancaster and Worcester, where such literacy was highest, people seemed generally proud of their walking, and happy to notice and talk about it; but at the other extreme, in Leicester and Leeds 'ordinary' everyday walking seemed stigmatised, and sometimes psychologically repressed – it is better to overlook the fact that one sometimes walks. The degree to which this was the case varied from place to place (and indeed from person to person), but it can be argued that the lack of recognition that walking is for many a legitimate and important means of everyday transport, which has to be planned and provided for, contributes to the poor quality walking environment experienced in most British cities.

The place of walking in the four contrasting ethnographic study areas is now briefly described from field observations made by the researchers. Remember, these areas are not representative of the cities from which they are drawn, but were selected to reflect four different types of living environment that are found widely across all British urban areas. In the middle-class neighbourhood of Lancaster most people walked to some degree. They walked for recreation and with their dogs (most housing is relatively close to open countryside), and many people walked into town or to the railway station (a five- to fifteen-minute walk depending on location). Some children also walked to school on a regular basis as there were both primary and secondary schools nearby. In talking to people, walking was recognised as being good both for health and the environment. In the morning and evening rush hours the streets could be quite busy and thus felt safe. In this area it can be suggested that there was a 'green' or environmental discourse around walking. However, most families in this area were also car owners and use of the car often took precedence simply because it was more convenient. Thus, although walking took place, and was to some extent recognised, most households in this locality were also locked into the system of automobility which meant that car use remained the first choice for many trips, including some that could perfectly easily be achieved by more sustainable means.

Whereas the largely middle-class area studied in Lancaster was within easy walking distance of the town centre, the suburban middle-class area chosen in Worcester was a little more distant from most facilities (though it is possible to walk to town in 25 minutes). The combination of distance and of lifestyles that seemed to require a substantial number of longer-distance journeys (for work, shopping and so on) to other communities, meant that this was the most car-dominated area that was studied. For much of the day walking was barely visible on the streets of this quiet suburban community. Some children walked to and from school (usually with their parents), and some people walked to the small parade of local shops, but otherwise almost all travel was undertaken by car. The narratives that we collected from this community suggest that most people see this as unproblematic. They have made a deliberate decision to live in a suburban location (just as others in Worcester and elsewhere have chosen to live in a location that allows minimal use of the car), and the car is a taken-for-granted aspect of life in this community. We suggest that in this area the discourse around walking can be characterised as one where although walking may be seen as potentially good (for health and the environment), it was not perceived as being relevant to the lives of residents. We suggest that this is typical of many, if not most, suburban communities across Britain where walking is seen as an activity that is (at best) undertaken rarely, mostly for leisure purposes, or for very short journeys within the immediate neighbourhood.

The study locality in Leicester has a strong South Asian heritage and forms a close-knit community with most services and facilities being relatively close by. In some ways it is a neighbourhood in which walking should be the norm: many everyday needs can be accessed on foot. However, while walking does occur in this neighbourhood, and at certain times of the day the streets are busy with people, walking is not constructed as a usual means of everyday travel. The main concept of walking is as an activity designed to improve health: this is usually done in the local park or on a treadmill in the gym. Both locations are normally driven to although they are within walking distance for most people. Utility walking does take place: to school, to local shops, to visit neighbours (mostly by women in daylight). However, it is barely recognised as an activity or as a means of transport: it is simply something that is done; tends to be viewed as something that is endured when there is no alternative; and the preference and aspiration of most people is to travel by car whenever possible. Consequently many very short trips are undertaken by car. Paradoxically walking is thus both visible and invisible in this locality. We saw it on the street; we watched people going about their everyday activities on foot; and we saw them exercising in the park. However, such movement is barely recognised by the local community that constructs a strong discourse that walking is good for health (and this is a neighbourhood where health problems such as diabetes and heart disease are common), but which otherwise relegates walking to a marginal and un-noticed activity.

The ethnographic study area in Leeds was the most deprived locality studied: here walking was common but was mostly done from necessity as car ownership was low. The area was also close to the city centre and hence most facilities, so that many tasks could be accomplished on foot. This was also the location in which walking was most contingent on other external factors. Two types of walking were observed. First, people travelling on foot within the housing estate to take children to school, to shop locally or to go to the community centre; second, journeys off the estate to the city centre (for work or shopping) or as part of a longer multi-mode journey. During daylight hours some pedestrians could be seen, but few people ventured out after dark (defined as after about 3 pm in winter), and both the times and places that people walked were circumscribed by concerns about safety (see below). Thus although almost everyone spoken to walked to go about their everyday business (the only exceptions were respondents who could not walk for health reasons), when asked why they walked the question was often met with puzzlement or incredulity. Although walking was a common practice it was barely noticed as an activity: it was simply something that was done to facilitate everyday life and did not require conscious decision making or thought beyond that of route choice and safety. It was in effect present but invisible. Effectively, there was no discourse around walking in this locality.

How people walk

Questions of how and why are obviously closely linked and the previous paragraphs also give clues to how walking was accomplished in the urban areas studied. In this section we focus especially on the ways in which walking was incorporated into the lives of people we spoke to, the experience of walking in urban areas, and on the creation of individual walking identities. For many walking is a social activity and is normally, or preferably, done with others rather than alone. Although we talked to some lone walkers who valued the opportunity to have time to themselves while walking (for instance) to or from work, and to others who walked alone from necessity for at least some journeys, for many companions were seen as at least desirable and in some cases essential. Walking with others could provide a motivation and reason for walking, could make what might be viewed as an arduous journey more enjoyable, and could provide protection against perceived risks. Issues of safety are dealt with in the third section of this chapter, here we focus especially on the ways in which existing cultures of walking to some extent required the participation and approval of others to make it acceptable, pleasant and normal (Box 7.8). Thus Kirsty intimated that she only walked regularly when her daughter was at home and she had someone to accompany her on leisure walks, and both Joe and Polly commented that they preferred walking to cycling because it was a more sociable activity. It is more difficult to carry on a conversation or to stop and talk to others when cycling.

Jen, Sandra and Kay all stressed the sociability of walking when comparing it to driving, and Neela said she preferred to walk to school rather than use the bus because it allowed her to travel with friends. For many who walked for some journeys company was important, particularly for leisure walks that did not have any other purpose. In the absence of human companions the need to walk a dog could be a good substitute. This was especially obvious in suburban areas relatively close to open land where recreational walks could take place. The sociability of walking can also extend beyond the walk itself and encompass other aspects of life. This was expressed clearly by Percy (Box 7.8) who found that the common experience of walking created a 'bond' with a work colleague. It can also be suggested that this common experience to some extent legitimised an activity that otherwise might have been perceived by work colleagues as unusual.

Box 7.8: The sociability of walking

When my daughter's home we go out for a walk in the park every day, just to get out. (Kirsty, Lancaster, interview)

We like walking at the same speed, whereas cycling I go faster than her, so for that reason it's, yeah, walking has become the favoured leisure time activity. (Joe, Leicester, interview)

There would be no point in getting the bus [to school] because everyone walks it and you've got all your friends with you. (Neela, Leicester, interview)

I think, like I say, I like to walk now because, I find, in a car you don't socialize do you as much? (Sandra and Kay, Leeds, ethno)

When you're walking as well, which is a slight advantage to the cycling is you've got more chance of stopping and talking to somebody haven't you? (Polly, Worcester, go-along)

I meet people I know when walking which is what you miss if you drive. (Jen, Worcester, interview)

There is a colleague in personnel who walks maybe slightly further and we have a bonding, we like to talk about it together that we both walk and how much we enjoy it. (Percy, Worcester, go-along)

It can also be argued that all of the above respondents were to some extent describing their walking identities: they had begun to construct a narrative of how and why they walked and the circumstances in which they did so. In this section we explore the concept of walking identities in more detail. Identities are complex, multi-faceted and much discussed in the academic literature (Anderson, 2006; Jenkins, 2008; Graham and Howard, 2008). They can be voluntary or imposed, displayed or hidden, and can be expressed through many different actions and experiences. For most people the way in which they undertake their everyday travel is unlikely to be a major part of their identity – which is more probably constructed around concepts such as religion, language, social class or identity with place – but it may be a secondary aspect that, while often hidden, emerges as important under certain circumstances. Travel identities may also interact with other more dominant aspects of identity: for example, if the norms or customs of a particular religious or social group impose constraints or create expectations about how it is acceptable to travel. If walking is uncommon among the group with which you identify, and among the neighbours with whom you live, then it may be less likely to be practised on a regular basis. Conversely, if others around you walk then you may be more willing to travel on foot for at least some journeys.

For a small number of our respondents walking was a central part of their identity. Lance, who formed part of the ethnographic study in Leeds, was one such person. Lance was 82 at the time of our interviews with him and he had lived in a tower block on the estate for the past 50 years. The following brief extract from observation notes made during the ethnography (interview and accompanied walk) summarise the extent to which walking was, and remained, a central part of his life:

> Lance is a legend as 'he walks everywhere' and every day he walked around ten miles (in two hours), now he does two mile walks. He had an operation on his foot a few years ago, now has a hammer toe and his feet get sore. He does not want to use a stick. He just sets off from his flat (needs to get out of the house) and walks, he has a weekly route. He used to cycle to work 40 years ago, but that was just transport, he would not do it for leisure. He has never driven or had a car. (Field observation, Leeds)

Thus for Lance independent travel without a car, and without significant use of public transport, is important. For longer journeys in the past he cycled but his preferred form of travelling is on foot, and he has continued to walk despite increasing age and infirmity because it forms an important part of who he is. Because he has lived in the area so long he also has a reputation as someone who walks everywhere: although viewed as unusual it is accepted in the community and has to some extent become a badge of pride for Lance.

Relatively few respondents showed the commitment to, and the need for, walking that Lance has; but many did find ways of embedding walking into their everyday routines, even though it was combined with other forms of travel and conditional on local circumstances. Audrey is a typical example of one such regular walker. She lives, with her husband, in a residential area on the edge of Lancaster in an area that is within walking distance of the town centre but which is also at the top of a steep hill that could be a disincentive to walking. At the time of our interview she was about 60 years of age, still working, and in good health. During the interview she expressed a strong walking identity in that it was her preferred mode of travel for all short trips within the urban area, including travel to work. She believes that she derives real benefits from walking in terms of exercise, relaxation, thinking time, speed and convenience:

> Walking is an easy way to take exercise and feel better…When I'm walking to and from work I like my mind to be completely on something else and so if I walk the same route to work and back every day then my mind can be doing something else…I often think through what I'm going to be doing, on the way to work I am usually thinking what I am going to do at work and prioritising things so that when I arrive at work I am ready to start. Coming home is the opposite it is clearing my mind of all the things so that when I get home I can just switch off…The journey from home to work is across town and therefore, at a busy time of day you are as quick to walk; especially when you think about parking at the other end, which there isn't any. (Audrey, Lancaster, interview)

Walking clearly gives her a sense of satisfaction as she feels 'very smug when I'm walking to and from work because the cars are just absolutely nose to nose and it is mad' and the ability walk to most everyday destinations formed an important part how she and her husband determined where they should live:

> One of the ways we chose where to live was that we wanted to be within walking distance of town. That was important to us… Everything is just so much easier if everything is within walking distance…I love living in town, it's very convenient to be able to just pop in to the chemist or if you go to the doctor's or just to the shop. (Audrey, Lancaster, interview)

Elsewhere in the interview she states that they have considered moving out into the country but decided that the advantages of the countryside were readily outweighed by those of the town, and that the car dependence that country living creates was major disincentive for such a move. However, Audrey and her husband are car owners and although it may go several days without being used there are some purposes, including walking in environments that are more attractive than those of the town, for which she deems a car to be essential:

> I very, very, rarely take the car; the car sometimes can be outside for three or four days, without moving. It's practicality, it's partly green and it's partly I am certainly more conscious of the physical benefits of walking. We own a car because there are certain things you can only do in a car, to go walking in the countryside, our weekly shopping trip, to take my mother out. (Audrey, Lancaster, interview)

Although Audrey is a keen and confident walker there are things about walking through town that she does not like. She varies her route to avoid what she perceives to be hazards and there are some routes that she only uses at certain times of the day when she views them as safe. In very bad weather she might use the car (or more often ask her husband to give her a lift), and to avoid carrying heavy books to and from work she often extends her working day. Like most people her walking is to an extent conditional and she adjusts her behaviour accordingly:

> I like walking through town when it's very quiet. But if town is busy, around 4 pm, I'll avoid it simply because it's too much dodging people…Where the paving stones are very uneven and slippery, I don't like the unevenness so I don't go that way…As a pedestrian I get very annoyed about people parking on the pavement…If it is raining, throwing it down and you don't really want to end up at work soaking wet, or if it's icy and slippery, yes then I will get a lift in the car…I would never walk along the canal in the dark. It can be a bit intimidating because there aren't many people there and the people that are there can sometimes be a bit odd…Because I am walking I can't really take heavy folders with me to work on at home, so therefore I stay at work until they are shut and then I don't have anything heavy to carry, so that's a conscious decision, to make long working days. (Audrey, Lancaster, interview)

Audrey made it clear in the interview that her commitment to walking also extended to encouraging others to adopt more active and sustainable forms of travel.

> When I talk to people at work and say, 'Why do you come in your car?' If people are coming from somewhere where they could come by other means then you say, 'Well, why don't you cycle?' or whatever, and some people say, 'Well, you would arrive at work very sweaty and you wouldn't be able to wear your other clothes', but there are – I do have colleagues who cycle in different clothing and then they change and it's not a big deal…As soon as kids are 7 or 8 they can walk to school on their own. (Audrey, Lancaster, interview)

It can be surmised that such views do not always go down well with colleagues, that to an extent Audrey's commitment to walking is seen as eccentric, and that her views on the acceptability of young children walking alone to school reflect a period (some 20 or more years earlier) when the attitudes of most parents towards child safety were very different from those expressed by the majority of young parents today. We argue that Audrey's high degree of self-consciousness about her walking, the way in which she incorporates walking into her everyday routine, and the conditions that she imposes on this activity, are fairly typical of many people who embrace walking as part of their travelling identity. But the degree of commitment described by Audrey remains a minority view: for most people walking trips were kept to a minimum and, although walking occurs, it is socially and culturally almost invisible (apart from exercise for health) and certainly subservient to the car.

   This section has focused on how people walk: the ways in which they undertake this activity and the extent to which it forms a part of their personal identity. We now focus more directly on the experience of walking in the urban areas studied and reflect on the ways in which this influences how people walk in cities. There is an extensive literature on walking as an embodied activity, exploring the experiences of bodily movement and engagement with the environment in both urban and rural areas (Ingold, 2004; Wylie, 2005; Ingold and Vergunst, 2008; Middleton, 2009a; 2010; Scheldeman, 2011). We do not attempt to engage directly with these literatures in this chapter but, rather, we focus on the more practical aspects of walking through the city. What is a typical experience of negotiating the urban environments found in the four case study towns? Data are drawn from a combination of go-along interviews, observations and our own experiences of moving through the cities. Two general points can be made: first, the walking environments found in the towns studied varied enormously from place to place and thus generalisation is difficult and, second, that for the most part the people we spoke to paid relatively little attention to the quality of the walking environment through which they passed and consequently had very low expectations. In other words, generally poor conditions for walking across the four cities were taken for granted, and so were almost invisible to our research participants. On most journeys undertaken with respondents there were some stretches where the quality of the environment was high and the experience good, but there were other stretches where a combination of poor pavements, heavy traffic and lack of convenient crossing points made the experience unpleasant or frustrating. However, complaints from respondents were mostly muted, with the views of Bob being fairly typical: 'I really do think the provision for walking is fine and the pavements, although car parking on the pavement is a problem everywhere' (Bob, Leeds, interview). This acceptance of conditions that were often not ideally suited for walking was especially the case for utility travel (the main focus of our study); when people walked for leisure they were much more likely to demand a high quality environment in which to walk.

   Box 7.9 summarises our observations made during accompanied walks with selected female respondents in Leeds and Leicester. They illustrate the varied, and sometimes problematic, experiences that women (often with young children) face when walking through a British city. All these respondents enjoyed walking and made a positive decision to walk. Parts of their routes, usually through parks or quiet residential streets, were pleasant and could provide opportunities to allow children to engage in active play; but other parts of the routes were more difficult. These problems were created both by the available infrastructure (lack of pavements, difficulties with kerbs, lack of convenient crossings), and by the behaviour of others (speeding cars, vehicles on the pavement and fear of strangers). For these women while walking was something that they chose to do, and which they saw as a positive experience, the environment through which they passed presented a range of hazards and difficulties that had to be negotiated. It can be argued that this significantly restricted the quality of their experience of urban walking. We did also undertake go-alongs with male respondents, and in the smaller towns of Worcester and Lancaster. Despite their smaller size the walking environments presented similar challenges, and although male participants were less concerned about safety than women, and were also less likely to be travelling with children, they faced all the same inconveniences as their female counterparts.

Box 7.9: The experience of walking in Leeds and Leicester*

One child has autism and likes only to walk along set routes. This was a short walk (approx 10–15 minutes) from home to the park with three children. This is a walk the family frequently do in the school holidays. During term time they walk to school. As the children are all under seven, the walk went at a gentle pace. The weather began dry and started to rain briefly at the park… While this is not the quickest route to the park, H considered that it was preferable for involving less time on the main road. While the minor roads were quiet, they also involved sections where there was no pavement, and one section where the pavement was made of loose stones. (Observations during go-along with Hailey, Leeds)

This was a pleasant walk on a sunny May weekday afternoon. Part leisure walk (we took the dog) and part trip to the shops. We took the long way round through park and woodland. Distance, about two miles partly along residential streets, a long stretch through green and very pleasant parkland, up a hill (woodland) and then down… We took minor residential roads, and passed through the busy urban shopping centre. Some of the residential roads were semi-detached type housing, some terraced. E was conversational and open. She enjoyed walking and kept up a reasonable pace. She preferred walking to taking the same trip by car and was not concerned that some thought her travel habits a little unusual. (Observations during go-along with Eliza, Leeds)

Approximately 4km walk home from (work) via daughter's nursery. A works two days/week and makes this journey on each of those days. Rainy evening walk. A tends to walk regardless of weather. She was wearing a rain coat and trainers – this [footwear] is what she also wears in work. The walk to the nursery was mainly along city centre shopping streets, and a shopping centre, most of which are pedestrianised. A noted that she usually walks at a brisk pace for this part of the journey. After the nursery, A was accompanied by her 3-year-old daughter, and a pushchair. As her daughter has a long day at nursery, she goes in the pushchair for at least part of the journey home… A had substantial difficulty in getting the pushchair up and down kerbs, even where the kerb is dropped but still has a lip. A also noted concern about cars doing illegal U turns where she uses pedestrian crossings on some of the busy junctions, and she also noted a concern at the possibility that a car could go onto the pavement and present a risk to her daughter. A and her daughter use the walk home as time for talking and playing – and consequently sometimes it takes two hours to get home. A noted that talking could be difficult due to the noise of traffic, and she frequently stops walking in order to hear her daughter. A's daughter notices things such as cobwebs and leaves, and likes to run about on a patch of grass they pass, and uses a wall as a climbing frame. (Observations during go-along with Al, Leicester)

Sunny Friday evening walk home from work…Most of A's journeys are on foot. She suggested that a major reason for this was economy – buses are expensive. She does sometimes get lifts from friends. A walks briskly. She wears trainers for the walk, and changes into shoes at work. She tries to stick to main, busy roads with many cars or pedestrians due to concern for her personal safety. This seems to be her main concern, and this fear limits her evening journeys. She says that she feels less safe on quiet residential streets. A is also worried about joyriders/ speeding cars mounting the pavement particularly at the pedestrian crossing of S Road – in the moments we were at this crossing we saw speeding cars – there is also a substantial dent in the barriers at this crossing. (Observations during go-along with Annette, Leeds)

Note: *Observations are edited to remove route details and preserve anonymity

The barriers to walking

Previous sections have hinted at the difficulties and barriers that may be faced when walking in the urban environment. In this section we examine these in more detail using examples from all four towns studied. We focus on five main themes: problems associated with the urban infrastructure; issues of safety and risk; constraints imposed by families and lifestyles; the impact of weather and topography; and the influence of culture and image. Together, we argue, these factors combine to make walking both difficult and unpleasant for at least some people for some of the time. Those people who do walk regularly do so despite the conditions that exist. Complaints about the urban infrastructure related both to the physical environment itself and to the ways in which it was used by others (Box 7.10). Pavements were mostly thought to be adequate, though some complained about lack of space (forcing pedestrians too near vehicles), poorly sited crossings and lack of maintenance which led to pavements being slippery or uneven. Other inconveniences related to the level of crowding on some pavements which impeded progress, the quantity of dog dirt (especially a problem in residential areas), the inconvenience of pavement cyclists (see below), and to being hassled by others on the street. However, as noted above, the quality of the infrastructure used for walking seemed to be barely noticed by many people and they tended to accept without question what existed without considering that it could be better. Their expectations were low and were largely met, and for most people the quality of the infrastructure was not a major factor that prevented them from walking. This is understandable. If walking is an activity that is rarely consciously considered by most people, and when it does take place it is seen as mundane and routine, then critical appraisal of the environment for walking is likely to be absent. However, by spending a substantial amount of time in all four towns observing pedestrians at a variety of locations in which people regularly walked we were surprised, and to some extent shocked, by the poor quality of pedestrian provision that existed outside of central pedestrianized areas.

Box 7.10: Problems caused by the urban infrastructure

At peak hours there's too many people, there's not enough space on the pavement, too much traffic. I enjoy more walking when its quiet than when it's noisy. (Kapil, Leicester, go-along)

I don't like walking on busy roads. I hate the big lorries. It's the big vehicles that frighten me whether I'm on foot or on the bike. (Jan, Leeds, interview)

If I lived in a bit more of a scenic area I'd probably do a lot more walking than I do at the moment…

There are quite a few industrial estates round here. I wouldn't take a walk around those. (Jackie, Leicester, interview)

This road is seldom used so I walk in the middle of the road, aware that something might come behind me but unlikely…[later] For a pedestrianized street there's an awful lot of cars and things. (Harriet, Lancaster, ethno)

Two quite dangerous roads, even though they're quite narrow. They're not like big roads like the inner city ring road, but almost as dangerous to cross, just to go and get a pint of milk. (Heidi, Leeds, ethno)

[Attention should be paid to] the absolutely disgusting state of our pavement slabs. (Molly, Leicester, interview)

People do just walk off the pavement and onto the road because the pedestrian crossings are not where they want them to be…They've just put loads more pedestrian crossing on this road because before there wasn't that many and then they said that they'd put them where people want to cross but they haven't. (Steve, Leeds, ethno)

That road is awful, the pavement is very narrow, and in autumn it's covered in leaves so you slip over half the time, it's terrifying. But by car the road is fine. (Linda and Paul, Lancaster, ethno)

Whoever designed this estate didn't have pedestrians in mind…I have to go on a narrowish path with big piles of dog dirt on it. (Nancy, Leeds, interview)

> The only thing you have to worry about there is dog dirt, absolutely disgusting up there. (Bea, Worcester, interview)
>
> Negative effects of 'chuggers' [charity muggers] on walking – can't go anywhere without being asked for money and embarrassing to say 'No'. (Al, Leicester, go-along)

To give just some examples: we were struck by how commonly across all four cities people on foot, including very young children, are in close proximity to very fast-moving motorised traffic, including heavy goods vehicles and buses. At big and busy junctions it is normal for pedestrians to be forced to wait for long periods of time before they are able to cross, and then – when crossing bigger roads such as dual carriageways – often to be contained in small 'refuges' which, were they less taken-for-granted, would seem wholly inadequate. Time after time we witnessed older and/or less able people struggling to cross roads which the young and able-bodied might cross almost without thinking; and frequently we witnessed people taking a chance, jumping through moving traffic which, too often, made no concession to their plight. The more conscious we became of the sub-standard conditions for walking that predominated across the four towns, the more problems we began to see, to the extent that it began to seem completely inhumane that (especially during periods of peak pedestrian flows) so many people are contained on such narrow sections of our city streets, which are so dominated by (often solitary people in) potentially lethal motorised vehicles. Not only are the majority of most urban streets given over to motorised modes at the expense of pedestrians, but also pedestrians are expected to give way to those motorised modes at every non-signalled intersection (and pedestrians who challenge motorised modes' right of way are typically seen as deviant). Even when motorised vehicles are stationary, our research gaze shifted to seeing such parked cars, especially, as intensely problematic to the creation of more people-friendly streets, towns and cities.

A much more prominent factor that, while not necessarily preventing walking, certainly influenced when and where people walked was the perception of risk and safety held by the respondents to whom we spoke (Box 7.11). There were also interesting differences between the four urban areas studied. In the larger cities of Leeds and Leicester we identified relatively high levels of concern about safety focused on particular neighbourhoods and exemplified in the relatively deprived localities chosen for the ethnographic studies. In contrast, in the smaller towns of Lancaster and Worcester fears were more muted and tended to relate either to general perceptions gleaned from the media, or to specific quite limited localities to and through which people would not venture at particular times, especially after dark. Respondents expressed fears both for themselves and on behalf of their children, and concerns were raised by both men and women, though female respondents were likely to be much more forthcoming on this topic. They also restricted their movements to a greater extent than most men (as demonstrated by the predominance of quotes from women in Box 7.11). Most commonly, the fears that people expressed restricted their walking after dark, on empty streets, or in neighbourhoods and along routes which they considered had a reputation for being unsafe. Most people who did walk had adopted strategies to deal with these concerns: most commonly by varying their route to ensure that they remained where others were present or by travelling with companions. Others simply switched to using the car, a taxi or public transport if they travelled at night. Familiarity with a neighbourhood could bring a greater sense of security for some, for instance Lily who has lived for 30 years in the same deprived neighbourhood in Leeds travelled mostly on foot (though over very short distances) and felt reasonably secure because she felt she knew most people and that they would know her.

Box 7.11: Perceptions of safety and risk when walking

I think most parents are worried about their kids walking alone with the traffic. (Deidre, Lancaster, interview)

I certainly wouldn't walk down that bike track at night, no way. (Nadia, interview, Lancaster)

I wouldn't tend to go walking at night generally. (June, Worcester, go-along)

If I want to go to the Post Office, there's one quite close but I'll take the car because I don't like walking through the estate...I feel very vulnerable walking some places because I can't run...Walking through alleyways can be very claustrophobic and you feel a bit scared so I tend to walk the long way round on the road which adds journey time, but it's worth it. (Jen, Worcester, interview)

I don't feel safe out walking by myself. (Naomi, Worcester, ethno)

When it's light I walk across the park. (Abby, Leicester, go-along)

There's always dangers being [walking] in isolated areas. (Pierce, Leicester, go-along)

Like all cities you have to keep an eye out for antisocial people...It was safe if you were careful but to be careful you had to take your time. (Oscar, Leicester, interview)

I know the good areas and the bad areas in the city and I always make sure I am walking with someone, or that I am walking at the right time...I don't feel I have to be aware of anything at all when I am walking around. I pretty much know everyone in the area. It's just being familiar with faces, we're not a close knit community but I think people would look out for each other if there was a problem. (Anju and Pooja, Leicester, ethno)

> It's OK when everyone walks it and you've got all your friends with you, I wouldn't want to go on my own so I would get the bus. (Neela, Leicester, interview)
>
> I feel safer going through that street where there's a lot more people around, rather than that road where you've got the cars but you don't really have many people walking it…I think you've just got to be vigilant whatever you do, and not be too complacent about things. But if you let your fears of walking places get the better of you then you're never going to do anything…In the winter months people don't come out, as they don't like to be going home in the dark…I prefer to walk on streets with more houses because I think you feel a bit more safer when there are more things. And that's the main reason for walking this route in winter when it's dark. (Steve, Leeds, ethno)
>
> It's just because there's so much fear and you just get scared no-one's about. But I suppose I don't know. It's not safe when there's no people about. (Group discussion, Leeds, ethno)
>
> I more or less know everybody round here so I could take the chance to walk. With it being dark anything's possible though, isn't it? (Lily, Leeds, ethno)

The other major safety concern of pedestrians was the conflict that frequently arose between walkers and pavement cyclists (Box 7.12). The specific reasons why so many cyclists routinely use the pavement for at least parts of their journeys are explored in Chapter Eight, but the fact that this emerged as a major concern of pedestrians both reinforces the issues of safety associated with cycling, and underscores the ways in which cycling and walking should be viewed as very different types of travel that make distinct demands upon the urban environment. It is also interesting to note that these concerns were expressed both by pedestrians and by cyclists, many of whom recognised that pavement cycling posed problems for pedestrians, but who also felt that they had little option but to do so, given the current cycling infrastructure found in most British towns. Conflicts between pedestrians and cyclists occurred mainly on standard pavements adjacent to highways but also on some of the off-road routes that did exist in the towns studied. These were normally shared spaces for cyclists and pedestrians, usually with a white line nominally separating the two, but both pedestrians and cyclists who used these routes sometimes felt that there was insufficient separation between the two groups and that this could lead to conflicts. What is clear, certainly from the perspective of pedestrians, is that walkers and cyclists are incompatible users of the same space and that if the needs of both groups are to be satisfied then they must have clearly separate urban spaces. The degree of concern that pedestrians expressed about pavement cycling also varied between the four case study towns. The problem was most strongly recognised, and objected to, in Worcester and Leicester: our observations confirmed that rates of pavement cycling were indeed high in both localities though, as explained in Chapter Eight, the nature of pavement cycling was rather different in these two towns. In Lancaster and Leeds complaints from pedestrians we interviewed were present but more muted, though as in Worcester and Leicester the issue was sometimes picked up in the local press, and especially in the letters pages, but the relative lack of pavement cycling was borne out by our observations. Likely reasons for this are different: in Leeds rates of cycling were low and thus the visibility of cycling overall was less; and in Lancaster the Cycle Demonstration Town status had both provided a somewhat enhanced network of cycle routes and had also educated cyclists on appropriate cycling etiquette. These factors are also explored in more detail in Chapter Eight.

Box 7.12: Conflicts between pedestrians and cyclists

I just get cross with some cyclists because it's basic good manners to let people know you're coming. (Moses and Lisa, Worcester, interview)

When I'm a pedestrian I sometimes feel a bit threatened by cyclists that they're going a bit too fast and they do sort of, you know, weave in and out a little bit sometimes...They [have] pedestrianised this town but they're cycling and they don't seem to take an awful lot of care, you know. (Sally, Worcester, interview)

I can understand some people having a go at you for cycling on the pavement. (Pete, Worcester, go-along)

My bugbear is cyclists on the pavement, that really gets me going, because I think it's dangerous, and some of them go too fast. (Kirsty, Lancaster, interview)

You step out of our front gate any morning and you're likely to be knocked over by somebody cycling. (Mary, Worcester, go-along)

The footpath is for people really. (Raj, Leicester, ethno)

The fact that there's no clear delineation for cyclists from pedestrians along this section here does cause problems sometimes. (Jason, Leicester, go-along)

Pavement cycling is a problem for most disabled [blind] people. (Evan, Leicester, interview)

I've always felt as a pedestrian, much more threatened by cyclists...I have a fear because a lot of the cyclists don't seem to obey rules of the road, especially when it comes to traffic lights and chopping and changing between being on the road and being on the pavement and so I've almost been hit far more times with a bicycle [than by a car]. (Tim, Leicester, go-along)

When people cycle on the pavement, I side up and let them go through. If I told them off they might give me a back hand. I'm not taking the chance am I? (Lily, Leeds, ethno)

The third major set of barriers to regular walking for utility travel, and ones that occurred more-or-less ubiquitously across all groups and study areas, were the constraints imposed by twenty-first century family life and associated lifestyles (Box 7.13). Although many people enjoyed walking under at least some circumstances, and recognised its value both for personal health and for the environment, the way in which they lived their lives, or the locality in which they lived, meant that for much of the time walking – even for short trips – was simply incompatible with carrying out their everyday tasks and with fulfilling the role of good parents. While this is perhaps expressed most simply by Jack and Deidre in Leeds, respondent after respondent told us a similar story and elaborated on the reasons why fitting walking into everyday routines was hard. The presence of children was a key factor: when young they are too tired to walk and as they get older walking is seen as unfashionable, while a large family spanning different ages is especially problematic. As several respondents stated, although in one sense walking is a very simple activity, if you have a family it needs careful planning – an activity that is not always possible – and if there are school bags or shopping to carry walking becomes even more problematic. Several people simply stated that, with the demands of work, home and family, they were simply too tired to walk (or to plan to walk), and thus using a car (when available) or public transport was the obvious easy option that enabled them to get through the day and to accomplish the tasks that had to be done. Although less problematic than cycling, walking also requires the storage and ready availability of a range of equipment including outdoor shoes, coats and umbrellas for all the family. Where these were not readily available – and our mobility inventories showed this often to be the case – then there were further barriers to walking. Such problems were felt especially acutely in families where both parents worked (the norm), or in single parent families; and in those situations where the age and activities of children meant that many journeys were complex and multi-purpose. As this was the normal state for many respondents, even with the best of intentions walking was relegated to a lowly place on the family's list of priorities. In effect, not walking had become habitual with this condition constructed and reinforced by the multiple barriers outlined in this section.

Box 7.13: Family and lifecycle constraints

I enjoy walking – always have done – but we don't have time to do it. (Jack and Deidre, Leeds, interview)

The boys moan a bit walking home from school sometimes, because they get tired, sometimes I take the car to pick them up. (Linda and Paul, Lancaster, ethno)

Children influence walking routes (both through wanting (insisting) to go a particular way and through parents wanting to take them a nicer/safer/less polluted way)... Distance is important for walking, especially if with kid or if carrying stuff. (Hailey, Leeds, go-along)

As the kids got older they liked it [walking] less and less. (Dick, Leicester, interview)

[When you have children] you don't have any sleep and you just can't do it [three-quarters of an hour journey each way]. You can't get up at half six every day and go to work. (Cassie, Leicester, interview)

With the demands of family and work and everything there's not much time or energy [for walking]. (Percy, Worcester, go-along)

I think time between activities makes a difference, even though it may be a short journey, we probably wouldn't walk or cycle because we've only got so much time to get from one place to another. (Pete, Worcester, go-along)

I would probably walk, you know, if I've got the time I'd walk any distance. (Liam and family, Worcester, interview)

[There is] need for a fair degree of planning for walking, especially if you are intending to carry something. (Eliza, Leeds, go-along)

I always try and walk everywhere I can, except if I can't possibly carry all the shopping. (Dan and Catrina, Lancaster, interview)

I wouldn't normally use the bus, unless I have bought something too heavy to carry home – I would always choose to walk. (Kirsty, Lancaster, interview)

Usually I go with the car because of convenience, less time, because sometimes J [age 3] is tired when I pick him up from nursery and I would have to carry him, and I have my books as well, and when there's two of them... In the week [I use the car] for two days a week, at some point I might even try just walking with the kids, but it's usually because with the two kids they have different energies, and R runs and J is a bit more like staying here and hanging round here and there, so that creates some kind of tension and also I'm on pressure to get on time to work, then it's really much more convenient to just strap them in the seats and take them and leave them and that's it. Apart from that I would just walk. (Donald, Lancaster, ethno)

The attractiveness of walking on any particular occasion is also affected by external factors such as the weather and the difficulties presented by a particular route. Although regular walkers were rarely put off by rain or hills, as evidenced by the testimonies of Kirsty and Abigail (Box 7.14), most respondents admitted to being fair weather walkers at best. In the questionnaire survey (Chapter Six) the weather was also identified as a significant barrier to regular walking. Bad weather was especially problematic for journeys at the start of the day – to work or to school – when getting wet could mean spending all day in damp clothes, whereas for a one-off trip or a journey home when it was possible to quickly dry out and change, walking in rain was not so problematic (Box 7.14). Of course the ability to cope with wet weather interacts with the household and lifestyle factors outlined above. Modern outdoor clothing is very efficient at providing protection from all types of weather, but to be of use it has to be available for all family members (and equipping a family of rapidly-growing children can be expensive), and also readily to hand. Such outdoor clothing may also not be seen as fashionable by older offspring, or as compatible with work-wear by some adults. It is perhaps of note that two of the respondents who expressed least concern about the weather both came from Lancaster which is the study location with the highest rainfall. Thus, it can be suggested that if you live in an area with relatively infrequent rain you are much less likely to have wet weather clothes available and handy than if you live in a town where rain is more common. In the north-west of England the wettest areas have in excess of 3,000 mm of rain a year with 50 to 60 days of rain in winter and 40 to 45 in summer. In contrast much of eastern England receives less than 700 mm of rain per year with fewer than 30 rainy days in winter and 25 in summer (Met Office website). If you are expecting rain, and see it as a normal part of everyday life, you are much more likely to be prepared for it. Comments on the impact of local topography were mostly quite muted: as with weather those who were committed to walking were happy to walk up hills and for others the presence of hills was probably not the major factor that prevented them from walking. Lancaster is probably the hilliest of our case study towns, but even here many routes are relatively flat and, with good local knowledge, some of the worst hills can be avoided. One Lancaster respondent who lives on the hilly side of town put this especially clearly: 'The basic principle is to minimise the height gain and steepness coming from town to here…there is a lot of up and down and these roads round here all slope in two planes and so there are innumerable different versions' (Anthony, Lancaster, interview). Thus, although both the weather and local topography can influence the amount of walking undertaken, and the route chosen, we argue that the effect of these (fixed) factors is much less than the impact of other variables over which we do have some control.

Box 7.14: The influence of weather

I walk down for my papers unless it's pouring down with rain. (Ron and Julie, Leeds, interview)

If I'm walking and it rains then I'll take a taxi or a bus. If it's a sunny day I'll probably walk. (Kev, Leeds, ethno)

It depends on the weather really, if it is good I would normally walk, and if it is miserable I'd just take the bus. (Neela, Leicester, interview)

I have walked home from work a couple of times in horrible weather but if it is really bad I'll catch the bus. (Jackie, Leicester, interview)

If you are going to be soaked in the rain you're going to feel all horrible and you are going to have to come back home and get changed and it just makes you think, shall I just not go out at all…I've got a long walk into work, about ten minutes, and I really dread it when it's absolutely raining. (Anju and Pooja, Leicester, ethno)

I'm a fair weather walker. I don't walk in the rain. (June, Worcester, go-along)

If it's pouring down wet, no we don't [walk]. But if it's, you know, a chance of the odd shower or something, a little bit of drizzle, it doesn't stop us from walking. (Polly, Worcester, go-along)

I probably wouldn't necessarily embark on a shopping trip if it was raining but just to go for a walk in the rain then yeah, definitely. We quite like it don't we. (Bea, Worcester, interview)

I can't bear the thought of [my children] walking to school and getting wet, to then sit in wet clothes all day. (Angie, Worcester, interview)

Bad weather doesn't affect me, I quite like walking in wind and rain. (Kirsty, Lancaster, interview)

I walk in all weathers. (Abigail, Lancaster, go-along)

The cumulative impact of all the above perceived barriers to walking for everyday travel in urban areas has led to a society in which utility walking is not usual, and in which it is almost seen as abnormal unless undertaken for recreation in particular locations such as parks and off-road paths. This then becomes self-reinforcing as the less visible that utility walking is the less normal it appears. What is clear from talking to those respondents who do walk regularly is that once established as a habit or routine walking can quite quickly become incorporated as a normal part of everyday life. As shown in Box 7.15, those people who walked usually had a long history of doing so, had often been encouraged to walk by their parents when they were children, and had a strong commitment to bringing up their own children in the same way. Sometimes forming the habit of walking was something that came initially from necessity – it was the only affordable way of moving around – but once established it could become routine even though other forms of transport could be afforded. In other cases regular walking was undertaken for health or environmental reasons, or simply because it was enjoyed, but once established as a routine it had become normalised and accepted as the most sensible and convenient way of undertaking at least some journeys. In our interviews with respondents the abnormality of walking was often implied rather than stated explicitly, but it did come through quite forcefully in some testimonies (Box 7.16). Comments varied from those who simply saw walking as abnormal because it was uncommon, to those who had experienced really negative comments about the fact that they walked regularly, such as Steph in Leeds. Some respondents constructed their view of the abnormality of walking in relation to the perceived normality of driving and these views were especially clearly expressed by Lara and Bob in Leeds and by Jim in Lancaster. We feel that this is probably a crucial point. It is not that people by and large are opposed to walking, they will walk on some occasions and under certain circumstances they enjoy walking. In this sense the barriers to walking are relatively muted, especially when compared to those affecting cycling (Chapter Eight). However, when an alternative form of transport is seen as more commonly used – more normal – and this form of transport also offers advantages in terms of (usually) speed, comfort and security, then it is not surprising that even for short trips the car is preferred to travelling on foot.

Box 7.15: Habit, lifestyle and identity

I'm happy enough, I've sort of settled into being a pedestrian, being mainly a pedestrian and public transport sort of person. (Oscar, Leicester, interview)

My mum and dad didn't drive so we grew up without a car. (Jackie, Leicester, interview)

We never had a family car when I was young and I didn't learn to drive till later in life, and then only because it was a necessity. My mum dragged us out walking, we always walked. (Kirsty, Lancaster, interview)

I prefer walking, we always walked as kids, and we did cycle quite a lot when we were younger as well. (Dan and Catrina, Lancaster, interview)

I see my legs as a mode of transport. (Wanda, Lancaster, interview)

A long history/experience of walking helps. (Peter, Lancaster, interview)

I'm going to walk most days because I need to get into the habit of walking again. (Abby, Leicester, go-along)

We have always been walkers. We have always enjoyed walking…I have plenty of wet weather gear that I put on. (Vince, Leeds, interview)

It's a puritan ethic I think. I always would have walked in preference to driving. (Nancy, Leeds, interview)

I wouldn't even think of going in the car into town. I would rather walk. (Moses and Lisa, Worcester, interview)

Any condition I will walk. I used to do it in the time I lived in Russia. So it wasn't a winter to me, it was just something really nice and pleasant. (Molly, Leicester, interview)

Box 7.16: The 'normality' of walking

You don't see a lot of people walking around my neighbourhood. (Thomas, Worcester, ethno)

We do know a lot of people who are quite committed to walking and cycling. (Liam and family, Worcester, interview)

People still assume that there's something wrong with you if you don't drive…I would walk a lot more if I could. Often I don't have the right shoes with me. (Lara (and Bob), Leeds)

You feel unusual walking. (Eliza, Leeds, go-along)

I have lots of high heels in a cupboard but I never wear them unless I'm just getting a taxi because you know they're just there for special occasions because I'd like to wear them but I just can't, I cannot [walk]. (Heidi, Leeds, ethno)

Walking boots and skirts and bare legs in summer are out – in winter I'll wear boots with trousers. (Jan, Leeds, interview)

I get called the bag lady, because I walk everywhere and I have quite a lot of stuff with me. (Steph, Leeds, ethno)

The whole thing with transport and not having a car, I do feel like a second class citizen, there's definitely a sense that as a pedestrian and a cyclist you are definitely second class citizens. (Jim, Lancaster, interview)

Conclusions: building walking cultures

In this chapter we have demonstrated what could be characterised as the paradoxical relationship that many people in Britain seem to have with walking. When viewed from an international perspective levels of walking in Britain are quite high compared to other rich nations: certainly much higher than those in

North America and Australasia and comparable with many countries in continental Europe (Chapter Three). This contrasts markedly with the situation for cycling. These positive messages are confirmed by the fact that, in our case study towns, attitudes towards walking were mostly positive and walking was used for at least some trips by most people. Excepting only those with major health problems, it was rare to find someone who never walked. However, this picture needs to be tempered with the strong evidence that most walking is conditional on a range of factors including timing, location, companions, purpose and weather; and by our view that, despite relatively high levels of use, the walking environment in most British towns is often poor. We were particularly struck by the low expectations that people had of the facilities and environments provided for pedestrians and we attribute these low expectations to three main factors. First, walking, when done, is barely noticed as an activity: it is a means of carrying out simple local tasks but it is not really registered as a means of transport. Thus most walkers have no real expectations that a transport infrastructure should be provided for them. Second, and perhaps most crucially, almost all the walkers we spoke to were also car drivers and as such they viewed the urban environment through the eyes of a motorist. Although strategies to improve the urban environment for pedestrians (see Chapter Nine) might make their short walking trips more enjoyable the constraints that such changes might also impose on them as motorists meant that criticisms of the infrastructure provided for pedestrians was muted. This was even true for those who walked regularly and over relatively long distances, let alone for those for whom walking was an occasional and marginal activity. Third, and following from the above, we argue that over the last half century most people living in English cities have simply become used to spending their everyday lives in car-heavy environments. The car's dominance over urban space (both stationary and moving vehicles) has proceeded gradually, and people have adapted to it, almost to the extent that they no longer notice.

Our research suggests that adopting walking as a convenient and normal thing to do is, for most people, contingent on a combination of circumstances coinciding: a family situation that provides a degree of freedom; services and facilities nearby; a neighbourhood that is perceived to be safe (or at least familiar) and pleasant; and, preferably, friends and neighbours who also walk. Respondents who walked regularly were all in situations where walking was possible and thus, to some extent, they had been able to create walking cultures: that is, life situations where walking was normal for many (though not all) everyday purposes. It can be argued that if such travel choices are to be more widely adopted it will be necessary to create a society and environment where a majority, rather than a minority, perceive the opportunities and advantages of walking outlined by those respondents who engage in walking, who find it easy to incorporate walking into everyday routines, and who enjoy so doing. In Chapter Nine we begin to outline the strategies that we believe will be necessary if such changes are to occur. We recognise that many of the barriers to walking outlined above are strongly embedded and hard to change. We also have demonstrated, however, that most people do have a broadly positive attitude towards walking. Thus it can be suggested that relatively small changes may be sufficient to shift at least some people away from car dependence towards greater use of walking as a means of everyday travel.

EIGHT

The role of cycling in
the urban environment

Why people cycle

First, it is important to re-state that most people do not cycle. Second, we note that most of those people who do cycle do not engage in the kind of urban, utility cycling with which we – as well as transport planners and policy-makers – are here primarily concerned. On the contrary, most people cycle only under a quite specific set of conditions, including being at leisure, in daylight and fine weather, and removed from motorised modes. These conditions tend not to prevail in urban centres. However, it is also clear that many people do enjoy cycling when they choose to ride, and they do so for a wide range of reasons, but mainly to do with health, fitness and the opportunity to unwind. For example, Dick, a middle-aged sales representative from Leicester, described with unselfconscious enthusiasm his love of a summertime bike ride at the end of a day's work (which usually entails much driving): he gets home, gets changed, and pedals out into the nearby countryside, to clear away the stresses of the day, feel the fresh air, enjoy the wildlife, get some exercise and work up an appetite for dinner. He never rides towards the city centre, nor does he undertake any of his more necessary journeys by bike, but regular bike rides, especially in summer, are for him constitutive of a particular image. He wants to keep himself in shape and not drink too much: 'I mean it keeps me a bit fit. I don't want to get old and unfit.' He has a couple of regular mainly off-road routes, each about ten miles long, and which get him into good bird-watching territory: 'One of my hobbies is bird watching…so, yeah, I like to get out and do something.' His cycling, though, is contingent on his mood:

> I've got to be very disciplined with my cycling…So I have to come home from work, take my suit off, get my shorts on, get my tee shirt on, go out to the garage, get my bike out and go off before I've really thought about it. If I don't do that I won't do it.(Dick, Lancaster, interview)

We met people in all four towns who spoke positively about their personal experiences of cycling, especially when that cycling was a leisure practice over which they had a good deal of control in terms of when, where, how and with whom it took place. However, people who enjoyed recreational cycling rarely considered, let alone found similar pleasures in, utility cycling. The most common exception to this was when and where such utility cycling shared some of the characteristics of leisure cycling. For example, we spoke to people who enjoyed cycling to the local shops to buy a newspaper early on a Sunday morning, when the roads were especially quiet, or who would cycle between their home and allotment because the entire route was along quiet back roads, and they made the journey at quiet times of the day. However, we did interview and ride alongside people in all four towns who enjoy urban cycling. Box 8.1 contains a selection of quotes from such people, who rode regularly in order to accomplish the different tasks of everyday life: cycling to work, to shops and to other activities. These quotes demonstrate the diversity of reasons people give when asked to explain their cycling. Talking to people who have established cycling as an ordinary means of moving around, it was also clear that their cycling was something that they simply did, and was largely taken for granted: cycling had become for them as habitual and ordinary as driving has become for the majority of people. The comments of Kyle – a keen cyclist from a committed cycling family – were typical: 'it's just the obvious way of getting around; for me the question is not why do I cycle, but why do other people not cycle?' (Kyle, Leicester, interview). When such cycling enthusiasts were pushed to account for their cycling, the motives most commonly recited were based around the concepts of autonomy and control, health and fitness, saving money, and fresh air and direct contact with nature.

Box 8.1: What people like about cycling

I have a 4x4 so it gas guzzles so obviously, driving in five days a week it can get quite expensive, so starting to cycle was partly to cut down on that. But partly just, you know, nice weather, fresh air and exercise either end of the day, it's just pleasant, and I got a new bike in June so I was sort of wanting to start using it a bit more. (Sonya, Leicester, cycling go-along)

This is the new, upgraded cycle route – if I've got plenty of time, if it's a pleasant day, nice sunshine and all that and I'm not in a hurry, it adds another two or three minutes going this way, to my journey. (Dylan, Worcester, ethno)

I started by accident. I don't think it would ever have occurred to me to go on a bike. I borrowed a bike, it was a man's bike, so it wasn't ideal, but it was the only way I could think of getting to work. It built up gradually, I do it four times a week, because I work Monday to Thursday…I can't bear going in the car now. I've really got into cycling. I love it…my confidence levels, my energy levels, they're much higher than they used to be. And I say to a lot of people, I do my best thinking on a bike in the morning. I can de-stress. You know, after running around with the kids in a morning, this is just completely selfish time for me. It's something I've not really had before, with having children so close together. It's always been really busy…I've surprised myself just how much I enjoy cycling. And how much quicker it is an important thing…My kids are really proud of me, and that's been really nice. (Nadia, Lancaster, go-along)

I actually cycle to make myself feel young. (Percy, Worcester, go-along)

I much prefer cycling [to being in a car]; it's just so, you know, you're not enclosed, you can smell the fresh air. (Liam, Worcester, interview)

We do cycling sometimes, we did one like last week. If the weather's good, 'cause my cousins live in Rushymead area so we just get together and go to Watermead park. It's good exercise…I love cycling, it's quite good I think; good for your heart, good for your legs…once you know what you are doing it gets more better actually so I do use my cycle quite a lot…leisure trips, mostly it's leisure, have fun on the cycle and you are with everyone so…Mostly it's pavement – it's easier. On the road you have to watch out for cars and I can't ride with one hand so even if I want to signal I have to stop the bike and then put my hand out so it's better if we just like ride on the pavement I think. Mostly it's pavement. (Neela, Leicester, ethno)

I get a buzz when I come to work having cycled. If I just get in my car in a morning and just coast down the road in a lovely warm car, there's no pleasure in that. (Andy, Worcester, go-along)

Unlike most people to whom we spoke, for this group current urban cycling conditions did not prevent enjoyment of a wide range of benefits from cycling. Cycling for short trips was for these cyclists more 'obvious', because they tended not to see the equally 'obvious' barriers that others did. Indeed, as Kyle's question above demonstrates, many of these cyclists struggle to understand why more people do not cycle, believing that if they can do it, then surely everyone else can, too. We would argue that the collective failure of experienced and enthusiastic cyclists to recognise their accomplishment, to cycle successfully in the city, is today one of the barriers to developing strategies that would get many more, rather than a few more, people onto bikes for ordinary, everyday journeys, in ways that do not demand the development of a strong cycling identity. Yet strikingly, and somewhat paradoxically, these enthusiastic urban cyclists did mention the difficulties of urban cycling: problems that in some cases (such as storage solutions, and best routes) they had overcome; and in others (such as motorist behaviour, and poor infrastructure) they had learned to negotiate and/or tolerate. Their tolerance and acclimatisation to current urban cycling conditions meant that such conditions had to them become 'normal', and to some extent acceptable. For instance, on his return home from work, Peter rides downhill towards the city centre along a narrow stretch of main road; during a go-along he described to the researcher how he had twice been knocked off and had several more near-misses along this part of his journey, but that it was 'best to get your head down, take your space, and get it done quickly' (Peter, Worcester, ethnography). Peter was tenacious, and had developed an assertive riding style in the face of conditions that most would perceive as far from conducive to cycling. We would suggest that his negative experiences had directly contributed to the development of a powerful cycling identity. However, many experienced cyclists (understandably) do not consciously recognise how their travel identities have become constituted through their urban cycling experiences. This ensures that at the same time as they espouse the advantages of cycling as an 'ordinary' mode of transport, they inadvertently develop and perpetuate their identities as 'elite'. We argue that the main reason why many cyclists continue to cycle, despite what we see as widespread difficult cycling conditions, has to do with identity, however this is formed.

Many times during the qualitative fieldwork we were struck by the lengths to which people went as part of their work in 'becoming a cyclist'. As we saw in Box 8.1, Nadia enjoys cycling and rides to work in Lancaster regularly. During our time with her, however, we learnt that Nadia's husband worries about her riding to work, and is particularly concerned about the stretch of her journey along a big, fast, busy and exposed road, which often carries heavy goods vehicles. Rather than not ride because of her husband's concerns, Nadia agrees to him taking her and her bike in his van for the first half of her journey, to a point where she can continue, largely off-road for the rest of it: 'It's a kind of a compromise because he's not very happy with me on the bypass.' Nadia also described how she is seen as something of an eccentric by other parents in the school playground, when dropping off her children and wearing her cycling attire: 'Everyone in the playground, this is how they usually see me in my cycling stuff and they're all, "Why do you do it on the bike? How can you put up with it?"' (Nadia, Lancaster, go-along). Another participant in Lancaster had only recently returned to cycling following a break of three years, after being knocked from his bike by cars twice in quick succession. In the second collision Fabian had been badly injured, and he had developed a fear of bicycles and of cycling. He had managed to pursue a claim for damages which resulted in compensation, which he had used for therapy to re-build his confidence to cycle:

> It made me feel sick to be near a bike so it was quite a few sessions of just going into a bike shop and saying 'Hello' to the guys who were in there and saying, 'Right, I'm just going to stand with a bike again' and spend 15, 20 minutes in a bike shop and then go again, and then, it was like, right, can I just hold on to one of the bikes, held on to the rack, sat on one of the bikes, week by week building that up until it was a case of, right, I think I can do this. (Fabian, Lancaster, go-along)

To summarise, most people are only willing to cycle under quite specific conditions. When those conditions do not hold, most people we spoke to are simply unprepared to cycle. The main reason people refuse to cycle short urban journeys is the requirement to ride in conditions dominated by fast, motorised modes of traffic. Time and again during our qualitative fieldwork in all four cities people told us either that they had once cycled but had now stopped because they found it too scary, or that they cycled away from roads, but would not cycle on roads, and certainly not urban roads. An example of the former is provided by Catrina from Lancaster during an interview:

> I used to bike, I did really enjoy biking…But once, I was biking in the road and a car beeped at me and it really put me off. I didn't do it much after that, it was one of my last times I think, because I really didn't like that. I lived in a little town and the pavements are really narrow so people don't like you biking on the pavements, but people don't like you on the road either, so I had to be in the road and I didn't like it, I don't like cars being behind me, and having to stop when cars stop and all that…I don't want to do it on these roads, there's no chance. (Catrina, Lancaster, interview)

People's enjoyment of cycling for leisure in 'traffic-free' environments came across strongly and consistently, but this preference is of course contrary to the intentions of much current government policy, which aims to encourage utility cycling in order to reduce car travel, rather than recreational cycling, which so often depends upon the car to reach the start of a ride. We return to current urban conditions as the key barrier to utility cycling later, in the third section of this chapter, and a selection of relevant quotes is given in Box 8.7.

A few people we met through the research cycled out of necessity. This was the case for some recent immigrants with whom we conducted ethnographic fieldwork in Leicester. The most common scenario was lack of a car, combined with a workplace beyond comfortable walking distance, and a pattern of shift-work that made use of public transport not just expensive, but awkward. The people who cycled out of necessity still spoke of its other benefits, but their style of cycling was distinct from the 'voluntary', and usually more obviously committed cyclists whom we met. These 'forced' cyclists tended to ride relatively cheap machines, to have little knowledge of how best to maintain them, and to ride on the pavement, both because they perceived it as safer and because they felt they should stay out of the way of cars, which had a greater right to road space. These people, then, are as reluctant to cycle in currently dominant urban conditions as the rest of the population – but their specific circumstances give them very little option: the choice that they do have some control over is where to ride, and for the most part they choose to do so off the roads, on the pavements. That these attitudes and practices were widespread beyond the people we talked to was confirmed by broader ethnographic observation of cycling in, especially, the Leicester neighbourhood, where many young men of south Asian origin could be seen moving around by cycle, but almost never on the road. The cycling of this group seemed particularly fragile. For example, people we spoke to did not know how to inflate tyres to the correct pressure, nor how to fix a puncture; consequently their cycling experience seemed likely to be both sub-optimal and short-lived. These people tended also to live in high-density terraced housing, with no designated area for cycle storage; their bicycles occupied already crowded and precious living space. The issue of cycle storage is particularly pressing in inner-urban areas, where housing tends not to have garages, where gardens or yards tend to be non-existent or very small, and where security and theft of cycles are significant issues. Our research confirms earlier findings that secure and convenient residential cycle parking is a key requirement of high-density housing areas in particular (Ryley, 2005). In general, however, lack of car ownership did not result in an increased likelihood to cycle, and our research supports recent findings that levels of cycling are highest among car owners (Borjesson and Eliasson, 2012).

There were clear differences in both attitudes towards and practices of cycling across our four ethnographic study areas. In the middle-class area of Lancaster cycling was seen as 'a good thing'. However, the majority of people we spoke to there, although they owned a bicycle, cycled only occasionally, and then as a leisure-time activity, typically along one of the car-free cycle routes that follow the river Lune out from Lancaster into the surrounding countryside. Cycling, then, was a predominantly weekend activity, particularly on sunny days in the summertime. A few people living here did cycle to work and for other everyday journeys, but such utility cycling was exceptional, with the majority of people expressing deep concern – often incredulity – about the city centre roads as places to cycle. These people did not express a concern that this situation should be otherwise; rather they accepted current conditions, while describing them as inappropriate for cycling. Despite this neighbourhood lying within what is widely considered to be 'ideal cycling distance' of the city centre, that journey was much more likely to be driven or walked than it was to be cycled. Interestingly, Lancaster was the place that we found to have the highest degree of reflexivity about car use, and awareness that to reduce car use, and even to reduce the number of cars owned by the household, was a worthwhile thing to do. To give just one example, Anthony says about his household's car use: 'it's always consciously done…we do try to manage our car use consciously' (Anthony, Lancaster, interview).

The situation in the suburban middle-class neighbourhood of Worcester was broadly similar, although the increased distance between it and shops and services, combined with a flatter topography, theoretically make cycling a clearer option for more journeys here. Again, however, we found very few people made everyday journeys by bike, rather more enjoyed cycling on nearby car-free routes such as the River Severn path as a form of fine weather leisure, and most people lived lives firmly centred on the car as the ordinary, default, means of moving around even locally. In general, the car was firmly entrenched and accepted in the patterns of everyday life of almost everyone we met and spoke with in Worcester, although as in Lancaster there was also often recognition of the problems cars cause. During the day, a few retired people could be seen cycling the quiet and wide residential streets between their homes and the nearby parade of shops, but during the morning and evening rush-hours, especially, such cycling seemed simply to disappear under the sheer weight of cars. Probably the key difference between our Lancaster and Worcester ethnographic field sites on the one hand, and those in Leicester and Leeds on the other, was in attitudes towards cycling. Most of the people we met in our middle-class neighbourhoods understood cycling's significance as a more sustainable alternative to the car, even while they continued for the most part to make their own journeys by car. In our Leicester and Leeds communities, however, this sense of cycling as a 'sensible' and 'sustainable' mode of transport was largely absent: government policies promoting urban cycling seemed not to have registered at all and cycling was mainly seen as trivial and/or irrelevant. Bicycle ownership was in these places lower; partly this can be attributed to lack of storage, but it can also be attributed to the bicycle's very low status among most adults, who correspondingly have little incentive to own one (Box 8.2).

Box 8.2: The stigma of cycling

Other people might think I'm trying to save money...So it's almost like I should be ashamed to cycle – it's because I can't afford a car...When the elderly are riding a bicycle, the young ones make fun of them. That's one part. I've seen it, I don't know if anybody's seen it, when elderly people are riding bicycle, young ones you know, make fun of it. (Devaraj, Leicester, ethno)

I don't cycle locally because I think the area, and the young people and stuff might take the mickey a little bit, or have a good laugh about it...there'd be people maybe having a laugh and a joke about, you know, 'she's a bit old to be using a bike' and stuff...my daughter's friends saying 'I saw your mum on a bike earlier' and stuff – it might be a bit of an embarrassment for her as well. (Sadie, Leeds, ethno, focus group)

I don't know anyone that bikes. (Catrina, Lancaster, interview)

Anju: It's not a cool thing for a girl to be on a bike.
Pooja: Yeah.
Researcher: Right.
Anju: Just an observation.
Researcher: Is that changing or not?
Anju: I don't think it is … A lot of my friends…when we all go out together, everybody is either getting a bus or everyone is getting a taxi or everyone is walking; you'd never get everyone on a bicycle and going out together.
Researcher: Do you have friends who cycle?
Anju: No, no, none at all.
Pooja: No.
(Anju and Pooja, Leicester, ethno)

I was talking to my Mum and she goes, actually she'd feel a bit embarrassed if she did ride a bike; she goes it would be a bit embarrassing, you know, riding a bike at this age. (Neela, Leicester, ethno)

In Leicester we worked mainly with people of South Asian heritage. Here, car ownership and use were high, and – perhaps what is more important – aspirations towards the car were still very powerful. To own and drive a car demonstrates that you've 'made it', in one key respect at least (on different motives for car use, see Steg, 2005). In contrast, aspirations towards the bicycle seemed almost non-existent. The bicycle seemed especially stigmatised among the older generation of south Asian households in Leicester. As Devaraj's comments (Box 8.2) make clear, the bicycle often seemed synonymous with poverty, and riding one a particularly visible way of announcing one's poverty. Of those we met, some people could understand cycling as a healthy practice, and there was very limited uptake of it as a recreational activity or for health reasons. More commonly cycling was an indoor health practice, done away from the public gaze in a gym on a static bicycle. To ride a bicycle in order to get somewhere communicated something bad; it demonstrated to others in a particularly clear way that you were unable to afford a car. As we have already noted, this understanding seemed borne out by the number of people who seemed mainly to cycle out of necessity and whose cycling is very different from the kind of fast, confident, fully-equipped commuter cycling that a few of our respondents in Lancaster and Worcester practised; the person seen cycling in our Leicester field site tends to wear their 'normal' clothes (perhaps supplemented with a helmet and hi-viz vest, but no more than that), and their cycling tends to involve the bare minimum of equipment (so, for example, luggage is carried in a plastic bag swinging from the handlebars rather than in a pannier attached to a rack), to be much slower, and to take place primarily on the pavement rather than the road. Ironically, it is of course something akin to this style of cycling that needs to be encouraged if cycling is to become a more mainstream mode of urban mobility. Two obvious ways to make such cycling more plausible are the provision of appropriate space for cycling, and an improvement in the quality of bicycles that people ride: together these would do much to improve people's overall cycling experience. Across younger generations in Leicester, attitudes towards cycling did appear generally more positive, although unlike Lancaster and Worcester, there did not seem to be even an embryonic construction of a culture of 'the bicycle as a good thing'.

Cycling barely registered among the people we spoke to in our Leeds fieldwork neighbourhood. A place of sometimes acute deprivation, most people here have much more pressing concerns than thinking about how they move around, so talking about cycling was obviously well down their list of priorities. That said, cycling was still visible in three main ways. First, some children from the area rode around locally, mainly on BMX bikes. We spoke to some of these children – their main issue was having their bikes stolen, usually under force by older children while they were actually riding them; they did not use locks, or any extra equipment of any kind. This use corresponded to how most people talked to us about cycling (see, for example, Sadie's comments in Box 8.2) as a childhood activity to be left behind with adulthood. Second, a few men – mostly young or middle-aged – could also be seen riding bikes; however, there is an obvious and significant stigma attached to such riding, given how often people we met talked about cycling as the preferred mode of transport of drug dealers and the criminal fraternity. Men riding a bike clearly risked being categorised in these ways. Third, lycra-clad commuters who lived outside the locality could be seen pedalling through the area, mainly during the morning and afternoon rush-hours; these people corresponded to local people talking about cycling as something that other people do. Overall, cycling had an 'othered' status – it was something that certain kinds of people did, but none of these 'others' were considered worthy of emulation; indeed cycling was for children, delinquents, or eccentrics.

How people cycle

People incorporate cycling into their lives to very different extents, and in very different ways. People also ride bicycles in different ways – the machines they ride, the clothes they wear, the equipment they feel they need, the routes they take, the distance over and speed at which they travel, where and when they are and are not prepared to cycle, all these things vary. This section explores in more detail the various ways in which people cycle. For the small minority of committed cyclists we met, cycling is almost a way of life, or lifestyle. Any journey that can be cycled will if at all possible be cycled. Fred from Lancaster, for example, said:

> It's my normal mode of transport. If I want to go somewhere, my first thought is I go on a bike. Shopping, going to see friends, whatever... It's mainly convenience because I can go anywhere I want, when I want...I just prefer going on my bike...I can't imagine a time when I won't cycle. (Fred, Lancaster, go-along)

Distance was less of an obstacle than time for such people. Indeed, for a few of the cycling enthusiasts we met, the struggle was how to fit more cycling (as training) into their busy schedules; ideally they would like to ride further than they do. People belonging to this group clearly participated in a 'culture of cycling'. They recognised themselves, and could recognise others, as 'cyclists'. They had strong cycling identities. Most spoke fondly of belonging to this group, and some actively participated in it by reading relevant magazines, holding club memberships, taking part in organised rides and so on. Belonging to a more dispersed cycling culture is probably important in sustaining a person's commitment to cycle in the face of local indifference or even hostility. Indeed, we would argue that one reason why these people have such strong cycling identities is due to the harassment and intimidation that they systematically suffer at the hands of motorists. By riding on the roads at all, they are asserting their right to the road, but as we will see more clearly later when looking at pavement cyclists, this right is not widely recognised even by people who ride bikes. Box 8.3 provides evidence of some of the ways in which committed cyclists tend typically to talk about their use of the roads. The overall impression is that being a cyclist in a car-dominated world is difficult.

Box 8.3: Assertive cycling

I think you've got to be quite confident really, to cope with traffic coming so close to you. (Rosa, Worcester, interview)

As an observer I feel that the cyclists who are safest are the ones who make themselves big and 'I'm here and I'm keeping up with the traffic and I know what I'm doing' and you make yourself obvious. (Andrew, Lancaster, ethno)

If pressured by vehicles I will sit in the middle of a lane and make them wait. You're not pushing me off the road. (Lisa, Worcester, interview)

I don't mind riding in traffic. Erm, I'd prefer it if there was none. But I'll claim my space, move up on the outside of queuing traffic…I suppose I've always made my own advance stop line. (Kyle, Leicester, go-along)

The only thing you can do is just behave like a car. You know, cycle down the middle of the road and then make them overtake you like a car. If you get in the gutter they'll just squeeze you out. (Mary, Worcester, go-along)

It's a bit of a battle up here except that most times the traffic's not moving very fast and so I'm going a lot faster than the traffic, so I'm going on the outside of the traffic and riding up the middle of the road basically, passing all the traffic for a lot of the way… obviously you've got to be pretty careful, you've got to be pretty sharp and pretty aware, but I ride and I expect, I'm almost expecting somebody to do something stupid, I don't ride and expect everybody to do what they should do, I always ride expecting them to get in my way, or I'm going to get in their way; it's not the best thing, it's not what you'd want to do…but I guess it's a compromise between that and [a longer route]… Then it starts to flow and the traffic's passing me as you go up the rest of this hill, up here, which is not that pleasant I have to say, especially if you've got a big lorry behind you going up the hill and who can't get past…I just keep going, I just keep the proper distance from the kerb but I just keep going…I'm a confident cyclist so I'll do battle with the traffic. (Rhys, Worcester, ethno)

For a much larger, but still relatively small, group of respondents, cycling is an occasional means of moving around. People in this group still identify with, and speak fondly of, cycling. Although they might ride primarily for leisure, they nonetheless make some of their everyday journeys by bike. Their decisions to do so, however, are much more influenced by external conditions than is the case for more committed cyclists, whose internal drive to cycle tends usually to outweigh external circumstances. People in this category find ways of coping with an urban environment that is generally hostile to cycling, through making both spatial and temporal adjustments. Stella from Worcester provides an example of this kind of more 'conditional cyclist'. She is in her early 70s, lives with her husband, and has two grown-up children who live elsewhere. Stella moves around locally by bike – cycling to her part-time job as a charity shop volunteer in Worcester, and to the local shops in her neighbourhood. She also cycles for pleasure with her husband. Stella is a keen and confident cyclist, but there are things about cycling that she does not like. Most significantly, she dislikes cycling in traffic, but her relatively relaxed daily schedule means she can avoid busy times, and she also is happy to dismount from her bicycle and push it along pavements. She also selects routes that keep her away from the busiest and most intimidating roads. She is less likely to cycle at night, but then she has little need to do so. She will cycle in most weathers, although does not like to ride in icy conditions. Her more leisurely semi-retired lifestyle, and particularly the flexibility it affords, means that Stella can make cycling work for her. Busy and potentially scary road conditions are less of a disincentive to cycling for Stella than they might be for many other people. Her preference for cycling and her lifestyle have also co-evolved, however, so that – similarly to Audrey whose walking-centred lifestyle we examined in the previous chapter – cycling has helped to shape the contours of her life, in which cycling is correspondingly relatively easy. She has always cycled, and it continues to be her preferred mode of travel for all short trips within the urban area, including travel to work; but cycling has not become a rule, and Stella will use other modes of transport when she feels that it makes more sense to do so. For this respondent cycling is good exercise, environmentally-friendly, practical and convenient. Cycling is clearly an important part of her identity. In her own words:

> I've never not ridden a bike. I mean, I never stopped as a teenager, so that I'm used to riding a bike. I cycle into town; I'm afraid I use the pavements an awful lot when, you know, I mean obviously if there are people walking on the pavement then I just push, get off my bike and push it. (Stella, Worcester, ethnography)

Off-peak cycling is one strategy by which people make cycling work for them; people who are able tend to choose to make journeys by bike at quieter times. Carole in Lancaster, for example, notes: 'Because I have to use the A6 for a few metres, that's one of the reasons I prefer to go (to work) quite early because it's quiet. A bit later, the cars tend to get so close, you can almost knock on their windows' (Carole, Lancaster, go-along). Similarly Jason, a regular cyclist in Leicester, takes advantage of flexible working hours to cycle to and from work:

> I tend to time my journey to miss most of the traffic…It's lovely that I have the flexibility of my job at least sometimes, on some days, to travel after 9 o'clock in the morning on the way into work, and you know, well after at least 6 o'clock in the evening in order to miss the main traffic on the busier sections. (Jason, Leicester, go-along)

Such contingent cycling was common across our research areas: people were prepared to cycle if conditions were right, or could be made right, but not otherwise. Ideal conditions tended to be off-road, in good weather, for sociable, recreational purposes. The further from such an ideal conditions became, the less likely were people to cycle. Furthermore, the majority of people do not have the privilege of being able to adjust the temporal and/or spatial aspects of their day to fit in cycling.

As we have seen, by far the biggest group of contingent cyclists is formed by people who are happy to cycle for leisure, or under leisurely conditions, but not for everyday journeys that require them, either alone or with others, to negotiate the urban transport environment by bike. Overall, our research suggests that over the last few decades, as car ownership and use has expanded, cycling has become more powerfully framed and cemented as a leisure rather than as a utility practice. People utilise bicycles not in order to reproduce everyday life (through, for example, cycling to the shops, to school or work), but in the construction of healthy, productive and enjoyable leisure time. The incorporation of cycling as a break from the everyday, rather than as part of that everyday, was nowhere more apparent than in Worcester, where we spoke to many people about the (then under construction but since completed) new walking and cycling bridge across the River Severn at Diglis Basin. Almost everyone we spoke to welcomed the bridge, but always because it gave them extra options for leisure walking and cycling around their local area. We met no one who planned to use it either to facilitate their current utility cycling journeys, or to encourage new utility trips by bike. The weather, daylight and seasonality are also important factors affecting cycling: Box 8.4 contains statements from participants in our research on their influence. Sometimes these effects can be contradictory: for example, many people are happy to cycle during daylight but not after dark, and Carole does not cycle into Lancaster at night because she worries about her bike being stolen; yet Cari considers cycling to be a safe night-time form of transport:

> Cycling, from a woman's point of view, is much safer than walking home…Women will say, 'Oh, I feel safer in my car', and I'll be thinking, 'Well, you've still got to park your car somewhere and walk to it and get in it', and if it is a slightly dodgy area or you're feeling a bit, you know, whereas with a bike you can literally park it outside wherever you are, or even inside. (Cari, Worcester, interview)

For the greater proportion of people participating in our research, cycling is barely considered at all. Or rather, it is more likely considered to be an irritating practice that others do, often on the pavement, rather than as a practice that they might themselves one day adopt. Most strikingly in our Leeds and Leicester ethnographic neighbourhoods, cycling is almost invisible. In these places particularly, to ride a bike involves visibly stepping (or pedalling) outside of local norms and expectations, something it is hard both to imagine and to do. As the examples in Box 8.2 make plain, cycling is here much more likely to expose a person to ridicule than to positive affirmation. So any incorporation of cycling into everyday life requires active effort. It is not something that is automatically done, but rather something people must want to do, and which takes effort to make part of their lives. Because of its differential status effects, to do this work is more plausible in our Lancaster and Worcester ethnographic fieldwork sites than it is in the Leeds and Leicester communities studied in detail. Wherever someone cycles, and to whatever extent, to do so means going a little against the grain. However, to the extent that a person incorporates cycling into their lifestyle, then, they tend also to develop a cycling identity. Meanwhile, most people 'simply' drive – to drive is the norm, it requires little if any active effort; and there is less decision-making involved. Until the same is true of cycling, it will continue as a mode of urban transport to have the marginal status that we have described here.

Box 8.4: The influence of weather, daylight and seasonality

I've never used it for like travelling to shops and stuff; I just use it on a weekend and stuff, go for bike rides and stuff, getting out of the area…we just sort of go on the park for an hour or so and then ride back down, 'cause I've got a teenage daughter as well as nieces and nephews, so like a line of us, but that tends to be in the nicer weather, summer time and stuff. I don't use it in winter, I get lazy. (Sandi, Leeds, ethno)

Because of bad weather since mid-December until now I haven't used the bike much recently…I don't like cycling when it is wet actually, so I am more likely to walk…I've got out of the habit of using the bike since the bad weather which started, if you remember, about a week before Christmas. We've had pretty rotten weather off and on since then, it's not been cycling weather…I had a meeting at County Hall a couple of weeks ago, I used the car…if it was really decent, if it was in the summer I might well have cycled, but it was a snowy morning, an unpleasant morning. (Dylan, Worcester, ethno)

My behaviour changes with the weather, which is quite interesting. Sometimes I will cycle relatively slowly, when it feels hot and sticky. When it's a bit cooler, I'll belt along. When it gets really cool I abandon the bicycle altogether, and walk. (Percy, Worcester, go-along)

I always go to work on my bike, whatever the weather. So I never opt to go in the car to work, I always go on my bike. (Rhys, Worcester, ethno)

You're often vulnerable when it's raining, I always feel – you know, the roads; you can't stop so quickly, and people I think are less careful when it's raining. (Mia, Worcester, interview)

We are fair-weather cyclists – not in the rain, and not in snow, obviously. (Sally, Worcester, interview)

I quite enjoy cycling when the weather's good. (Don, Worcester, interview)

A lot of cars don't see you, especially at night. You might have all the lights...I wouldn't go cycling at night, bloody hell! (Dan and Catrina, interview, Lancaster)

I don't like cycling in the dark on the roads...I avoid cycling home from work in the dark, so I don't cycle to work in the winter. (Adam, interview, Lancaster)

[During winter] there's just no gritting, there's nothing going on. The roads are frozen, the paths are frozen, there's loads of ice about, it's totally unsafe. So at the point, you get your car back out and you drive like everyone else. (Andy, Worcester, go-along)

I prefer not to leave my bike at a time when people are drinking in all of the pubs. So if I go to the cinema or theatre I prefer to walk there and not bike. (Carole, Lancaster, go-along)

The barriers to cycling

Previous sections have hinted at the difficulties and barriers that people confront when cycling in the city. This section examines these in more detail, using examples from all four towns studied. As in the last chapter, we focus on five main themes: problems associated with the urban infrastructure; issues of safety and risk; constraints imposed by families and lifestyles; the impact of weather and topography; and the influence of culture and image. Together, we argue, these factors contribute to making cycling both difficult and unpleasant for most people for most of the time. Those few people who cycle regularly do so despite, not because of, the conditions that exist. Although they remain restricted mainly to leisure cycling, designated off-road cycle facilities – paths that might be shared with pedestrians but from which motorised vehicles are excluded – were easily the most favoured cycling environment. Such provision is not without problems; it can create conflicts between cyclists and other users, particularly pedestrians, and most particularly dog owners. Such provision is typically what people think of, and talk about, when contemplating good places to cycle, however. We found designated beside-road and on-road (as opposed to off-road) cycle routes to be much more problematic. Such routes have been increasingly installed across the UK over the last two decades in an attempt to create space for cycling, particularly along bigger and busier roads. Beside-road cycling infrastructure typically converts what was formerly a pavement for the sole use of pedestrians to a space that cyclists can share; sometimes such use is divided by means of a white line, with cyclists supposed to keep to one side, pedestrians the other. Respondents' views of current cycling infrastructure are given in Box 8.5.

Box 8.5: Problems of urban infrastructure

The new crossing and lights for the benefit of pedestrians and cyclists...the time it takes for the lights to go green for cyclists is ridiculously long. The traffic has passed by the time they go red; that is not the way. (Dylan, Worcester, ethno)

The way that cycle lanes have been developed around here it's very hard not to feel a certain cynicism about it, and feel that cynicism has crept in somewhere. There's a large number of places in Morecambe I can think of where you cycle along, there's a cycle lane and you get to somewhere where it's difficult – traffic lights or bus stops – and suddenly it disappears. Well this is only playing at it, isn't it?...I sometimes wonder with these odd bits of cycle track we've got just painted on the side of the road, then people say, 'Oh, we've got 50 miles of cycleway.' Well, you've got 50 miles of road where cyclists can still be knocked down. (Adam, Lancaster, interview)

I don't like going on the road, particularly the A6, which is, I find it the most dangerous, frightening experience...This sounds quite cowardly but at Scotforth traffic lights and down at Penny Street Bridge I'll get off my bike and walk it through because I don't like going through that amount of traffic. I'd much rather stay off the road and away from the vehicular traffic. (Rick, Lancaster, interview)

The cycle paths in my area seem to be a roundabout way of getting somewhere, rather than being functional or direct...The actual marked cycle routes just go out of the way. They seem to be more for leisure than for actually getting where you want to go...Certainly if there were the major routes in and out of town, if they had cycle routes as well, you know...then I'd be more inclined to use them. (Noah and Natalie, Worcester, go-along)

I would be very wary of cycling in Leeds. I prefer walking to cycling and I wouldn't cycle...I think motorists have a complete disregard for cyclists...The cycle lanes are very haphazard – they start then stop, people park in them. (Vince, Leeds, interview)

My ideal would be, if it were possible, transport wise, for cycle paths to be absolutely physically removed from roads, as in a proper kerb separating cyclists from the traffic so that cyclists didn't have to use the pavement but weren't sharing the roads with cars. Then cycling would definitely be an option, and I'd find ways around the other inconveniences of cycling. But as I say, with cyclists having to mix with traffic it just seems crazy...All this work that seems to be going on in the middle of Lancaster is to paint cycle paths on the road. You know, that's just not going to do it because there's no physical barrier between the cyclists and the traffic. (Holly, Lancaster, interview)

I did not like cycling on the outside of a line of parked cars, and in Lancaster (laughing) there is always a line of parked cars, erm, and I just gave up...I felt I was too far out

> into the middle of the road, and there were other cars coming past me, and I, I just didn't like it. So I gave up the bicycle. (Jennifer, Lancaster, ethno)
>
> There's an alleyway which we'll actually go on just before the end of the journey which is actually marked not for cyclists. There are many such alleyways in this area, but it actually saves about a third of a mile or something, and it's a very short section, so what I usually do is basically just walk with my bike through there. (Jason, Leicester, go-along)
>
> There's an issue with the trailer, which we're finding out. It's as wide as a wheelchair and there's a lot of places we can't go through...there are good cycling routes we can't really have access to because of the trailer. (Isla and family, Worcester, go-along)

Experienced cyclists invariably saw such provision as irrelevant to their journeys. They disliked it because they tended to feel it created an expectation in the minds of motorists that they should be using it, and so be off the road when they wanted to stay on the road because to do so best facilitated their journeys. Such cyclists looked a bit more kindly upon on-road cycle lanes, but still tended to resist what they felt to be an imposition of a correct cycling position; they indicated to other road users where cyclists ought to be, without always reflecting where these experienced cyclists actually wanted to be. These attitudes towards beside-road and on-road cycling provision tended to be reversed for less experienced cyclists and non-cyclists, who saw on-road cycle lanes (which in the UK very rarely provide any sort of physical separation from flows of motorised traffic) as not giving them the kind of protection that they felt they needed to cycle safely and comfortably. These cyclists and non-cyclists looked more kindly upon beside-road provision, but typically considered such provision to be far too piece-meal to be useful. Roads with no designated space for cycling are accepted, and sometimes even preferred, by committed cyclists who, rather than being put into a particular part of the road, can instead adjust their road position according to the speed, scale and their sense of motorised traffic; but they present real difficulties for others, especially on bigger and busier roads. Rick from Lancaster, for example, cycles regularly, including to move around as part of his job as a peripatetic carer of housebound elderly people. He cannot face cycling along the main road which forms an important part of the route for most of his journeys, as he finds the road too intimidating; to negotiate this section of his journey, he gets off his bike and pushes it along the pavement.

In the tradition of ethnography of the street (Whyte, 1955; Hamilton, 2002; Lefebvre, 2004), we spent long periods making detailed observations of people negotiating urban space, and particularly junctions, by bike. More than anywhere else, it is clearly junctions, and especially complicated junctions, where cyclists feel confused, at risk and on their own. More confident cyclists might approach and negotiate the junction in the same way as would a motorist, but like Stella and Rick, many cyclists effectively become pedestrians, getting off and pushing their machines, while others take to the pavements without dismounting. In Worcester we made multiple observations of one stretch of road linking our ethnographic neighbourhood with the shopping centres of St John's and central Worcester. This stretch is narrow, with very limited carriageway widths, and is usually congested with motorised traffic. We noticed early on in the fieldwork that the number of cyclists taking to the pavement along this stretch of road was unusually high, and repeated observations made clear why they did so. To remain on the road meant sharing very limited space with long queues of motorised traffic, including heavy goods vehicles and buses, and it also required extreme vigilance in moving through this traffic as vehicles turned on to or off the road at many different junctions. Suffice to say, there is no dedicated space or special provision for cycling at any point. As Rhys, a hardened cyclist who rode a bike for sport as well as for commuting to work, said: 'St John's centre as a cyclist is a bit of a nightmare'. Like the minority of experienced and confident cyclists, however, Rhys stuck to the road when negotiating this stretch; it was the majority of less experienced and less confident cyclists who felt compelled to develop a range of alternative strategies. By far people's greatest fear, whether in contemplating cycling or in actually moving around by bike, was the fear of co-existing with motorised traffic which, they felt, did not or would not account sufficiently for their vulnerabilities as a cyclist. These fears held for a large majority of adults we spoke to, but they were even more powerfully articulated by parents when contemplating the prospects of their children cycling.

When accompanying people on their cycling journeys we were struck time and again by the ways in which people shifted from the road to the pavement and back again, according to the requirements of making their journeys as safely and smoothly as they could. This jumping around of cyclists between different infrastructures within the urban environment clearly demonstrates how for many people riding bikes there is, quite literally, nowhere obvious to go and stay. We saw in the last chapter how pavement cycling is a major concern for many pedestrians. All the people we spoke to who rode on the pavement understood and appreciated this, but felt they often had little alternative (Box 8.6). Many were unable to see how they could possibly negotiate many junctions on the road: it was not simply that the prospect seemed daunting; it seemed impossible. Others thought it was possible, but were unwilling to do it because it seemed so dangerous. It was not only junctions that persuaded people to ride on the pavements. As we have indicated already, many people we spoke to also saw fast, busy roads as inappropriate for cycling. While riding along a main road in Leicester, one go-along participant commented 'You can see why people would choose to ride on the pavement, because you are constantly pressured by the traffic. On the busier roads in Leicester it kind of feels like it's always on your shoulder trying to get past, about to come past' (Kyle, Leicester, go-along). Many people we spoke to saw cycling along such roads as impossible: they pointed to the domination of the carriageways by trucks, buses and cars, and could see no space for cycling; some of these people were incredulous at the very idea they might cycle on the road.

Other people understood that cycling on the road was practically possible, but trusted neither themselves ('too wobbly') nor motorists sufficiently to feel safe putting themselves into those kinds of spaces. A selection of the fears expressed by respondents is given in Box 8.7.

Box 8.6: Pavement cycling

To go to the city centre now and back, it is really tricky. There's one way streets, too much traffic – got to go on the pavement…I don't like cycling on the pavement, I feel I'm a nuisance. But people never say anything. (Isla and family, Worcester, go-along)

I know I shouldn't cycle on the pavement but I'm quite prepared to – say if there's no provision for cyclists, and it's better than getting killed. (Sonya, Lancaster, interview)

This bit here, we went out, my wife and my daughter, we went out for a little ride the other Sunday and we came round this way…but this bit is a nightmare here, you see, because you've got no option but to go on the [very fast, with no space for cycling] road or on the pavement, which is not designated for use. (Rhys, Worcester, ethno)

I cycle mainly on the road, I try and cycle as much as I can on the road, but if there are obstructions or if the cars are too close to the kerbs, I do then come onto the pavements, you know? Some of the traffic is not aware, you see? (Akhilesh, Leicester, ethno, go-along)

From my house to the park I would cycle on the pavement and then, obviously when I was in the park I was OK. (Anju and Pooja, Leicester, ethno)

My journey through town is quite hairy really. It's not ideal by any means, so and I go on the pavement for a little bit…If there is just the two of us, I'll often take to the pavements, and part of me is quite bolshie about it, and I think if anyone wants to, you know…and we cycle carefully, we don't ever hit anyone or anything! You know, and I'm very conscious of people who may be elderly or really frail or something, we'll stop…I don't think it does cyclists any favours when you see some cyclists hop onto the pavement just a bit when there's a traffic light, and then go back the other side. (Liam and family, Worcester, interview)

I'd say you see more cyclists on the pavement [in Leicester] than you do on the road…I can see exactly the pedestrian's point of view they don't expect to see a cyclist. (Richard, Leicester, go-along)

If you want to be really safe and that then you'd have to ride on the pavement. (Neela, Leicester, interview)

Box 8.7: Fears of cycling

In winter, in the dark, you have to be much more aware; not every car driver is bike aware. I need my lights in good working order and protective clothing for the weather… It's quite scary on the ring road on a bike – people come down at 60, 70, 80 mph. (Katie, Leeds, interview)

I just think that the majority don't really appreciate what it's like to be on a bike on a road and about how much room you should give people and all the rest of it. And you get the very occasional ones who get irritated … I do have an occasional shout at some people (Rhys, Worcester, ethno)

I used to cycle, but because I got knocked off twice early on, that puts you off…Cars always want to overtake you…they don't feel that you're another vehicle on the road; they just see you as a pedestrian on the road, and an inconvenience. (Andy, Worcester, go-along)

I don't cycle because it's not safe, it's very risky (Raj, ethno, Leicester)

Car drivers and cyclists don't mix. I'm frightened to cycle on the roads, I'll only cycle on the cycle track. (Wanda, Lancaster, interview)

I like cycling and I've got a bike but I am terrified of cycling because of the traffic around here – narrow winding roads and cars go very fast. (Ron, Leeds, interview)

My main issue for not cycling would be because I don't want to go on the roads; that would be my issue really…I've heard of enough accidents on roads, I'm not too confident on the road. I don't even like driving, so cycling on the road would be a different question. (Anju, Leicester, ethno) I find cycling around here incredibly dangerous. (Brian, Leeds, interview)

I did have a bicycle. I did try to cycle but I am not comfortable at all with cycling…I'm always scared of the traffic around me. (Molly, Leicester, interview)

I wouldn't cycle on the roads because it's far too dangerous. (Aidan, Leeds, ethno)

I think you've got to be quite confident really, to cope with traffic coming so close to you. (Clive, Worcester, go-along)

I used to bike, I did really enjoy biking…But once, I was biking in the road and a car beeped at me and it really put me off. I didn't do it much after that, it was one of my last times I think, because I really didn't like that. I lived in a little town and the pavements are really narrow so people don't like you biking on the pavements, but people don't like you on the road either, so I had to be in the road and I didn't like it, I don't like

> cars being behind me, and having to stop when cars stop and all that…I don't want to do it on these roads, there's no chance. (Catrina, Lancaster, interview)
>
> I did my cycling proficiency at primary school and I took a bike with me when I first went to university in St Andrews, but I'm a complete coward when it comes to cycling on roads…I just, everybody I know who does a considerable amount of cycling at some point has been knocked off and hurt themselves in some way, and as a driver, cyclists on the road just seem so vulnerable that I just don't want to join them, and although the university cycle path is really good as far as it goes, erm, even so you can't avoid cycling on the road at some point, and if not cycling on the road then cycling on the pavement, which isn't legal and does expose pedestrians to risk, which I can't justify. So, you know, it's just not something that I'd consider. (Holly, Lancaster, interview)
>
> I am not a happy cyclist…I gave my bike away, to someone who was going to use it and get benefit from it…I'm not comfortable in traffic, so the kind of bike riding I'd prefer to do would be away from traffic completely. I know we have lovely cycle paths. I could go to Morecambe and then even along the prom, but I would have to get there on a bike, and I couldn't face that. (Alison, Lancaster, go-along)

Many people felt guilty and apologetic about cycling on the pavement, but nonetheless rode there because they felt they had no alternative. This arguably suggests significant repression of cycling: if cycling had a clear and coherent place within the transport infrastructure, many more people who currently either do not contemplate cycling at all, or else think about cycling but are reluctant actually to do it, might be encouraged to do so. If the majority of people who do ride bicycles have quite literally been pushed off the road, what does this say about the state of cycling more generally? There are also many ideal cycling short-cuts along which cycling is theoretically prohibited. To cycle however respectfully along such routes, which often form important connections between stretches of quieter road and so constitute important resources to urban cycling, is to risk being seen as 'deviant'. We argue that the prohibition of cycling along these stretches contributes to a generalised (if also overlooked) discrimination against urban cycling; although, as Jason's comments in Box 8.5 make clear, some people do manage successfully to incorporate such routes into their cycling journeys.

Another major barrier to regular cycling for utility travel, and one that occurred more-or-less ubiquitously across all groups and study areas, was the difficulty involved in getting multi-person households – often including people of different ages, interests and abilities – to make their individual and collective ordinary journeys by bike. Chief among these is probably storage and maintenance in a roadworthy state of (for a family) multiple machines, so that they are ready-to-ride at any time. For safe and smooth cycling, these machines need to be equipped with lights, locks, racks, panniers and mudguards; and the kind of wet weather gear that makes walking more of an option is also required for cycling. We met families who moved by bike, and who had organised their homes and their lives in ways that facilitated regular and routine cycling, but they represented a tiny minority of all those people who participated in our research. In Leicester, for example, Kyle and Sashi live with their children, Ray, who is 15 and Tania, who is 11. All the family are keen cyclists, and make most of their everyday journeys by bike. Cycling has become for this family the habitual way of moving around, in the same way that most families use the car. They have a large shed full of different machines, which emerge according to requirements. For example, if Tania needs to be dropped somewhere but will get a lift home later in a friend's family's car, Kyle and Tania will ride the family tandem, on which Kyle can return alone. The family is a musical one, and play an assortment of instruments, so they have a bike trailer, on which even the largest (a cello) can be transported. Only in exceptional circumstances does the family's car get used; but in a world organised predominantly by and around the car, this family is exceptional, and continues to cycle in the face of its unusual status. As we argue in later chapters, for them to become normal, the world, and so other people's lives, needs to become different. Added to these barriers at the material level are a range of potential physical, psychological and emotional barriers. The various family members, who are required to cycle in order to get around, need similarly to be ready-to-ride; fit, strong, fresh and enthusiastic enough to make a journey requiring both some physical exertion and technical competence. Additionally, if moving by cycle is rarely practised, it never becomes habitual and will remain difficult and awkward. If one or more is available, the car remains the default option, and the 'good sense' of using it is continuously, perhaps many times daily, reproduced. Of course if cycling could be routinely done more sedately in safe surroundings then these fitness factors would become less important. We have already cited examples of quite elderly people cycling, and cycling has very high ergonomic and energy efficiency.

When talking about cycling, perhaps surprisingly, people expressed concerns about wet weather and hills much less than they did about heavy and fast-moving traffic. Unless they were competitive sports cyclists, people who cycled for leisure tended to cycle only in fine weather, and to choose reasonably 'easy' routes that included few, if any, hills: canal towpaths, sea-front promenades (such as Morecambe, near Lancaster), river and estuary paths, and disused railways – many of which have been converted to walking and cycling use by Sustrans – were all especially popular (many commuter routes used for everyday cycling also take advantage of such flat and traffic-free corridors). More regular cyclists, however, were rarely put off by rain or hills, as evidenced by some of the testimonies in Box. 8.1; this is because by-and-large they rode bicycles with a good range of gears that could cope with even severe climbs, and over time they had developed a level of fitness that sustained cycling. They also invested in good quality waterproof clothing that kept them warm and dry in even the wettest and coldest weather. The conditions most likely to put off these committed cyclists were snow and ice. Even the most committed cyclists admitted to finding cycling much easier and more pleasurable in the longer, lighter and warmer days of summer than during the short, dark and cold days of winter. People who did not cycle but who were required by our research questions to think about the prospects of their cycling did sometimes mention the weather (and especially rain), and topography (and especially any steep local hills that they knew of) as reasons why they would be unlikely to do so; but our general and strong impression was very much that weather and hills are not the most important reasons why people do not cycle. In Lancaster, which is perhaps the wettest and hilliest of our case study towns, the profile of cycling is probably highest. So as with walking, weather and local topography might influence the amount of cycling undertaken, and the route chosen, but we argue that the effect of these (fixed) factors is much less than the impact of other variables over which we do have some control.

The various barriers to cycling ensure that it remains a very marginal means of urban travel. Outside of specific times and places cycling is unusual, and so are those who do it. As we saw with the situation of walking in the last chapter, so with cycling we have entered a self-reinforcing and downward spiral, in which barriers to cycling ensure it remains unusual, and its unusual status deters and/ or sabotages efforts to make it more normal and mainstream. If fear was the biggest barrier to cycling in our Lancaster and Worcester study neighbourhoods, in the communities to which we got up close in Leicester and Leeds issues of image and identity were more significant. It was as though most people in these places had not really contemplated the idea of themselves cycling, and so had not yet thought about how afraid they might be to do so. Cycling simply was not contemplated as a potential practice by most of the people we spoke to in these places; it was so stigmatised that the idea of practising it was faintly absurd. In many communities cycling is quite simply not taken seriously as an ordinary, everyday mode of mobility. We agree that under present road conditions such an attitude makes sense, reflecting as it does the still dominant wider attitude towards cycling and the ways in which motor vehicles dominate our streets. We have, however, seen that some people, including families, do establish cycling as a habit, so that cycling successfully connects and integrates the different aspects of their ordinary, everyday lives. We argue that the existence of such individuals and families amply demonstrates that wider cycling-based lifestyles are possible, and we consider how they might best be more widely encouraged in the remaining chapters of this book.

Conclusions: building cycling cultures

Cycling is a relatively popular form of recreation across contemporary Britain, but as a mode of urban transport it is virtually irrelevant. In line with established trends, only a very small minority of the people who participated in our research used a bicycle as a means of making their ordinary, everyday urban journeys; but as we saw in Chapter Three, other European countries have much higher levels of urban cycling. It thus seems reasonable to suggest that levels of urban cycling in Britain could be a great deal higher. How, however, do we get from here to there?

How do we build a mainstream culture of cycling? Many people like cycling and would like to cycle more, but feel hampered by what they perceive as a real lack of a cycle-friendly urban environment. Other people, and particularly those from more disadvantaged backgrounds and who are much less versed in the concept and importance of sustainable transport, are indifferent towards cycling, although we would argue that this indifference is born in large part from that same lack of a cycle-friendly urban environment. People are unlikely to want to cycle if the message they receive from their wider environments (not just the urban transport environment, but also the ideological environment, including media discourses, government policies and everyday talk) is that cycling is not taken seriously. Whatever views to the contrary might emerge from time to time from national and local government, our research indicates that rather than feeling encouraged to get on a bike, most people are discouraged from urban cycling.

Over the last half century most people living in urban Britain have become used to living their everyday lives in car-heavy environments. The car's dominance over urban space (whether those cars are stationary or moving) has proceeded gradually, and people have adapted to it, almost to the extent that they do not notice. The car's taken-for-granted centrality to urban life will become both more obvious, but probably also more cherished, only as it is challenged; but our research clearly indicates that in order to create more cycle-friendly urban environments challenged it must be. What a few people are able to achieve at the individual and/or family level requires, if it is to be achieved at a societal level, some very big changes: changes of a scale and significance that the majority of people have never personally experienced. Over the final two chapters we spell out in detail what these changes are, and how they might be achieved.

Section III

POLICY PERSPECTIVES

NINE

The future of walking and cycling in British urban areas

Strategies for making walking normal

Our research shows that there are currently some situations where most people do indeed perceive walking to be a normal and expected means of travel. However, these tend to be restricted to trips that are undertaken for leisure and pleasure rather than those that are required for work or other essential everyday activities. The main exception to this is travel to school, especially for children of primary school age, where travelling on foot remains a common experience. Given that walking is something that most people associate with enjoyment, and that it is often a voluntarily-undertaken leisure activity, it ought to be reasonably easy to shift more short-distance everyday travel to walking. However, our research shows that most respondents only associate pleasurable walking with certain environments. When our respondents walked for pleasure they most often did so in urban parks, on off-road tracks, or in the countryside, usually with other family members or with a dog that was seen as providing a legitimate reason for walking. Many of these walking trips first required a car journey to reach a destination in which walking was seen as acceptable, pleasurable and a normal thing to do. Probably the most extreme example of this was in the small area in Leicester where ethnographic research was focused. Here, it was relatively common for residents to use the local park to walk for exercise, but rather than walk (sometimes only a few hundred metres) from their home to the park along local streets they would drive to and from the park. Thus there was a clear separation in respondents' minds between walking for health and pleasure, in the park with others who engaged in a similar activity, and walking on the streets to get to and from a destination. The former was normal but the latter was not. Although rarely quite so visible within a small area, similar values and behaviours were observed and recorded in all study areas.

Apart from walking for pleasure and/or health, most people who walked occasionally did so out of necessity. Thus those who could not drive (children, the elderly) walked more than those with access to a car; and those on low incomes who either did not own a car or who wished to restrict car use walked more than those with fewer financial constraints. Thus walking was common in the deprived area of Leeds studied in detail (either to a local destination or as part of a multi-mode trip), but it was done from necessity and usually only at certain times of the day when it was perceived to be safe. Walking from necessity also occurred when respondents' normal form of transport ceased to be possible. Thus people walked in snow and ice when driving was deemed too dangerous, or if the car was in the garage for repair. Sometimes respondents noted that they found they enjoyed these enforced walks, but they rarely continued once usual conditions were restored. Walking was also an activity associated with childhood: partly because young people have fewer alternative options so are forced to walk for some everyday activities, but also because it was associated with going out to play. In this sense, walking could be seen as something that you grow out of as you get older and then only participate in for particular purposes or in the company of others as a social activity.

We identify five sets of factors that collectively inhibit walking for everyday travel in British towns and cities. These are the issues for which strategies need to be derived that will address concerns and reduce barriers to greater levels of walking. In summary the five are: the quality of the infrastructure for walking; the unpleasantness of the urban environment; concerns about personal safety; the difficulty of reconciling walking with family and household routines; and the taken-for-granted expectations created by a largely sedentary society. Time after time we were told by respondents that the infrastructure for walking in their neighbourhood was very poor and that this deterred them from walking, even for short trips to local shops, services or friends. In part these concerns related purely to the physical environment, and in part they interacted with external conditions that were perceived to make the infrastructure less attractive. Key concerns included the narrow width of pavements; their unevenness; the extent to which they were cluttered with street furniture (signs, bollards, bins and so on); and the difficulty of finding safe and convenient crossing points. This was confirmed by our observations in the four towns where all too frequently pavements were narrow and crossing points were restricted and inconvenient. Although most urban streets did have segregated pavements, whenever the available space was restricted by topography or buildings it seemed to be pavements that suffered with road space left largely unaltered. The unattractiveness of pavements was heightened by a number of external factors. These included lack of maintenance (holes and cracked paving stones not repaired); the existence of parked cars that often obstructed pavements; and the impact of weather. Many respondents commented on the way in which pavements became very slippery in wet weather, especially in the autumn when leaves were on the ground. Almost all commented on the difficulty of walking in winter when there is snow and ice: although local authorities clear and grit many roads this is rarely the case for pavements. This can leave some people, especially the frail or elderly, effectively housebound as they are unwilling to walk even to the local shops or the nearest bus stop. Pavements could also be made unattractive by the activities of other people: most obviously by pavement cyclists creating a risk for pedestrians, but also by the impact of crowds or large groups who, without necessarily doing anything anti-social, by their presence in a confined space made the pavement an unpleasant place to be. Dog walkers could also make the pavement problematic both through poorly-controlled pets and failure to clear up mess left by their animal. In almost all these situations better infrastructure in terms of wider, less cluttered, and better maintained pavements, together with better segregation from cyclists, would make walking a much more attractive proposition. Such changes alone will not greatly increase either the amount or enjoyment of walking, but strategies to improve infrastructure for pedestrians should be one part of a larger package of measures.

A related, but separate, factor that deters people from walking is the quality of the environment through which they would have to pass. Again, we can identify two distinct elements: the built environment itself and the impact of other road users. Unsurprisingly, people prefer to walk in a location that they find attractive: hence the concentration of walking activities in parks and quiet lanes. Definitions of what is an attractive urban environment are likely to be quite personal but people are much more likely to feel comfortable walking in an area where property is clean and well-kept and where there are things of interest along the way. They are also most likely to walk in good weather, though committed pedestrians will be prepared for all conditions and, if other reasons for walking are strong enough, weather alone is unlikely in most circumstances to be a major deterrent. There is a long history of research that has stressed the importance of an attractive and 'imageable' urban environment if people are to use it (Lynch, 1960; Jacobs, 1972; Appleyard et al, 1981). If the townscape is bland or ill-kept then people are likely to be deterred, not necessarily through fear (see below), but simply because they find the environment unattractive. For people unfamiliar with a town good signing for pedestrians is also essential. While all towns and cities have excellent, standardised, signage for motorists, signage for pedestrians is highly variable. Major tourist centres that expect a large number of visitors often have good pedestrian signage in the city centre and to major attractions, but elsewhere finding a pedestrian route in a strange town can be problematic. Walking in the city is usually made even less attractive by the proximity of other road users. Walking next to a busy road, even on a segregated pavement, creates an environment that is noisy, smelly and in which the pedestrian will be subjected to pollution from petrol and diesel fumes. Irrespective of whether or not people are specifically aware of the potential health effects of exposure to vehicle exhaust emissions (Buckeridge et al, 2002; Burr et al, 2004), this is likely to be perceived as an unattractive environment due to the noise, smell and fumes created by traffic. Most cities have few pedestrian routes that are well segregated from traffic, apart from city centre shopping precincts, and provision of more such routes could greatly enhance the attractiveness of walking in the city. This could be approached from two separate directions. In some circumstances there may be scope to provide new (signed) pedestrian routes that are well away from traffic (and that do not also involve significant detours), but in most places there will also be a need to regulate and reduce traffic volume so that the impact of cars and lorries on pedestrians is minimised. Strategies to improve the quality of the environment through which pedestrians pass should be a second aim of any package of measures to increase levels of walking in urban areas.

Although concerns about personal safety while walking were much more muted than those expressed about cycling (see below), many respondents did state that fear was a factor that either sometimes prevented them from walking, or which made parents restrict their children's walking. The fears expressed by pedestrians (and even more by potential pedestrians) did not relate primarily to dangers posed by motor vehicles or even pavement cyclists – though clearly both do pose risks (especially at road crossing) – but rather they focused on fear of attack from others while walking. Whereas many of the findings from our research were quite consistent across social groups and between areas, the ways in which fear of walking was expressed did vary quite substantially. In particular, parents were more concerned about the risks strangers might pose to their children if they were allowed out alone, rather than expressing concern about their own safety; women were more likely to express concern than male respondents; and the elderly tended to be more fearful than young adults. In middle-class districts fears were mostly muted and rarely prevented a journey on foot, though respondents might vary their route or ensure that they were accompanied on certain journeys and late at night; but in the more deprived districts fear of assault and theft of belongings was a real disincentive that could severely inhibit movement. This was particularly evident among women of South Asian heritage in Leicester where there was a strong view that the gold jewellery that they customarily wore made them especially vulnerable. The other fear that respondents expressed did not relate to the potential for physical harm, either from traffic or from potential assailants, but rather to the fear of being perceived as odd. In an environment where walking is rare then being on the streets can be seen as aberrant behaviour: most people prefer to fit in with the community in which they live and if walking is seen as eccentric then only the most committed will walk regularly. There are many ways in which these fears can be tackled. Streets can be made to feel safer and more secure through better lighting, while improvements to the built environment as outlined above can also make a neighbourhood feel more friendly and safe. In some situations CCTV cameras may be appropriate, and can be a deterrent to crime, though there are concerns both about their overall effectiveness and the ethics of widespread surveillance (Gill and Spriggs, 2005; Taylor, 2010). However, it can be argued that the best way to reduce people's fears when walking is to increase pedestrian footfall. Busy streets are generally safe streets and it is only when someone is walking alone down a deserted road that they begin to feel truly fearful. Thus other measures to increase walking, if successful, could also have the effect of reducing perceptions of risk. In this way different strategies to increase pedestrian movement in cities could be mutually reinforcing.

So far we have considered factors over which local authorities, planners, and others concerned with managing the built environment have some control: widening pavements, managing traffic flows, improving security are all things that it is within the power of local authorities to tackle (though they are not without their own problems of implementation). However, probably the most significant set of factors that deters people from walking, or at least prevents them from walking as often as they might otherwise do, is the impact of family and household constraints. Respondents who lived alone had the most freedom in this regard: usually they had the ability to organise their daily routine in the way that suited them best and could, if they wished, plan to carry out many of their shorter journeys on foot. For respondents with families and multiple commitments relating to family, work and homecare, life was usually much more complex. As outlined in Chapter Seven, most respondents could give some examples of times when travelling on foot, even for short journeys, was simply not feasible. The most common constraints included the presence of small children who were unable (or unwilling) to walk; the amount of time it took to get all family members dressed appropriately for walking in inclement weather; the need to carry school bags and/or shopping; the necessity of speed (often because other family circumstances meant that they had lost time and at least one family member risked being late for school or work); and the necessity of linking together several different activities which meant that walking would be too slow or complicated. We spoke to many families in all four areas where walking for at least some trips was viewed as desirable, often because it saved money, was good for health, or was seen as good for the environment, but where such trips were more often than not undertaken by car due to the sorts of family and household constraints outlined above.

While all households experienced such constraints to some degree, there were considerable variations in how they were handled and the strategies that people adopted. In some households, although there was recognition that it might be good to walk more often, there was little evidence of active engagement to make this possible, but in others at least some trips were constructed in such a way that walking was possible. This was most noticeable in the more middle-class study areas where, on average, families had more flexibility and control over their everyday activities. In the more deprived districts everyday mobility seemed to be rarely considered as anything other than a necessity that was completed as quickly, cheaply and safely as possible; such decisions were certainly secondary to the more pressing needs of surviving in an often hostile economic and social environment. Strategies to tackle such factors that inhibit everyday walking clearly need to operate at a number of levels: at a societal level to facilitate economic and social changes that make more sustainable travel choices easier (to be considered further in Chapter Ten); at the community level (for instance through neighbourhood schemes of child minding and shared escorting to make it easier to fit walking into everyday routines); and at the individual level of household management and day-to-day organisation. In most circumstances it is not impossible to walk short distances with small children, and children can often enjoy walking and engagement with the outdoor environment, but it does usually require some degree of prior thought and planning.

The final factor to be considered is probably the most intractable to tackle. We live in a society in which many of the attributes that are both taken for granted and perceived by most to be advantageous, conspire to encourage us to lead sedentary lives. As outlined in Chapter Two, in the past many people had little alternative but to walk for most of their everyday business. Since the nineteenth century, and especially from the late-twentieth century, the balance has changed so that today if we wish to walk we must make a positive effort to do so. There are many examples of such changes: increasing affluence means that most people can afford to own and use a car if they wish, so the opportunity not to walk is usually parked outside the front door; almost instant mobile communication systems mean that activities and transactions that used to require face-to-face meetings (and thus movement by at least one party) can now be conducted without physical movement; the availability of almost unlimited in-house entertainment from television, video and computers means that going out for social activities has declined; and access to on-line services has removed the need to travel to shop or to gain access to information. If we wish, we can live a full life while rarely leaving a chair. Increasing affluence and the year-round availability of foods from across the globe has also enabled us to increase levels of consumption, contributing to a high incidence of obesity. This produces a vicious circle in which weight gain makes walking physically harder, potentially more embarrassing, and thus less attractive, leading to lower exercise levels and further weight gain. This combination of factors has produced what have been termed 'obesogenic environments' in most rich nations (and increasingly in many poorer ones). Given such societal conditions, where sedentarism is the norm, it is not surprising that many people rarely seriously consider walking as an option when planning a journey (Hinde and Dixon, 2005; Booth et al, 2005; Lake and Townshend, 2006). While the development of an increasingly sedentary society also contributes to feelings of abnormality and eccentricity among those who do walk, the disincentives go much deeper than this. It can be argued that what comes through in the views expressed by many respondents is the acceptance, often barely recognised, of the powerful influence of what have now become deeply embedded societal structures. Our lives, and the things that we depend on to make those lives work in the twenty-first century, are increasingly constructed in ways that makes walking seem redundant. It is, in one sense, an old technology that has been overtaken by later developments: if we can talk, travel, shop and gain information while remaining seated (at home or in a car) why use a means of transport that takes longer, expends more effort, is less comfortable and has increasingly become associated with fitness and leisure rather than everyday travel. Strategies to change such views will require a major shift in societal priorities.

Strategies for making cycling normal

Whereas walking is an activity that almost everyone still does some of the time, even if it is mainly restricted to walking round the house and garden, or to the car; as shown in Chapter Eight, cycling in Britain is an activity that is undertaken by only a small minority of the population. As demonstrated by our survey, although most households own a bike, and most people were taught to cycle when young, few continue to do so into adulthood. Cycling is primarily viewed as an activity for specialists and experts, or for children for whom a bike is a plaything. As with walking, cycling for health, leisure and pleasure has increased in frequency in recent years among at least some portions of the population, but this is almost exclusively done off-road (or on quiet country lanes), often requires transporting bikes by car prior to a cycle ride, and rarely leads to the bike also being used for utility travel in urban areas. As outlined in Chapter Three, this is very different from the situation in much of continental Europe. In this section we draw together evidence presented in Chapter Eight to identify the key factors that inhibit cycling in Britain, and which make British cities different from so many other European towns. As with walking, we also identify the areas where strategies might be developed to increase levels of utility cycling: specific policy recommendations are given in Chapter Ten.

Cycling in British towns and cities currently takes place in four main locations. The most visible cyclists are those who use the road and thus share road space with motor vehicles. Although the number of regular cyclists has increased in some British towns, especially in central London and other places where there have been initiatives to increase more active and sustainable travel (Sloman et al, 2009; CPRE, 2010; DfT/DoH, 2010; Redfern, 2011), on-road cycling in urban traffic remains an activity that even those who cycle elsewhere rarely contemplate. Sharing the road with motor vehicles is just too daunting for most people to consider. Second, much cycling in urban areas takes place on pavements. These are perceived (rightly or wrongly) by adults and children alike to be a safer option for moving around town on a bike but, inevitably, pavement cycling leads to conflict with pedestrians. It is also illegal for older children and adults, though this is rarely enforced. Third, where there are off-road cycle routes that are fully segregated from traffic these can be quite heavily used for utility cycling. However, their use is clearly restricted to those journeys that coincide with the off-road route which, given the paucity of such facilities in British towns, is likely to be a minority of all journeys. Fourth, cycling as a sport and leisure activity is booming in Britain, boosted by the international success of the Great Britain cycle team, but such activity is often restricted to off-road locations such as sports' centres and purpose-built cycle tracks. When public roads are used then cycling is often undertaken in a sizable group, thus increasing visibility and safety, or during a race that is well marshalled and during which traffic is to some degree controlled. Most longer-distance leisure cycling is undertaken on quiet country roads, often designated as cycle routes. Although carrying relatively light traffic volumes these are also not without their hazards to riders (CPRE website). Clearly these are not discrete categories, and one individual may use a variety of different routes depending on the purpose, location and timing of a journey but, with the exception of off-road cycling, all the options are likely to bring cyclists into conflict with other travellers. In this sense it can be suggested that cycling is a more difficult and complex form of everyday transport to accommodate than is walking: it makes more demands upon the environment (off-road cycling can be a significant source of erosion) and given current urban infrastructure in Britain is more likely to lead to conflict with other users of urban space.

The factors that prevent greater use of cycling as a means of everyday transport in British towns are at one level similar to those outlined above for walking, but our research has shown that they are structured in distinctly different ways and that strategies to increase cycling are likely to be very different from those used to promote walking. In part this is because there is much greater public antipathy towards cycling: whereas walking is something most people would consider some of the time, cycling is an activity that many people refuse to engage with in any way. In Britain there are also much higher levels of walking than of cycling, and thus any strategy to increase cycling is starting from a much lower base. Proper provision for cyclists also makes more demands on the urban environment than does the provision of facilities for pedestrians (if only because pavements already exist in most towns); while cycling arguably places more demands on the individual traveller in terms of skill and equipment thus making it harder to achieve. As research by Aldred (2010, 2012a) has shown, cycling cultures also vary substantially from place to place, and thus strategies to increase cycling that work in one location may not be effective elsewhere. In this section we focus on four main factors that emerge from our research as key barriers to the greater use of bikes for everyday travel: safety, inconvenience, effort and identity. In addition, we more briefly consider the ways in which some of the factors identified as barriers to walking also have an impact on cycling, but in subtly different ways.

The overwhelming message that emerges from our study of everyday travel in four English towns is that, with the exception of a small minority of committed cyclists, most people are deterred from cycling regularly on urban roads because of fear of traffic and their perception of the risk of serious injury. Even those who do cycle expressed concerns but they have developed strategies to negotiate the risks encountered on a daily basis. These concerns relate to both our adult respondents themselves and, especially, to the concerns that parents have about their children. Even adults who have a strong commitment to cycling may be reluctant to allow their children to cycle on public roads. This further reinforces a culture in which people, who may have received cycle training as children (for instance through Bikeability schemes) are deterred from cycling regularly for everyday travel. These views were expressed consistently in all four towns and were common to all social groups. Although female respondents were more likely than males to express feelings of fear, and unwillingness to cycle on public roads, most male respondents also said that they had real concerns about the safety of themselves and others. For both men and women life cycle stage was also a factor that influenced the degree to which such concerns had an impact on actual behaviour. Whereas those who were single or childless might be prepared to take risks, parents of young children felt that they had a greater sense of responsibility to ensure their own safety because the consequences of a serious accident could be devastating for the whole family. Thus even those who cycled while young also restricted their use of public roads later in life, possibly using their bike mainly for off-road leisure cycling. In most families children were encouraged to learn to ride a bike, but this was done in public parks, on pavements, and in other locations that were deemed to be relatively safe. Existing cycle facilities, such as the narrow strip of intermittent red cycle lane along many urban roads, were mostly felt to be totally unsatisfactory as they still allowed traffic to pass very close to a cyclist and did not provide adequate protection at road junctions. There are really only two ways in which such concerns can be addressed. Either cyclists must be provided with fully segregated cycle lanes, and with properly engineered junctions, so that cycling through a town rarely requires interaction with motor vehicles; or urban vehicle traffic must be severely restricted to create road space on which cyclists feel safe and are respected by other road users. In reality a combination of the two strategies is likely to be necessary depending on local circumstances and street architecture. What is clear is that efforts to increase levels of utility cycling in British towns will have limited effect unless concerns about safety are adequately addressed.

Although for most respondents other issues were secondary to those of safety, there were many other factors which, in combination, made it difficult for individuals and families to cycle regularly even in situations where safety was not a major issue. Many respondents reported that they found the process of organising their lives to include cycling difficult in comparison with the ease of travelling by car. This can be constructed as a series of, often minor, inconveniences, which cumulatively militate against cycling as an activity. First, in many houses there are limited places in which bikes can be conveniently stored. While less of an issue in the middle-class study areas, where most people lived in detached or semi-detached houses or bungalows with garages and gardens, for those who lived in terraced houses or in high-rise flats (as was predominantly the case in the ethnographic study areas in Leeds and Leicester) there was simply nowhere convenient and secure that bicycles could be kept. Even the act of having to wheel a bike through the house from a backyard could be a significant disincentive. Second, although travelling by bike can be very simple, requiring no special clothes or equipment other than the bicycle itself, most respondents' perceptions of cycling as an activity linked it with the requirement to have (and wear) a helmet and special (often high visibility) clothing for reasons of safety. Lights, a lock, and panniers all created extra clutter with the perceived need to remove easily stolen items whenever the bike was left. Thus for many cycling became a complicated activity, requiring a level of organisation that was hard to fit into a busy household routine. This was especially the case if travelling with children or when undertaking complex multi-purpose journeys. In short, issues of storage, convenience and organisation all conspired to make cycling difficult for many people. Even where a bike was readily available in a garage the hassle of having to keep it roadworthy, and the need to gather together special clothes, could be sufficient deterrent to make cycling a rare activity. Using a car was simply an easier and more convenient option. While there were some households where committed cyclists organised their household routines in such a way that cycling became natural and easy, for the majority this was not the case. Thus, in addition to making cycling feel safe, there is need to develop strategies that will enable families to easily create living arrangements into which cycling fits as comfortably as the car does for most people today.

In addition to the difficulty of fitting cycling into everyday household routines and living arrangements, many people simply found the whole experience of cycling too much effort to undertake on a regular basis. There was often a perception that such effort was acceptable (even enjoyable) for mainly off-road leisure cycling at weekends when time constraints were few, but that it was unacceptable on a regular basis when travelling to work or school against a tight deadline. This related not only to the physical effort of pedalling, exacerbated in hilly areas, but to concerns about cycle maintenance, the carrying of luggage, the perceived need to have a change of clothes, the impact of helmet wearing on hair, and the lack of shower and changing facilities at a destination. In heavy traffic cycling could also be seen as a stressful activity that could lead to someone arriving at work in a condition such that they could not immediately get on with their everyday work activities. Perceptions of the effort required to cycle are interesting, and it can be suggested that some of the cultural attitudes and expectations associated with cycling in Britain exacerbate this problem. One popular perception of cycling as an activity in Britain is that it is something for which you must wear special clothes, that you must cycle quickly (almost competitively), and that to be safe you must be assertive in traffic. Such cultures of cycling do require considerable effort. However, in countries such as Denmark or the Netherlands, where rates of cycling are high, there is a much stronger culture of cycling slowly, in everyday clothes (including office wear), and of arriving at a destination in a state where it is easy to transfer straight to a work environment (Pucher and Dijkstra, 2003; Aldred, 2012a). Few of our respondents mentioned electric bikes, which can deliver many of the advantages of cycling with reduced effort, and this is a technology which as yet has not had a significant impact at least in the towns that we studied. This contrasts sharply with the situation in, for instance, China or parts of continental Europe, where use of the e-bike is growing rapidly (Sangani, 2009; Rose, 2011). Concerns about the impact of weather on cycling were relatively muted in our interviews, possibly because most respondents were put off cycling by other factors and those who did cycle were committed to do so in all conditions, but the need to carry luggage was a significant deterrent for some. Again, this was exacerbated by the perception that it was necessary to shower and change clothes after cycling to work, and therefore there was a need to carry a full change of clothes. It can therefore be argued that shifts in the dominant cycling culture in Britain could make cycling more attractive and easier for a large number of people to achieve on a regular basis. Strategies to promote cycling as an activity that can be done slowly, with minimal effort, without special clothes, and in most situations could reshape popular perceptions of cycling as a means of everyday travel.

The other powerful disincentive to cycling in much of Britain is the degree to which many respondents viewed cycling as aberrant behaviour. Cycling marked you out as someone who was rather odd and eccentric, and it was felt that cycling could be construed as a deliberate marker of a particular set of (green, environmental) values. This contrasts markedly with walking, as even those who walked little saw this as a relatively normal way of moving around for at least some activities. Cycling was perceived by many respondents as distinctly abnormal (and risky) behaviour and thus not something to be contemplated. It can be suggested that there are two sets of (related) factors operating here. Most people prefer to fit in and to be seen as normal. Thus fear of ridicule for doing something perceived by much of society as odd is understandable. Only those people who operated in an environment where others with whom they associated regularly (family, work colleagues, friends) also cycled regularly seemed truly comfortable with the idea of cycling. In other words the extreme minority status of cycling in Britain means that it only becomes an acceptable (and easy) activity when done in the context of a community of like-minded individuals. Thus, although you may still stand out as odd to most of the population, in the environment in which you operate cycling becomes normalised. In our study this is, to at least some extent, the case in Lancaster where the combination of Cycle Demonstration Town status and cycle to work policies have led to quite a strong community of local cyclists. They remain a small minority, but within this segment of society cycling is normalised and expected. Second, it can be argued that the extent to which cycling is seen as abnormal is directly related to the visibility of cycling in the locality. All four study areas in the UWAC research had relatively low levels of cycling, but it can be argued that in places such as Cambridge, where levels of cycling approach those found in many continental European cities, cycling does to an extent become normalised. A combination of the presence of large numbers of cyclists on the roads, and local societal expectation that cycling is the normal means of travel, mean that people who may not cycle elsewhere do so in places where there are high levels of cycling and a strong cycling culture (Aldred, 2010, 2012a). Thus, it can be argued that any strategies that succeed in increasing levels of cycling may also have the additional impact of normalising cycling. This should then become a self-reinforcing process: the more that people view cycling as safe and convenient, the more that they will cycle, and the more that cycling will then be perceived as a normal and expected form of everyday travel. While cycling remains an activity undertaken by a tiny minority of enthusiasts it will be viewed as abnormal (and thus unacceptable) by most people.

Other disincentives to cycling are broadly the same as those that affect walking. A poor quality urban environment is less attractive to cycle through than one that is clean, attractive and pollution free. Although fear of attack while on a bike was much less than when walking (some female respondents in particular saw cycling at night as much safer than walking), this concern was not absent, especially in deserted, poorly-lit and run-down neighbourhoods. Exposure to traffic pollution, with consequential health effects, can be a real concern for some urban cyclists: something that can only be significantly altered (given present vehicle technology) by the separation of bikes from cars and through reductions in vehicle density. All of the more general household and time constraints that inhibit walking can also apply to cycling, and the sedentary nature of contemporary society militates against cycling in the same way that it influences levels of walking. Where cycling does perhaps have an advantage over walking is that it can possibly be more easily made attractive, at least to some, than walking. Walking is so mundane that for the most part it is hardly noticeable whereas cycling has some of the attributes that make motoring attractive to many. As outlined in Chapter Two the reasons why many people cycled in the 1930s and 1940s can be compared directly to the reasons why people use cars today. Many people (especially men) are attracted to machines and the technology that goes with cycling, and bikes and cycle clothing can become fashionable (see, for example, the Cyclechic website). The promotion of cycling as something that is trendy may have some positive effects. However, it can also be argued that any association of cycling with particular groups or values could be detrimental to the wider adoption of cycling as an activity. The great advantage that car use has is that it offers almost universal appeal and is not associated with particular segments of society. This is the great power of automobility. If cycling is an activity that becomes associated with certain values, fashions or groups it is likely to repel others (as is arguably the case already). To achieve high levels of cycle use in Britain it is necessary for cycling to be as homogeneous and all-embracing as is currently the case for cars.

Making it all happen: issues of implementation

It is obvious from the above discussion that generating an environment and culture in which both walking and cycling are viewed as safe, convenient, easy and normal will be difficult, yet this has been achieved in some continental European countries. In this chapter we have focused on the broad strategies that need to be developed. In Chapter Ten we suggest some specific ways in which these strategies might be achieved, but we recognise that there are likely to be many different routes to the same ends, and that different approaches are likely to be appropriate in particular places. Existing urban conditions and cycling cultures vary across the UK and policies need to be developed in the light of such local circumstances. In this section we identify and discuss some of the key implementation issues that are likely to be faced if the above strategies are put in place, whatever the specific policies adopted. We also try to identify how such barriers may be overcome. It is important to emphasise that the arguments developed in this book are not anti-car (though some may perceive them to be so). We accept completely that the private motor vehicle (in some form) is an embedded and for many people necessary part of modern society, and that it is not going to disappear, although there may be significant changes in technology that mean that cars of the future are rather different from those of today (Nieuwenhuis and Wells, 2009). However, what we are arguing for is a change in attitudes to car use so that where the distance and nature of the journey permits, such as short trips in urban areas, walking or cycling are seriously considered as a means of transport and the car is left parked by the house. The strategies discussed in this chapter are all designed to make such decisions easier: they do not prevent or reduce car use for longer journeys or trips that cannot realistically be undertaken by other means.

One argument against change is the perceived cost of implementation. This is particularly persuasive in conditions of weak economic growth and high national debt. However, the costs of inaction are also high. We have not attempted any detailed economic appraisal of the costs and benefits attached to the creation of a society in which walking and cycling are common for short trips in urban areas and, indeed, an accurate assessment is probably impossible. The variables involved, incorporating issues of health, time, convenience and capital investment, among other factors, are so complex and subject to individual variation that any meaningful economic assessment would be futile, though many cost–benefit analyses of specific interventions have been undertaken (Sælensminde, 2004; Cavill et al, 2008; Gotschi, 2011; Beria et al, 2012). Rather, we accept as read that shifting at least some short journeys from cars to walking or cycling has benefits for both personal health and the urban environment, and seek to demonstrate that at least some of the strategies outlined above could be implemented at relatively low financial cost.

We argue that it is necessary to place some restrictions on motorised traffic in urban areas if conditions for walking and cycling are to be made more attractive. Such restrictions are not necessarily high cost. A report for Transport for London that calculated the cost–benefit effects of 20mph speed limits on reducing road casualties used a figure of around £60,000 per kilometre for the full cost of implementing 20mph zones, and concluded that, when compared to the savings from reduced road casualties, there were real economic benefits (Grundy et al, 2008). It should be noted that this report only focused on a cost–benefit analysis in relation to road safety, and did not take into account other benefits of lower traffic speeds in towns. Implementation costs in London are likely to be higher than in smaller and less congested towns: for instance in Dunstable (Bedfordshire) the cost of implementing 20mph zones in 72 residential streets was estimated at just £40,000 (Jackson, 2012). Other measures to regulate and slow urban traffic also have modest implementation costs and can contribute significantly to creating an environment where walking and cycling are seen as more possible. The introduction of new infrastructure, such as segregated cycle lanes, obviously has much higher capital costs and these can vary enormously depending on the local environment: for instance Transport for London estimates an average cost of £100,000 per km but with a range from £10,000 in suburban locations to over £1m per kilometre where there are many complex junctions (TfL website, London Cycling Design Standards). However, even in such extreme cases the costs remain significantly below those of major road improvements. For example, the government has recently committed £88.6m to improving 6.5 miles (10.5 km) of the M4 and M5 around Bristol by converting the hard shoulder to create an extra lane and through the introduction of a variable traffic management scheme. This is part of a £2.1bn investment in motorway improvements across the country (Cook, 2011). Other interventions to make walking and cycling easier can also be relatively low cost. These include publicity, information and cycle training (as already promoted through the government subsidised Bikeability scheme), together with the provision of improved bike storage facilities in homes that currently do not have them. Although all of the strategies outlined above will have some costs associated with them, when placed against the money expended to support the systems of automobility that currently dominate British cities, they mostly seem modest.

A larger problem of implementation may relate to the physical difficulty of back-fitting a new cycle or pedestrian infrastructure into British towns and cities. We argue that in addition to regulating traffic flows and speeds there is need to provide fully segregated cycle routes on all busy roads. Given that the urban infrastructure in British cities has developed over many centuries, with some urban roads very constrained for space, this is not always easy. In practice, the creation of wider pavements to facilitate walking and segregated cycle routes with integrated junctions will often require the reallocation of road space away from motor vehicles and towards pedestrians and cyclists. To achieve this, without also creating unacceptable levels of congestion, will also require the implementation of other programmes to both reduce and restrict the volume of cars in towns. This has been done in other countries, and not only in those such as Denmark or The Netherlands that have a relatively long history of being cycle-friendly. For instance, the city of Paris has recently introduced an extensive network of segregated cycle lanes, has widened pavements and has created pedestrian spaces mostly at the expense of other road users. On some major boulevards the space allocated to vehicles has been significantly reduced and restrictions have been placed on car use within the central city to create 'espaces civilisés' (Apur, 2003; Mairie de Paris website). Although Paris remains a largely car-dominated city there have been significant steps to provide improved walking and cycling environments within a fixed and historic urban infrastructure. To fully accommodate increased levels of cycling urban space also needs to be allocated to cycle storage. While cycle hire schemes such as the Barclays Bikes in London or Velib in Paris are popular and well-used, they are mainly appropriate for occasional bike users. Regular cyclists require secure bike parking at workplaces and transport termini. The latter is particularly important if cycles are to be used as part of a multi-mode commuting journey: for instance cycling to the station and then travelling by train to a destination. The large bike park at Amsterdam Central Station is a good example of what can be provided. In many inner urban areas it may be difficult to remove vehicles completely or to provide total segregation. In such circumstances mixed use space is another option: creating an environment where motorised transport is severely restricted but shares space with pedestrians and cyclists. Although not always popular, especially among those with disabilities (Gant, 1977), this concept has been used in the busy Exhibition Road in London where formal barriers between walkers, cyclists and cars have been removed and the streetscape has been redesigned to improve the flow of pedestrians and minimise the impact of cars

(Royal Borough of Kensington and Chelsea website). It is one example of how imaginative urban design allows street space to be used differently.

While financial and physical constraints do present barriers, there are usually identifiable ways in which they can be overcome. More problematic, we suggest, are the societal constraints that hinder the implementation of strategies to increase levels of walking and cycling in urban areas. We live in a society that has a long history of car dependence and which is locked into what Urry (2004) has termed a 'system of automobility'. Because so much of what we do, and what we expect to do, is bound up with the motor vehicle, implementing any strategies that are perceived to threaten this system is difficult. Such views are not restricted to committed motor enthusiasts, expressing what might be termed 'Top Gear' values (Top Gear website), but are much more deeply held across society. Our research showed that relatively few people are totally committed to the car; but most people do find it hard to envisage life without it, or even a life in which the car is used less. As demonstrated in Chapter Two, as early as the 1930s when car ownership was still confined to a small minority of the British population, the Minister of Transport expressed the view that 'the luxury of the few had become the necessity of the many' (*The Times*, 28 March 1934, p 9). If that was perceived to be the case in the 1930s it is even truer almost 80 years later. This is reflected in the unwillingness of most British politicians (from any major party) to commit to policies that are perceived as targeting motorists: they are happy to support strategies to promote more sustainable forms of travel so long as the freedom of the motorist is not affected. One recent example of this is Transport Minister Norman Baker's reaction to increased evening and weekend parking charges in Westminster which he dubbed a 'war on motorists' (London Evening Standard website). The impact of such rhetoric combined with the path-dependent nature of automobile use, means that these values are widely accepted and held within British society. They become an embedded and taken-for-granted part of the social world that it is hard to challenge. Given these circumstances it can be argued that the biggest barrier to implementing measures to increase walking and cycling – which necessarily means restricting cars and the reallocation of road space – will at first, at least, be the opposition that such schemes will generate from politicians and public alike. This is reflected in the fact that in every British town where the public has been consulted about the use of congestion charging this strategy has been rejected. Most tellingly, in Greater Manchester all parts of the conurbation voted strongly against the charge (overall 78.8% were against), including residents in the central city areas who potentially had the most to gain from the scheme (Manchester Evening News website). In Britain only the Green Party has a set of policies that deliberately shift spending away from motorists and towards walking, cycling and public transport: at the 2010 general election the Greens polled just 1% of the total vote (Green Party website; BBC website, Election 2010). It can be argued that it is these societal factors that have led to the spending that has so far been committed to cycling having relatively limited impact on patterns of everyday travel. Unless there is fundamental change, which will require bold leadership from politicians and other public figures, strategies to produce more sustainable mobility in Britain are likely to continue to have limited success.

TEN

Conclusions: issues of society, economy and sustainability

Connecting walking and cycling to wider society

In this final chapter we briefly draw together the main themes of the book and link them back to some of the broader issues discussed in Section I. The aim is to demonstrate that creating an environment in which walking and cycling are seen as usual and easy ways of travelling short distances in urban areas is not just an issue relevant to concerns about urban transport, congestion or public health, but that they also have much wider ramifications for society. As demonstrated through the analysis in Section II, these connections operate in myriad different ways. For example, creating an environment in which walking and cycling are taken-for-granted and common means of everyday travel requires changes to urban structure so that goods and services can be accessed without a car; it necessitates changes to housing design so that the storage of bikes and outdoor clothing is unproblematic; it needs adjustments to working practices so that movement on foot or by bike can be fitted easily into everyday routines; it requires the re-design of public space to prioritise cyclists and walkers over motorised transport; and it needs new transport interchanges so that cycling can easily be integrated with travel by public transport. Such changes require quite fundamental shifts in the priorities of governments (both local and national) and in the mind-set of the majority of the population. Although such issues are more frequently discussed publicly than was the case a decade ago, there is little sign of significant change. For instance, a recent Joseph Rowntree report on minimum income standards in Britain, based primarily on what people considered to be necessary for a satisfactory living standard in the twenty-first century, assumed that a car was essential for families with children living in urban areas outside London. This had not been assumed to be the case in the previous survey carried out in 2008 (Davis et al, 2012). The implication is that we remain a very car-dependent society and that public transport, cycling or walking are seen by most people as either unacceptable or impractical methods of travel.

What is working now?

Despite the evidence cited above, there are many examples of good practice both in Britain and elsewhere in Europe. We argue that there are lessons to be learned from these examples that can be applied much more widely. As demonstrated in Chapter Three, levels of cycling in particular are a great deal higher in much of continental Europe than they are in the UK. If we want to know what a bicycle-friendly environment looks like we need go no further than many towns and cities in Denmark and The Netherlands. John Pucher and Ralph Buehler concisely sum up the key characteristics of a bicycle-friendly urban area as found in these countries (Pucher and Buehler, 2008, p 512). They list seven key areas where policy interventions in The Netherlands, Denmark and Germany have successfully promoted cycling and created an environment in which more people feel confident about using a bike for short trips in urban areas. The key features that they highlight are:

- extensive systems of separate cycling facilities in urban areas
- modification of intersections and traffic lights to prioritise and protect cyclists
- traffic calming measures, especially in residential neighbourhoods
- provision of ample and secure bicycle parking facilities
- coordination of bicycle systems with public transport
- traffic education and training to produce competent and confident cyclists
- traffic laws that protect cyclists and place obligations on motorists.

Given that the economies and societies of countries such as Germany, Denmark and The Netherlands are not markedly different from that of the United Kingdom, there seems no compelling reason why similar measures could not be implemented, and produce the same effects, in urban Britain. Of course the cycling environment in the above countries is not perfect, and levels of walking are no higher (and in some cases lower) than in the UK. The relative neglect in most policy measures of the promotion of walking as a means of transport is returned to below.

A recent study of four communities in England with relatively high levels of cycling (by British standards) sought to identify the key characteristics of cycling in Britain today, and to suggest policies for promoting cycling more widely (Aldred, 2012b). The research, carried out in Bristol, Cambridge, Hull and the London borough of Hackney, identified 15 key findings clustered around three themes of cycling experiences, cycling meanings and cycling promotion and policy; and from these identified 15 separate policy recommendations. Notable findings from the research included a focus on the emotional and social implications of cycling as an activity, the degree to which cyclists may be stigmatised and marginalised within society, and the importance of advocacy and embedded knowledge from existing 'everyday' cyclists in developing appropriate policy solutions. The research also highlighted the ways in which cycling cultures in England vary from place to place, even between communities that had initially been identified because they were places where cycling was relatively common. Thus Cambridge has a long tradition of cycling and is a city in which cycling, for many people, seems the obvious and normal way of moving around. In this respect Cambridge is unusual in the UK. Hull also has a long tradition of utility cycling, and though this has been declining in recent years there persists a culture of cycling both for health and convenience. Hull has also seen significant investment in traffic calming and dedicated cycle lanes thus facilitating the continuation of a cycling culture. In the London borough of Hackney high levels of cycling are relatively new and are mainly associated with a particular segment of the population who have deliberately adopted cycling as part of their everyday urban lifestyle and find it both convenient and sociable. However, cycling in Hackney was not always easy with bicycle storage a major issue. Bristol also has a relatively new cycling culture, still focused around particular segments of the population, but this has been particularly encouraged by the designation in 2008 of Bristol as a 'Cycling City' and associated development of improved infrastructure, workplace cycle schemes and cycle training in schools. Policy recommendations focus on the importance of recognising and promoting the benefits of cycling as perceived by those who do travel regularly by bike, the need to recognise the varied and subtle meanings associated with cycling, and the importance of building support networks from existing cyclists to assist in the promotion and maintenance of cycling cultures. Perhaps what is most striking about these research findings when compared with studies of continental Europe is the degree to which, even in places with relatively high levels of cycling, most cyclists still perceive themselves to be different and marginalised; and the fact that the nature of cycling cultures varies so much from place to place. In contrast, the research of Pucher and others clearly demonstrates that in countries such as The Netherlands and Denmark, cycling cultures are much more homogeneous, and that cyclists consider themselves to be conforming to a societal norm rather than sitting (and pedalling) on the fringes of society.

There is evidence of increasing levels of cycling, and provision for cyclists, in some other parts of Britain. The Cycling Demonstration Towns and Cities have seen (mostly) modest increases in cycling; while investment in both new cycle lanes, some limited improvements to road junctions, extensive publicity, improved cycle training, the Barclay's bicycle hire scheme and a mayor who cycles and promotes cycling have in combination led to a significant increase in levels of cycling in central London (TfL, 2010a). If current proposals are carried to fruition cycling could become even more firmly established in the capital (TfL, 2013). However, cyclists still form a very small minority of those who travel regularly in central London and there are continuing concerns about the safety of cyclists on the city's roads (London Cycling Campaign website; *The Times* cycling safety campaign website). In many ways the Welsh Assembly is ahead of the rest of the UK in formally recognising the importance of walking and cycling in its transport policy. A White Paper for the Active Travel (Wales) Bill was issued in May 2012 and after extensive consultation in conjunction with Sustrans Cymru, local authorities and a wide range of other bodies the Bill is likely to be approved in 2013 (Welsh Government, 2012; Sustrans Cymru, 2012; National Assembly for Wales website). This will place an obligation on all local authorities in Wales:

> To identify and map the network of routes within their areas that are safe and appropriate for walking and cycling; to identify and map the enhancements that would be required to create a fully integrated

network for walking and cycling and develop a prioritised list of schemes to deliver the network; to deliver an enhanced network subject to budget availability and following due process; and to consider the potential for enhancing walking and cycling provision in the development of new road schemes. (Welsh Government, 2012, p 2)

These measures are probably not sufficient on their own to raise rates of active travel in Wales to continental levels but, if passed, this Bill will be the first time that a British government has deliberately prioritised walking and cycling as part of its national transport policy. The leadership that the Welsh Assembly is showing can potentially be transformative in generating a shift in attitudes across wider society to enable the provision of improved facilities, create an environment where most people see walking or cycling as the obvious option for short trips in urban areas, and as a realistic option for parts of longer journeys undertaken by public transport. It is also notable that this White Paper gives equal prominence to both walking and cycling, thus rectifying some of the imbalance that has occurred so far with substantial sums being given to the promotion of cycling but with the needs of pedestrians largely ignored. Further support for such interventions comes also from the recent guidance on walking and cycling from the National Institute for Clinical Excellence (NICE, 2012) in which creating an environment where more active travel is easy and commonplace is presented as a key public health challenge, and from the report from the All Party Parliamentary Cycling Group (Goodwin, 2013)

What are the risks of doing nothing?

In twenty-first century Britain there is still a strong presumption that the car is a default means of transport, and that everyone has the right not only to own a car but to use it however and wherever they wish. We would not argue with the former contention (the right to car ownership) but would challenge the second (the right to use a car under almost all circumstances). Evidence presented in Section II clearly demonstrates that if walking and cycling are to be promoted as sustainable means of active travel in urban areas then cars must be regulated more strictly than they are at present. However, there are powerful voices arguing against this. While official motoring organisations such as the AA and RAC are relatively restrained, and recognise the need for responsible car use, other voices argue for fuel (and cars) to be taxed less, for speed restrictions to be lessened, speed cameras removed and the regulation of motor vehicles to be reduced (for instance: the *Telegraph*, Fair Deal for Drivers campaign (*Telegraph* website); on-line campaigns against speed cameras such as speedcameras.org; and the Drivers' Alliance). One argument often put forward by those opposed to investment in facilities for walking and cycling is that this is such a niche activity that it is irrelevant: it is much more important to cater for the majority for whom car use is both expected and demanded. This is a powerful argument when put to politicians who depend upon majority support to get elected and remain in power. What then are the risks of doing nothing?

As indicated in the introduction to this chapter, we argue that creating an environment in which walking and cycling is common will require significant societal change. Equally, we believe that not acting will have serious social, economic and environmental consequences that far outweigh any constraints or inconveniences that are placed on motorists. These risks are obvious, and were discussed in Section I of this book. Car-dependency is unsustainable in terms of resource use, global climate change, congestion and its impacts on human health both through lack of exercise and pollution. Even with the best possible (and at present extremely distant and unlikely) scenario of a wholesale shift to electric cars that can compete in terms of price and performance with the internal combustion engine, with electric power generated from renewable sources and a grid capable of supporting this demand, the problems of automobile dependency would not go away. Electric (or hybrid) cars are still vehicles: they continue to cause congestion, to create road safety hazards, especially for less powerful road users such as pedestrian and cyclists, and their presence would continue to make the urban environment an unpleasant place to be for non-motorists. Thus, arguments that future technological fixes will make cars unproblematic are not sustainable when it comes to considering the needs of other road users. The research presented in Section II has clearly demonstrated that current cyclists and pedestrians consider that the dominance of motor vehicles on British roads, and the lack of separate provision for other road users, is a major threat to those who do not travel by car. For potential future cyclists, in particular, the fear of being involved in a road accident is a major deterrent to getting on a bike for anything other than off-road travel. Moreover, the research also shows, through both a large-scale questionnaire survey and in-depth interviews and ethnographic study, that most people are well-disposed to walking and cycling and see these means of transport in a positive light: they convey good health, benefit the local environment, save money and are (mostly) enjoyable. Thus arguments that there is no public support for increased expenditure on walking and cycling, and for some restrictions of car use to benefit other road users, are misplaced. We would argue that potentially there is a large majority who would support better walking and cycling facilities, and who would be prepared to use these facilities, if the physical and social environment were different. The alternative is to continue a downward spiral in which congested roads, lack of pavement and dedicated cycling space create an ever more unpleasant urban environment for anyone not in a car, together with the frustration of slow-moving congested traffic for motorists.

What could be done?

In the previous chapter we outlined the key strategies that we believe should be implemented, and that follow from the analysis presented in Section II of this book. Here we summarise the specific policies that we consider are essential to create an environment where walking and cycling are seen as safe and easy options for everyday travel in urban areas. We stress again that many of these policy proposals could be implemented in different ways to suit local circumstances, and some require inputs from and coordination between several different bodies. We also argue that this is not a pick-and-mix list of policy options, but a set of minimum requirements all of which need action if the aim of substantially increasing levels of walking and cycling is to be achieved. Clearly they cannot all be achieved quickly, though some can, but we consider that a commitment to action on all fronts is necessary if real change is to occur. Our policy proposals can be summarised in seven bullet points:

- It is essential that the urban environment is made safe for cyclists and pedestrians. This requires the provision of fully segregated cycle routes on all arterial and other busy roads in urban areas. It is clear from the research that most non-cyclists and recreational cyclists will only consider cycling regularly if they are segregated from traffic and that pedestrians are hostile to pavement cyclists.

- Pedestrian routes must be made as welcoming as possible to increase footfall. This could include widening pavements, removing street furniture that obstructs pavements and ensuring that pavements are well lit, well maintained and kept free of leaves and ice.

- There need to be effective restrictions on traffic speeds, parking and access on all residential roads and other routes without segregated cycle and pedestrian paths so that both cyclists and pedestrians feel that they have a safe and convenient environment in which to travel. This could include 20mph speed limits, other traffic calming measures and resident-only access by car in some areas.

- The system of legal liability on roads used by the public should be changed to protect the most vulnerable road users (cyclists and pedestrians). One approach would be to adopt 'strict liability' so that pedestrians or cyclists injured in an accident involving a motor vehicle do not have to prove fault in seeking compensation. Forms of 'strict liability' are adopted in much of continental Europe and while not changing criminal responsibility they place a civil responsibility on drivers to obtain insurance that will pay vulnerable victims independently of fault. This could act as an incentive for car drivers to behave in a way that protects the most vulnerable road users.

- There need to be changes in the spatial structure and organisation of the built environment, enforced through planning legislation, to make accessing common services and facilities on foot or by bike easy. This would require the development of more neighbourhood shopping centres within walking or cycling distance of most people, restrictions on out-of-town developments, provision of secure bicycle parking facilities and the provision of cycle storage in most homes.

- There need to be wider societal and economic changes to give people the flexibility to travel more sustainably. Policies (that already exist in many countries) could include the greater use of flexi hours so that walking and cycling could be more easily fitted into a household routine, more family-friendly welfare policies so that in families with small children one parent could afford to reduce working hours and thus be less constrained by time commitments, and more equitable educational provision so that most children attended a school close to home.

- It is necessary to change the image of cycling and walking. To a great extent this should be consequential on the above changes: as more people walk and cycle then more people will accept it as normal. However, campaigns to promote walking and cycling as normal and something accessible to all, and not dominated by super-fit or unusually committed specialists, should also be adopted.

While such proposals may at first sight seem radical and hard to implement it is worth remembering that they are almost all things that already exist in some other comparable countries. However, to effect such changes in British society does require a change in attitude both from those with political power and more widely within society. We believe that three principles should underpin movement towards more sustainable and active travel in Britain. First, there must be awareness that it is not sufficient to change attitudes and make people more environmentally aware. It is necessary also to make the changes that enable people to translate these values into actions. Our research clearly demonstrates that even people with positive views and motivations towards more sustainable and active travel were often deterred from doing so by other factors. Second, it is important to base policies about walking and cycling not only on the views and experiences of existing committed cyclists and pedestrians, but also on the views of those who currently do not (or rarely) walk and cycle but who have the potential to do so. Existing cyclists in particular are, for the most part, a minority who have, against all the odds, successfully negotiated a hostile urban environment to incorporate cycling into their everyday routines. It is necessary to talk – as we have done – to non-walkers and non-cyclists, potential cyclists and walkers, former cyclists and walkers, recreational cyclists and occasional walkers to determine what would encourage them to make more use of these transport modes. Third, it should be recognised that while physical infrastructure is important, it is not on its own sufficient. There is also need for an integrated policy that embraces social welfare, employment, housing, health, and education among other policy areas to create a total environment that is welcoming for cyclists and pedestrians. We recognise that the scale of changes proposed may seem daunting. The measures proposed cannot be achieved overnight – though some could be implemented quite quickly – but achieving transition to a society where walking and cycling is normal should be seen as a long-term project that creates more sustainable urban environments for future generations.

Concluding comments

We have presented what we believe is convincing new evidence to explain why and how many people are reluctant to engage with walking and cycling for everyday travel, and from these findings have developed a set of policy proposals that we consider would make a real difference. A recent appraisal of the Cycling Cities and Towns programme also stresses the significance of life-course and contextual factors in influencing levels of cycling, and advocates multiple interventions to promote more sustainable travel (Christensen et al, 2012). Such changes have the potential to place Britain among the European nations with the highest levels of sustainable and active everyday travel. We have utilised novel research methods by integrating a range of quantitative and qualitative methodologies, and have contextualised these by reference to walking and cycling in other places and time periods. In particular, we argue that our use of in-depth qualitative and ethnographic research methods to seek to understand the complexities of everyday travel decisions adds significant new knowledge to our understanding of travel behaviour. While our policy proposals may be viewed by some as either unacceptably oppressing motorists, or of being unrealistically optimistic in terms of the likelihood of them being achieved, it is worth emphasising that many need only small changes to make a difference. The research and the proposals that follow from it are not against car ownership, but they do argue for different patterns of car use for short trips in urban areas. As demonstrated above, they are also policies that are already in place in many European countries.

Perhaps the most powerful argument against placing restrictions on car use in urban areas to promote active and sustainable travel on foot, by bike or on public transport, is that such measures are potentially discriminatory. It can be argued that those who will suffer most from restrictions on car use are those who have the fewest alternative options for everyday travel and who have the most complex routines: journeys that in current circumstances can only be reasonably accomplished by car. Women, those with restricted physical mobility and some low-income groups could be particularly adversely affected, and restrictions on car use could increase mobility-related social exclusion (Hine, 2003, 2012; Lucas, 2004, 2006, 2012). This is precisely why the policies that we propose must be implemented as a package. Restrictions on car use must be accompanied by (and preferably preceded by) improvements in the physical infrastructure for walking and cycling, changes in urban structure to enable access to most services and facilities without a car, and accommodation of different travelling practices by economy and society. Indeed, in creating a physical and social environment in which walking and cycling are seen to be both safe and easy – the obvious choice for most short trips in urban areas – restrictions on car use become much more acceptable and are likely to affect only a minority who continue to use their cars under any circumstances. The aim would be to create urban spaces where the only trips by car were undertaken by those who physically were incapable of travelling by other means and a small number of other journeys (for instance carrying very heavy loads) where a vehicle is essential.

Finally, it is worth remembering that many people in Britain today already manage perfectly well without a car, or with only occasional car use. At the 2011 census 25.6% of households in England had no access to a car or van, and many more individuals within car-owning households rarely make use of this mode of travel. If over one quarter of households can carry on their everyday lives without a car with the current limited provision of public transport and often adverse conditions for walking or cycling, any facilitation of non-car transport modes would make more active and/or sustainable travel even more attractive. It can also be argued that current car-dominated transport policies are actively discriminating against a significant minority of the population: those who do not own or have access to a car. Given current provision of public transport and conditions for walking and cycling it is not surprising that many (though not all) non-car owning households aspire to have a car. The policies proposed above aim to change such aspirations so that, in urban areas at least, car use is seen as unnecessary and difficult. In summary, we argue that when evidence from Britain and continental Europe is combined, there is a compelling argument for change and a clear vision of what needs to be altered. Many people in Britain already manage without a car, and many more are in principle attracted to more sustainable and/or active forms of travel including walking and cycling. In much of continental Europe there are examples of towns and cities where active travel modes have been successfully facilitated to the benefit of all urban residents, and there are a few places in Britain where there are signs of movement in the same direction. In sum, we argue that change is not as hard as it seems, and that creating a society and environment where walking or cycling are seen as the first choice for much urban travel is an achievable and desirable goal that should be embraced by politicians, planners and by the public at large.

References

Adams, J. (1999) *The social implications of hypermobility*, Paris: OECD (ENV/EPOC/PPC/T(99)3/Final/REV1), available at www.olis.oecd.org/olis/1999doc.nsf.

Adams, J. (2005) 'The limits to integration. Hypermobility: a challenge to governance', in C. Lyall and J. Tait (eds) *New modes of governance: Developing an integrated policy approach to science, technology, risk and the environment*, Aldershot: Ashgate, pp 123–38.

Adey, P. (2010) *Mobility*, Abingdon: Routledge.

Aizlewood, K. And Wellings, R. (2011) *High Speed 2: The next government project disaster?*, London: Institute of Economic Affairs, available at www.iea.org.uk/sites/default/files/publications/files/HighSpeed2-thenextgovernmentprojectdisaster(webversion).pdf.

Ajzen, I. (1991) 'The theory of planned behaviour', *Organizational Behaviour and Human Decision Processes*, vol 50, pp 179–211.

Ajzen, I. (2002) 'Perceived behavioural control, self efficacy, locus of control, and the theory of planned behaviour', *Journal of Applied Social Psychology*, vol 32, pp 665–83.

Aldred, R. (2010) '"On the outside": constructing cycling citizenship', *Social and Cultural Geography*, vol 11, pp 35–52.

Aldred, R. (2012a) 'The role of advocacy and activism', in J. Parkin (ed) *Cycling and sustainability*, Bingley: Emerald.

Aldred, R. (2012b) *Cycling cultures: Summary of key findings and recommendations*, London: University of East London.

Amin, Z. (2000) 'Q methodology: A journey into the subjectivity of the human mind', *Singapore Medical Journal*, vol 41, pp 410–14.

Anable, J. (2005) '"Complacent car addicts" or "aspiring environmentalists"? Identifying travel behaviour segments using attitude theory', *Transport Policy*, vol 12, pp 65–78.

Anderson, B. (2006) *Imagined communities: Reflections on the origin and spread of nationalism*, revised edition, London: Verso.

Anderson, G. (1976) *Victorian clerks*, Manchester: Manchester University Press.

Ansell, N. (2005) *Children, youth and development*, Routledge: Abingdon.

Ansell, N., van Blerk, L., Hajdu, F. And Robson, E. (2011) 'Spaces, times and critical moments: A relational time–space analysis of the impacts of AIDS on rural youth in Malawi and Lesotho', *Environment and Planning A*, vol 43, pp 525–44.

Appleyard, D., Gerson, S. And Lintell, M. (1981) *Liveable streets*, Berkeley: University of California Press.

Apur (Atalier parisien d'urbanisme) (2003) *Paris Projet 34–35: Paris 2020, elements pour un plan d'aménagement et de développement durable*, Paris: Apur.

Armstrong, J. (2000) 'From Shillibeer to Buchanan: Transport and the urban environment', in M. Daunton (ed) *The Cambridge urban history of Britain. Volume III 1840–1950*, Cambridge: Cambridge University Press, pp 229–60.

Arnold, D. And DeWald, E. (2011) 'Cycles of empowerment? The bicycle and everyday technology in Colonial India and Vietnam', *Comparative Studies in Society and History*, vol 53, pp 971–96.

Arthur, W. (1994) *Increasing returns and path dependence in the economy*, Ann Arbor, MI: University of Michigan Press.

Badland, H. And Schofield, G. (2005) 'Transport, urban design, and physical activity: An evidence-based update', *Transportation Research Part D: Transport and Environment*, vol 10, pp 177–96.

Baer, L. (2005) 'Visual imprints on the prison landscape: A study on the decorations in prison cells', *Tijdschrift voor Economische en Sociale Geografie*, vol 96, pp 209–17.

Baker, A., Hamshere, J. And Langton, J. (1970) *Geographical interpretations of historical sources*, Newton Abbot: David and Charles.

Bamberg, S., Ajzen, I. And Schmidt, P. (2003) 'Choice of travel mode in the Theory of Planned Behaviour: The roles of past behaviour, habit and reasoned action', *Basic and Applied Social Psychology*, vol 25, pp 175–87.

Banister, D. (2005) *Unsustainable transport: City transport in the new century*, London: Routledge.

Banister, D. (2007) 'The sustainable mobility paradigm', *Transport Policy*, vol 15, pp 73–80.

Barker, T. And Robbins, M. (1963–74) *A history of London Transport. Vols 1 and 2*, London: Allen and Unwin.

Barry, C. (1998) 'Choosing qualitative data analysis software: Atlas/ti and Nudist compared', *Sociological Research on-line*, vol 3, available at http://socresonline.org.uk/3/3/4.html.

Bassett, D., Pucher, J., Buehler, R., Thompson, D. And Crouter, S. (2008) 'Walking, cycling, and obesity rates in Europe, North America, and Australia', *Journal of Physical Activity and Health*, vol 5, pp 795–814.

Beck, M., Rose, M. And Hensher, A. (2011) 'Behavioural responses to vehicle emission charging', *Transportation*, vol 38, pp 445–63.

Bennett, T. And Watson, D. (2002) *Understanding everyday life*, Oxford: Blackwell.

Beria, P., Maltese, I. And Mariotti, H. (2012) 'Multicriteria versus cost–benefit analysis: A comparative perspective in the assessment of sustainable mobility', *European Transportation Research Review* (published on-line, DOI: 10.1007/s12544-012-0074-9).

Bianchi, S. (2000) 'Maternal employment and time with children: Dramatic change or surprising continuity?', *Demography*, vol 37, pp 401–14.

Birtchnell, T. And Büscher, M. (eds) (2011) 'An eruption of disruption', *Mobilities*, vol 6, pp 1–102.

Bissell, D. (2009) 'Conceptualising differently-mobile passengers: Geographies of everyday encumbrance at the railway station', *Social and Cultural Geography*, vol 10, pp 173–95.

Bissell, D. (2010) 'Passenger mobilities: Affective atmospheres and the sociality of public transport', *Environment and Planning D: Society and Space*, vol 28, pp 270–89.

Blomley, N. (2010) *Rights of passage: Sidewalks and the regulation of public flow*, London: Routledge.

Booth, K., Pinkston, M. And Carlos Poston, W. (2005) 'Obesity and the built environment', *Journal of the American Dietetic Association*, vol 105, pp 110–17.

Borjesson, M. And Eliasson, J. (2012) 'The benefits of cycling: Viewing cyclists as travellers rather than non-motorists', in J. Parkin (ed) *Cycling and sustainability*, Emerald: Bingley, pp 247–68.

Bräuchler, B. And Postill, J. (2010) *Theorising media and practice*, Oxford: Berghahn Books.

Breheny, M. (1996) 'Centrists, decentrists and compromisers: Views on the future of urban form', in M. Jenks, E. Burton and K. Williams (eds) *The compact city: A sustainable urban form?*, London: E & FN Spon.

Breheny, M. And Rookwood, R. (1993) 'Planning the sustainable city region', in A. Blowers (ed) *Planning for a sustainable environment: A report by the Town and Country Planning Association*, London: Earthscan.

Briggs, D., de Hoogh, C., Gulliver, J., Wills, J., Elliott, P., Kingham, S. And Smallbone, K. (2000) 'A regression-based method for mapping traffic-related air pollution: Application and testing in four contrasting urban environments', *The Science of the Total Environment*, vol 253, pp 151–68.

Briggs, D., de Hoogh, K., Morris, C. And Gulliver, J. (2008) 'Effects of travel mode on exposures to particulate air pollution', *Environment International*, vol 34, pp 12–22.

Brussel, M. And Zuidgeest, M. (2012) 'Cycling research in developing countries: Context, challenges and policy-relevant research', in J. Parkin (ed.) *Cycling and sustainability*, Bingley: Emerald.

Bryceson, D. And Bradbury, A. (2008) 'Roads to poverty reduction? Exploring rural roads' impact on mobility in Africa and Asia', *Development Policy Review*, vol 26, pp 459–82.

Buchanan, C. (1964) *Traffic in town*, Harmondsworth: Penguin.

Buckeridge, D., Glazier, R., Harvey, B., Escobar, M., Amrhein, C. And Frank, J. (2002) 'Effects of motor vehicle emissions on respiratory health in an urban area', *Environmental Health Perspectives*, vol 110, pp 293–300.

Buehler, R. And Pucher, J. (2009) 'Cycling to sustainability in Amsterdam', *Sustain*, vol 21, pp 36–40.

Buehler, R., Pucher, J., Merom, D. And Bauman, A. (2011) 'Active travel in Germany and the US: Contributions of daily walking and cycling to physical activity', *American Journal of Preventive Medicine*, vol 41, pp 241–50.

Burr, M., Karani, G., Davies, B., Holmes, B. And Williams, K. (2004) 'Effects on respiratory health of a reduction in air pollution from vehicle exhaust emissions', *Occupational and Environmental Medicine*, vol 61, pp 212–18.

Butcher, L., Codd, F. And Harker, R. (2010) 'Transport policy in 2010: A rough guide', *House of Commons Research Paper 10/28*, London: House of Commons.

Butlin, R. (1993) *Historical geography: Through the gates of space and time*, London: Arnold.

Cairns, S., Sloman, L., Newson, C., Anable, J., Kirkbride, A. And Goodwin, P. (2004) *Smarter choices: Changing the way we travel*, London: Department for Transport (DfT).

Campaign to Protect Rural England (CPRE) (2010) *Back-pedalling London's cycling revolution?* London: CPRE.

Cannadine, D. And Reeder, D. (eds) (1982) *Exploring the urban past: Essays in urban history by H.J. Dyos*, Cambridge: Cambridge University Press, pp 81–128.

Carpiano, R. (2009) 'Come take a walk with me: The "go-along" interview as a novel method for studying the implications of place for health and well-being', *Health and Place*, vol 15, pp 263–72.

Castro, F., Kellison, J., Boyd, S. And Kopak, A. (2010) 'A methodology for conducting integrative mixed methods research and data analysis', *Journal of Mixed Methods Research*, vol 4, pp 342–60.

Cavill, N., Kahlmeier, S., Rutter, H., Racioppi, F. And Oja, P. (2008) 'Economic analyses of transport infrastructure and policies including health effects related to cycling and walking: A systematic review', *Transport Policy*, vol 15, pp 291–304.

Chen, J. And Wang, L. (2007) 'Locus of control and the three components of commitment to change', *Personality and Individual Differences*, vol 42, pp 503–12.

Chin, G., Van Niel, K., Giles-Corti, B. And Knuiman, M. (2008) 'Accessibility and connectivity in physical activity studies: The impact of missing pedestrian data', *Preventive Medicine*, vol 46, pp 41–5.

Choo, S. And Mokhtarian, P. (2008) 'How do people respond to congestion mitigation policies? A multivariate probit model of the individual consideration of three travel-related strategy bundles', *Transportation*, vol 35, pp 145–63.

Christensen, J., Chaterjee, K., Marsh, S., Sherwin, H. And Jain, J. (2012) *Evaluation of the cycling city and towns programme: Qualitative research with residents*, Manchester: Report to Department for Transport (DfT) by AECOM, Centre for Transport and Society and the Tavistock Institute, available at http://www.cycling-embassy. org.uk/sites/cycling-embassy.org.uk/files/documents/cct-qualitative-research. pdf

Clark, D. (2011) 'Google discloses carbon footprint for the first time', *Guardian*, 8 September 2011, available at www.guardian.co.uk/environment/2011/sep/08/google-carbon-footprint?INTCMP=ILCNETTXT3487.

Commission of the European Communities (CEC) (1990) *Green Paper on the urban environment: Communication to the council and Parliament*, COM(90) 218 (1990), Brussels: CEC.

Committee on the Medical Effects of Air Pollution (COMEAP) (2010) *The mortality effects of long-term exposure to particulate air pollution in the United Kingdom*, Didcot: COMEAP.

Conley, J. (ed) (2009) *Car troubles: Critical studies of automobility and auto-mobility*, Aldershot: Ashgate.

Cook, A. (2011) *A fresh start for the strategic road network*, London: Department for Transport (DfT).

Cox, P. (2010) *Moving people: Sustainable transport development*, London: Zed Books.

Cox, P. And Van de Walle, F. (2007) 'Bicycles don't evolve: Velomobiles and the modelling of transport technologies', in D. Horton, D. Rosen and P. Cox (eds) (2007) *Cycling and society*, Aldershot: Ashgate, pp 113–32.

Cresswell, T. (2006) *On the move: Mobility in the modern Western world*, London: Routledge.

Cresswell, T. (2010) 'Towards a politics of mobility', *Environment and Planning D: Society and Space*, vol 28, pp 17–31.

Cresswell, T. And Merriman, P. (eds) (2011) *Geographies of mobilities: Practices, spaces, subjects*, Burlington: Ashgate.

Crossick, G. (1978) *An artisan elite in Victorian society: Kentish London 1840–1880*, London: Croom Helm.

Cullinane, S. (2003) 'Hong Kong's low car dependence: Lessons and prospects', *Journal of Transport Geography*, vol 11, pp 25–35.

Dargay, J. And Hanly, M. (2004) 'Land use and mobility', *Proceedings of World Conference on Transport Research*, Istanbul, Turkey, July 2004.

Davis, A., Hirsch, D., Smith, N., Beckhelling, J. And Padley, M. (2012) *A minimum income standard for the UK: Keeping up in hard times*, Cambridge: Joseph Rowntree Foundation.

Dawson, J., Hillsdon, M., Boller, I. And Foster, C. (2007) 'Perceived barriers to walking in the neighbourhood environment and change in physical activity levels over 12 months', *British Journal of Sports Medicine*, vol 41, pp 562–8.

de Boom, A., Walker, R. And Goldup, R. (2001) 'Shanghai: The greatest cycling city in the world', *World Transport Policy and Practice*, vol 7, pp 53–59.

De Certeau, M. (1988) *The practice of everyday life*, Berkeley, CA: University of California Press.

Deem, R. (1982) 'Women, leisure and inequality', *Leisure Studies*, vol 1, pp 29–46.

Dempsey, N., Bramley, G., Power, S. And Brown, G. (2011) 'The social dimension of sustainable development: defining urban social sustainability', *Sustainable Development*, 19, 289–300

Dempsey, N., Brown, C., Raman, S., Porta, S., Jenks, M., Jones, C. And Bramley, G. (2010) 'Elements of urban form', in M. Jenks and C. Jones (eds) *Dimensions of the Sustainable City 2*, London: Springer Science and Business Media.

Dennis, K. And Urry, J. (2009) *After the car*, Cambridge: Polity.

Department for Communities and Local Government (DCLG) (2007) *Manual for streets*, available at www.communities.gov.uk/publications/planningandbuilding/manualforstreets.

Department for Transport (DfT) (2000) *Transport ten year plan 2000*, London: DfT, available at http://webarchive.nationalarchives.gov.uk/+/http://www.dft.gov.uk/about/strategy/whitepapers/previous/transporttenyearplan2000.

Department for Transport (DfT) (2004a) *The future of transport*, London: HMSO, available at http://webarchive.nationalarchives.gov.uk/+/http://www.dft.gov.uk/about/strategy/whitepapers/previous/fot/.

Department for Transport (DfT) (2004b) *Walking and cycling action plan*, London: DfT, available at http://webarchive.nationalarchives.gov.uk/20100202100434/http://www.dft.gov.uk/pgr/sustainable/walking/actionplan/ingandcyclingdocumentinp5802.pdf.

Department for Transport (DfT) (2011a) *National Travel Survey 2010*, London: DfT, available at http://assets.dft.gov.uk/statistics/releases/national-travel-survey-2010/nts2010-01.pdf.

Department for Transport (DfT) (2011b) *Creating growth, cutting carbon: Making sustainable local transport happen*, London: DfT, available at www.official-documents.gov.uk/document/cm79/7996/7996.pdf.

Department for Transport (DfT) and Department of Health (DoH) (2010) *Active travel strategy*, London: DfT/DoH, available at www.dh.gov.uk/prod_consum_dh/groups/dh_digitalassets/documents/digitalasset/dh_113104.pdf.

Department of Energy and Climate Change (DECC) (2012a) *Renewable energy in 2011*, available at https://www.gov.uk/government/publications/renewable-energy-in-2011.

Department of Energy and Climate Change (DECC) (2012b) *Greenhouse gas emission data tables*, available at https://www.gov.uk/government/statistical-data-sets/env02-greenhouse-gas-emissions.

Department of Environment, Transport and the Regions (DETR) (1998) *A new deal for transport: better for everyone. The Government White Paper on the future of transport*, London: TSO, available at http://webarchive.nationalarchives.gov.uk/+/http://www.dft.gov.uk/about/strategy/whitepapers/previous/anewdealfortransportbetterfo5695?page=4#a1003.

Department of the Environment, Transport and the Regions (DETR) (1999) *Towards an urban renaissance: Final report of the Urban Task Force*, London: E & FN Spon.

Descartes, L., Kottak, C. And Kelly, A. (2007) 'Chauffeuring and commuting', *Community, Work & Family*, vol 10, pp 161–78.

Dill, J. (2004) 'Measuring network connectivity for bicycling and walking', *Transport Research Board Annual Meeting 2004*, available at http://reconnectingamerica.org/assets/Uploads/TRB2004-001550.pdf.

Dillard, J., Dujon, V. And King, M. (eds) (2009) *Understanding the social dimension of sustainability*, Abingdon: Routledge.

Dobbs, L. (2005) 'Wedded to the car: Women, employment and the importance of private transport', *Transport Policy*, vol 12, pp 266–78.

Dodge, M. And Kitchin, R. (2001) *Atlas of cyberspace*, Harlow: Addison-Wesley.

Dowling, R. (2000) 'Cultures of mothering and car use in suburban Sydney: A preliminary investigation', *Geoforum*, vol 31, pp 345–53.

Dyhouse, C. (1989) *Feminism and the family in England 1880–1939*, Oxford: Blackwell.

Dyos, H. J. And Aldcroft, D. (1969) *British transport: An economic survey from the seventeenth century to the twentieth*, Leicester: Leicester University Press.

Dyos, H.J. (1953) 'Workmen's fares in South London, 1860–1914', *Journal of Transport History*, vol 1, pp 3–19.

Ebert, A. (2004) 'Cycling towards the nation: The use of bicycles in Germany and The Netherlands 1880–1940', *European Review of History*, vol 11, pp 347–64.

Ebert, A. And Carstensen, T. (2012) 'Cycling culture in northern Europe: From "Golden Age" to "Renaissance"', in J. Parkin (ed) *Cycling and sustainability*, Bingley: Emerald.

ECOTEC (1993) *Reducing transport emissions through planning*, London: HMSO.

Eden, S., Donaldson, A. And Walker, G. (2005) '*Structuring subjectivities: Using Q methodology in human geography*', *Area*, vol 37, pp 413–22.

Edensor, T. (ed) (2010) *Geographies of rhythm: Nature, place, mobilities and bodies*, Farnham: Ashgate.

Ellis, G., Barry, J. And Robinson, C. (2007) 'Many ways to say "no", different ways to say "yes": Applying Q-methodology to understand public acceptance of wind farm proposals', *Journal of Environmental Planning and Management*, vol 50, pp 517–51.

European Conference of Ministers of Transport (2007) *Cutting transport CO2 emissions: What progress?* Paris: European Conference of Ministers of Transport.

Eurostat (2010) *Energy, transport and environment indicators*, Luxembourg: European Commission.

Evans, A. And Gough, J. (eds) (2003) *The impact of the railway on society in Britain: Essays in honour of Jack Simmons*, Aldershot: Ashgate.

Ewing, R. (1997) 'Is Los Angeles-style sprawl desirable?', *Journal of American Planning Association*, vol 63, pp 107–26.

Ewing, R. And Cervero, R. (2001) 'Travel and the built environment: A synthesis', *Transportation Research Record*, vol 1780, pp 87–114.

Ewing, R. And Cevero, R. (2010) 'Travel and the built environment: A meta-analysis', *Journal of the American Planning Association*, vol 76, pp 265–94.

Farag, S. And Lyons, G. (2010) 'Explaining public transport information use when a car is available: Attitude theory empirically tested', *Transportation*, vol 37, pp 897–913.

Farthing, S., Winter, J. And Coombes, T. (1996) 'Travel behaviour and local accessibility to services and facilities', in M. Jenks, E. Burton and K. Williams (eds) *The compact city: A sustainable urban form?*, London: E & FN Spon.

Featherstone, M., Thrift, N. And Urry, J. (2005) *Automobilities*, London: Sage.

Fincham, B. (2007) 'Bicycle messengers: Image, identity and community', in D. Horton, D. Rosen and P. Cox (eds) *Cycling and society*, Aldershot: Ashgate, pp 179–96.

Fincham, B., McGuiness, M., and Murray, L. (2009) *Mobile methodologies*, Palgrave: Basingstoke.

Fink, A. (2009) *How to conduct surveys*, London: Sage.

Freeman, L. (1977) 'A set of measures of centrality based on betweeness', *Sociometry*, vol 40, pp 35–41.

Freeman, M. And Aldcroft, D. (eds) (1988) *Transport in Victorian Britain*, Manchester: Manchester University Press.

Furedi, F. (2001) *Paranoid parenting: Abandon your anxieties and be a good parent*, London: Penguin.

Fyfe, N. (1996) 'City watching: Closed circuit television surveillance in public space', *Area*, vol 28, pp 37–46.

Fyfe, N. (2004) 'Zero tolerance, maximum surveillance? Deviance, difference and crime control in the late-modern city', in L. Lees (ed) *The emancipatory city? Paradoxes and possibilities*, London: Sage, pp 40–56.

Gant, R. (1997) 'Pedestrianisation and disabled people: A study of personal mobility in Kingston town centre', *Disability and Society*, vol 12, pp 723–40.

Gehl, J. And Gemzøe, L. (2004) *Public spaces – public life*. Copenhagen: Danish Architectural Press.

Gesler, W. (1992) 'Therapeutic landscapes: Medical issues in the light of the new cultural geography', *Social Science and Medicine*, vol 34, pp 735–46.

Gesler, W. (2005) 'Therapeutic landscapes: An evolving theme', *Health and Place*, vol 11, pp 295–7.

Giles-Corti, B., Wood, G., Pikora, T., Learnihan, V., Bulsara, M., Van Niel, K., Timperio, A., McCormack, G. And Villanueva, K. (2011) 'School site and the potential to walk to school: The impact of street connectivity and traffic exposure in school neighborhoods', *Health and Place*, vol 17, pp 545–50.

Gill, M. And Spriggs, A. (2005) 'Assessing the impact of CCTV', *Home Office Research Study 292*, London: Home Office Research, Development and Statistics Directorate, available at http://webarchive.nationalarchives.gov.uk/20110218135832/http://rds.homeoffice.gov.uk/rds/pdfs05/hors292.pdf.

Goeft, U. And Alder, J. (2001) 'Sustainable mountain biking: A case study from the south west of Western Australia', *Journal of Sustainable Tourism*, vol 9, pp 183–211.

Goetzke, F. (2011) 'Bicycle use in Germany: Explaining differences between municipalities with social network effects', *Urban Studies*, vol 48, pp 427–37.

Goodwin, P. (2004) 'The economic costs of road traffic congestion', *ESRC Transport Studies Unit Discussion Paper*, London: Rail Freight Group, University College London.

Goodwin, P. (2013) *Get Britain Cycling. Report from the Inquiry by the All Party Parliamentary Cycling Group*, London: APPCG.

Gordon, E. And Nair, G. (2003) *Public lives: Women, family and society in Victorian Britain*, New Haven, CT: Yale University Press.

Gotschi, T. (2011) 'Costs and benefits of bicycling investments in Portland, Oregon', *Journal of Physical Activity and Health*, vol 8, pp S49–S58.

Graham, B. And Howard, P. (2008) *The Ashgate research companion to heritage and identity*, Aldershot: Ashgate.

Green, D. (1988) 'Distance to work in Victorian London: A case study of Henry Poole, bespoke tailors', *Business History*, vol 30, pp 179–94.

Gregson, N. And Rose, G. (2000) 'Taking Butler elsewhere: Performativities, spatialities and subjectivities', *Environment and Planning D*, vol 18, pp 433–52.

Grieco, M. And Crowther, D. (2011) 'Identifying time–space constraints: A neglected element of the development discourse', *Social Responsibility Journal*, vol 7, pp 638–48.

Grieco, M. And McQuaid, R. (eds) (2012) 'Gender and transport: Transaction costs, competing resources and transport policy gaps', *Research in Transportation Economics*, vol 34, pp 1–86.

Grieco, M. And Urry, J. (eds) (2012) *Mobilities: New perspectives on transport and society*, Farnham: Ashgate.

Grieco, M. Ndulo, M., Bryceson, D. Porter, G. And McCray, T. (eds) (2009) *Africa, transport and the millennium development goals: Achieving an internationally set agenda*, Cambridge: Cambridge Scholars Publishing.

Grundy, C., Steinbach, R., Edwards, P., Wilkinson, P. And Green, J. (2008) *20mph zones and road safety in London: A report to the London Road Safety Unit*, London: London School of Hygiene and Tropical Medicine.

Haase, A., Steptoe, A. Sallis, J. And Wardle, J. (2004) 'Leisure time physical activity in university students from 23 countries: Associations with health benefits, risk awareness, and national economic development', *Preventive Medicine*, vol 39, pp 182–90.

Hadland, T. (2011) *Raleigh: past and presence of an iconic bicycle brand*, San Francisco, CA.: Van der Plas publications.

Hagerstrand, T. (1970) 'What about people in regional science', *Papers in Regional Science*, vol 24, pp 6–21.

Haixiao, P. (2011) 'Implementing sustainable urban travel policies in China', *Discussion paper 12*, Paris: International Transport Forum.

Haixiao, P. (2012) 'Evolution of urban bicycle transport policy in China', in J. Parkin (ed) *Cycling and sustainability*, Bingley: Emerald.

Hamilton, Peter (2002): 'The street and everyday life', in Tony Bennett and Diane Watson (eds), *Understanding Everyday Life*, pp. 91-138, Oxford: Blackwell.

Handy, S. (2005) *Critical assessment of the literature on the relationships among transportation, land use, and physical activity*, Transportation Research Board Special Report 282, available at http://onlinepubs.trb.org/onlinepubs/archive/downloads/sr282papers/sr282handy.pdf.

Harvey, D. (1989) *The condition of postmodernity: An enquiry into the origins of cultural change*, Oxford: Blackwell.

Hathaway, T. (1996) 'Assessing the costs and benefits of cycle networks', *World Transport Policy and Practice*, vol 2, pp 34–41.

Hensher, D. (2008) 'Climate change, enhanced greenhouse gas emissions and passenger transport: What can we do to make a difference?', *Transportation Research Part D: Transport and Environment*, vol 13, pp 95–111.

Hickman, R. And Banister, D. (2005) 'Reducing travel by design: What happens over time?', in K. Williams and E. Burton (eds) *Spatial planning, urban form and sustainable transport*, Aldershot: Ashgate, pp 102–19.

Higgs, G., Fry, R. And Langford, M. (2012) 'Investigating the implications of using alternative GIS-based techniques to measure accessibility to green space', *Environment and Planning B: Planning and Design*, vol 39, pp 326–43.

Hillman, M. (1996) 'In favour of the compact city', in M. Jenks, E. Burton and K. Williams (eds) *The compact city: A sustainable urban form?*, London: E & FN Spon.

Hillman, M., Adams, J. And Whitelegg, J. (1990) *One false move…: A study of children's independent mobility*, London: Policy Studies Institute.

Hillman, M., Whalley, A. And Henderson, I. (1976) *Transport realities and planning policy: Studies of friction and freedom in daily travel*, London: Political and Economic Planning.

Hinde, S. And Dixon, J. (2005) 'Changing the obesogenic environment: Insights from a cultural economy of car reliance', *Transportation Research Part D: Transport and Environment*, vol 10, pp 31–53.

Hine, J. (ed) (2003) 'Social exclusion and transport systems', *Transport Policy*, vol 10, pp 263–342.

Hine, J. (2012) 'Mobility and transport disadvantage', in M. Grieco and J. Urry (eds) *Mobilities: New perspectives on transport and society*, Farnham: Ashgate, pp 21–40.

Holtzclaw, J. (1994) *Using residential patterns and transit to decrease auto dependence and costs*, San Francisco, CA: Natural Resources Defense Council, available at http://docs.nrdc.org/smartGrowth/files/sma_09121401a.pdf.

Horton, D., Rosen, D. And Cox. P (eds) (2007) *Cycling and society*, Aldershot: Ashgate.

House of Lords Science and Technology Select Committee (2011) *Behaviour change report*, London: TSO, available at www.publications.parliament.uk/pa/ld201012/ldselect/ldsctech/179/179.pdf.

Hunecke, H., Haustein, S., Böhler, S. And Grischkat, S. (2010) 'Attitude-based target groups to reduce the ecological impact of daily mobility behaviour', *Environment and Behaviour*, vol 42, pp 3–43.

Ingold, T. (2004) 'Culture on the ground: The world perceived through feet', *Journal of Material Culture*, vol 9, pp 315–40.

Ingold, T. And Vergunst, J. (eds) (2008) *Ways of walking: Ethnography and practice on foot*, Aldershot: Ashgate.

International Transport Forum (2008) *Transport and energy: The challenge of climate change*, Paris: International Transport Forum.

International Transport Forum (2011) *Transport outlooks: Meeting the needs of 9 billion people*, Paris: International Transport Forum.

Jackson, B. (2012) *Report to Dunstable traffic management meeting on proposed 20mph speed limit zones*, available at http://www.centralbedfordshire.gov.uk/modgov/documents/s32899/Dunstable20mphzones-TMmeetingreportncmodifiedfinal.pdf.

Jackson, J. (1973) *Semi-detached London: Suburban development, life and transport, 1900–39*, London: Allen and Unwin.

Jacobs, J. (1972) *The death and life of great American cities*, Harmondsworth: Penguin.

Janelle, D. (1969) 'Spatial reorganization: A model and concept', *Annals of the Association of American Geographers*, vol 59, pp 348–64.

Jarvis, H. (2003) 'Dispelling the myth that preference makes practice in residential location and transport behaviour', *Housing Studies*, vol 18, pp 587–606.

Jenkins, R. (2008) *Social identity*, third edition, Abingdon: Routledge.

Jenks, M. And Dempsey, N. (eds) (2005) *Future forms and design for sustainable cities*, Oxford: Architectural Press.

Jenks, M., Burton, E. And Williams, K. (eds) (1996) *The compact city: A sustainable urban form?*, E & FN Spon: London.

John, P. (2011) *Nudge, nudge, think, think: Experimenting with ways to change civic behaviour*, Bloomsbury: London.

Jones, P. (2005) 'Performing the city: A body and a bicycle take on Birmingham, UK', *Social and Cultural Geography*, vol 6, pp 813–30.

Jones, T., Pooley, C., Scheldeman, G., Horton, D., Tight, M., Mullen, C., Jopson, A, and Whiteing, A. (2012) 'Moving around the city: Discourses on walking and cycling in English urban areas', *Environment and Planning A*, vol 44, pp 1407–24.

Jungnickel, K. (2011) 'The socio-politics of bloomers and lycra: Why cycling wear *still* matters', unpublished paper presented at AHRC History and Transport Policy seminar, Lancaster, 20 September.

Kasanko, M., Barredo, J., Lavalle, C., McCormick, N., Demicheli, L., Sagris, V. And Brezger, A. (2006) 'Are European cities becoming dispersed? A comparative analysis of 15 European urban areas', *Landscape and Urban Planning*, vol 77, pp 111–30.

Keeling, D. (2009) 'Transportation geography: Local challenges, global contexts', *Progress in Human Geography*, vol 33, pp 516–26.

Kellett, J. (1969) *The impact of railways on Victorian cities*, London: Routledge and Kegan Paul.

Kenworthy, J. And Laube, F. (1999) 'Patterns of automobile dependence in cities: An international overview of key physical and economic dimensions with some implications for urban policy', *Transportation Research Part A: Policy and Practice*, vol 33, pp 691–723.

Kitchin, R. (1998) 'Towards geographies of cyberspace', *Progress in Human Geography*, vol 22, pp 385–406.

Kunert, U., Kloas, J. And Kuhfeld, H. (2002) 'Design characteristics of National Travel Surveys: International comparisons from 10 countries', *Transportation Research Record*, vol 1804, pp 107–16.

Kusenbach, M. (2003) 'Street phenomenology: The go-along as ethnographic research tool', *Ethnography*, vol 4, pp 455–85.

Lake, A. And Townshend, T. (2006) 'Obesogenic environments: Exploring the built and food environments', *Perspectives in Public Health*, vol 126, pp 262–7.

Lake, A., Townshend, T. And Alvanides, S. (eds) (2010) *Obesogenic environments: Complexities, perceptions and objective measures*, Chichester: Wiley-Blackwell.

Laurier, E. (2004) 'Doing office work on the motorway', *Theory, Culture, Society*, vol 21, pp 261–77.

Law, R. (1999) 'Beyond "women and transport": Towards new geographies of gender and daily mobility', *Progress in Human Geography*, vol 23, pp 567–88.

Lefcourt, H. (1976) *Locus of control: Current trends in theory and research*, New York: Halstead Press.

Lefebvre, H. (2004) *Rhythmnanalysis: Space, time and everyday life*, London: Continuum.

Leicester City Council (2011) *Third local transport plan*, Leicester: Leicester City Council, available at www.leicester.gov.uk/your-council-services/transport-traffic/transportpolicy/transport-plan/third-local-transport-plan/.

Leslie, E., Coffee, N., Frank, L., Owen, N., Bauman. A. And Hugo, G. (2007) 'Walkability of local communities: Using geographic information systems to objectively assess relevant environmental attributes', *Health and Place*, vol 13, pp 111–22.

Llewelyn Davies, M. (ed) (1915) *Maternity: Letters from working women collected by the Women's Co-operative Guild*, London: Bell.

Lloyd Jones, R. And Lewis, M. (2000) *Raleigh and the British bicycle industry: An economic and business history 1870–1960*, Aldershot: Ashgate.

Lloyd, R., Parr, B. Davies, S. And Cooke, C. (2010a) 'No "free ride" for African women: A comparison of head-loading versus back-loading among Xhosa women', *South African Journal of Science*, vol 106, pp 50–5.

Lloyd, R., Parr, B. Davies, S., Partridge, T. And Cooke, C. (2010b) 'A comparison of the physiological consequences of head-loading and back-loading for African and European women', *European Journal of Applied Physiology*, vol 109, pp 607–16.

Lorimer, H. (2011) 'Walking: New forms and spaces for studies of pedestrianism', in T. Cresswell and P. Merriman (eds) (2011) *Geographies of mobilities: Practices, spaces, subjects*, Farnham: Ashgate, pp 19–34.

Lorimer, H. And Lund, K. (2008) 'A collectable topography: Walking, remembering and recording mountains', in T. Ingold and J. Vergunst (eds) *Ways of walking: Ethnography and practice on foot*, Aldershot: Ashgate, pp 318–45.

Lucas, K. (2004) *Running on empty: Transport, social exclusion and environmental justice*, Bristol: Policy Press.

Lucas, K. (2006) 'Providing transport for social inclusion within a framework of environmental justice in the UK', *Transportation Research* A, vol 40, pp 801–9.

Lucas, K. (2012) 'Transport and social exclusion where are we now?', in M. Grieco and J. Urry (eds) *Mobilities: New perspectives on transport and society*, Farnham: Ashgate, pp 207–22.

Lucas, K. And Stanley, J. (2009) 'International perspectives on transport and social exclusion', *Transport Policy*, vol 16, pp 19–142.

Lund, K. (2005) 'Seeing in motion and the touching eye: Walking over Scotland's mountains', *Etnofoor*, vol 18, pp 27–42.

Lynch, K. (1960) *The image of the city*, Cambridge, MA: MIT Press.

Lyons, G. And Urry, J. (2005) 'Travel time use in the information age', *Transportation Research Part A: Policy and Practice*, vol 39, pp 257–76.

Lyons, G., Jain, J. And Holley, D. (2007) 'The use of travel time by rail passengers in Great Britain', *Transportation Research Part A: Policy and Practice*, vol 41, pp 107–20.

Mackett, R. (2001) 'Policies to attract drivers out of their cars for short trips', *Transport Policy*, vol 8, pp 295–306.

Mackett, R. (2003) 'Why do people use their cars for short trips?', *Transportation*, vol 30, pp 329–49.

MacKinnon, D., Pirie, G. And Gather, M. (2008) 'Transport, the economy and development', in R. Knowles, J. Shaw and I. Docherty (eds) *Transport geographies: Mobilities, flows and spaces*, Oxford: Blackwell.

Maddox, H. (2001) 'Another look at Germany's bicycle boom: Implications for local transportation policy and planning strategy in the USA', *World Transport Policy and Practice*, vol 7, pp 44–8.

Magnusson, L. And Ottosson, J. (1997) *Evolutionary economics and path dependence*, Cheltenham: Edward Elgar.

Marsden, P. And Wright, J. (eds) (2010) *Handbook of survey research*, Bingley: Emerald.

Marshall, S. (2005) *Streets and patterns: The structure of urban geometry*, Abingdon: Spon.

McKenzie, A. (2011) 'Re-inventing the wheel', *Engineering Insight*, vol 12, pp 24–7.

McMillan, T. (2007) 'The relative influence of urban form on a child's travel mode to school', *Transportation Research Part A: Policy and Practice*, vol 41, pp 69–79.

Methorst, R., Monterde-i-Bort, H., Risser, R., Sauter, D., Tight, M. And Walker, J. (2010) (eds) *Pedestrians' quality needs: Final report of the EU COST 358 project*, available at www.walkeurope.org/final_report/default.asp.

Middleton, J. (2009a) 'Stepping in time: Walking time and space in the city', *Environment and Planning A*, vol 41, pp 1943–61.

Middleton, J. (2009b) 'The promotion of London as a "walkable city" and overlapping walks of life', in R. Imrie, L. Lees and M. Raco (eds) *Regenerating London: Governance, sustainability and community in a global city*, Abingdon: Routledge, pp 192–211.

Middleton, J. (2010) 'Sense and the city: Exploring the embodied geographies of urban walking', *Social and Cultural Geography*, vol 11, pp 575–96.

Middleton, J. (2011a) '"I'm on autopilot I just follow the route": Exploring the habits, routines and decision making practices of everyday mobilities', *Environment and Planning A*, vol 43, pp 2857–77.

Middleton, J. (2011b) 'Walking in the city: The geographies of everyday pedestrian practices', *Geography Compass*, vol 5, pp 90–105.

Migliore, E., Berti, G., Galassi, C. And 17 others (2009) 'Respiratory symptoms in children living near busy roads and their relationship to vehicular traffic: Results of an Italian multicenter study (SIDRIA 2)', *Environmental Health*, vol 8, pp 1–16.

Mitchell, R. And Maher, B. (2009) 'Evaluation and application of biomagnetic monitoring of traffic-derived particulate pollution', *Atmospheric Environment*, vol 43, pp 2095–103.

Moran, E. (2010) *Environmental social science: Human–environment interactions and sustainability*, Chichester: Wiley-Blackwell.

Moudon, A. And Lee, C. (2003) 'Walking and bicycling: An evaluation of environmental audit instruments', *American Journal of Health Promotion*, vol 18, pp 21–37.

Muhr, T. (1991) 'Atlas/ti: A prototype for the support of text interpretation', *Qualitative Sociology*, vol 14, pp 349–71.

Naess, P. (2006) *Urban structure matters: Residential location, car dependence and travel behaviour*, Abingdon: Routledge.

Nash, C. (2000) 'Performativity in practice: Some recent work in cultural geography', *Progress in Human Geography*, vol 24, pp 653–64.

National Institute for Clinical Excellence (NICE) (2012) *Walking and cycling: Local measures to promote walking and cycling as forms of travel or recreation*, Manchester: NICE, available at www.nice.org.uk/nicemedia/live/13975/61629/61629.pdf.

Needham, M., Wood, C. And Rollins, R. (2004) 'Understanding summer visitors and their experiences at the Whistler Mountain ski area, Canada', *Mountain Research and Development*, vol 24, pp 234–42.

Nelson, L. (1999) 'Bodies (and spaces) do matter: The limits of performativity', *Gender, Place and Culture*, vol 6, pp 331–53.

Newcomb, T. And Spurr, R. (1989) *A technical history of the car*, Bristol: Hilger.

Newman, P. And Kenworthy, J. (1989) *Cities and automobile dependence: An international sourcebook*, Brookfield, VT: Gower.

Newman, P. And Kenworthy, J. (1999) *Sustainability and cities: Overcoming automobile dependence.* Washington, DC: Island Press.

Nieuwenhuis, P. And Wells, P. (2009) *Car futures: Rethinking the automotive industry beyond the American model*, Westbury: Trend Tracker.

Njoh, A. (1999) 'Gender-biased transportation planning in sub-Saharan Africa with special reference to Cameroon', *Journal of Asian and African Studies*, vol 34, pp 216–35.

O'Connell, S. (1998) *The car in British society: Class, gender and mobility 1896–1939*, Manchester: Manchester University Press.

Oddy, N. (2007) 'The flâneur on wheels', in D. Horton, D. Rosen and P. Cox (eds) *Cycling and Society*, Aldershot: Ashgate, pp 97–112.

Ogilvie, D., Egan, M., Hamilton, V., Pettigrew, M. (2004) 'Promoting walking and cycling as an alternative to using cars: Systematic review', *British Medical Journal*, vol 329, pp 763–66.

Ogilvie, D., Foster, C., Rothnie, H., Cavill, N., Hamilton, V., Fitzsimmons, C. And Mutrie, N. (2007) 'Interventions to promote walking: Systematic review', *British Medical Journal*, vol 334, pp 1204–7.

Oliver, L., Schuurman, N. And Hall, A. (2007) 'Comparing circular and network buffers to examine the influence of land use on walking for leisure and errands', *International Journal of Health Geographics*, vol 6, pp 41–51.

Ordnance Survey (2011) *OS MasterMap Address Layer and Address Layer 2 User guide (v1.4, 01/2011)*, Southampton: Ordnance Survey.

Otter, C. (2008) *The Victorian eye: A political history of light and vision in Britain 1800–1910*, Chicago, IL: Chicago University Press.

Pain, R. (2001) 'Gender, race, age and fear in the city', *Urban Studies*, vol 38, pp 899–913.

Pain, R. (2006) 'Paranoid parenting? Rematerialising risk and fear for children', *Social and Cultural Geography*, vol 7, pp 221–43.

Pain, R. And Smith, S. (eds) (2008) *Fear: Critical geopolitics of everyday life*, Aldershot: Ashgate.

Papas, M., Alberg, A., Ewing, R. Helzlsouer, K. Gary, T. And Klassen, A. (2007) 'The built environment and obesity', *Epidemiological Reviews*, vol 29, pp 129–43.

Parkin, J. (ed) (2012) *Cycling and sustainability*, Bingley: Emerald.

Pawson, E. (1977) *The turnpike roads of eighteenth-century England*, London: Academic Press.

Peake, S. And Smith, J. (2009) *Climate change: From science to sustainability*, Oxford: Oxford University Press.

Perkin, H. (1970) *The age of the railway*, London: Panther.

Pooley, C. (1994) 'The mobility of criminals in North-West England', *Local Population Studies*, vol 53, pp 15–28.

Pooley, C. And Turnbull, J. (1999a) 'The journey to work: A century of change', *Area*, vol 31, pp 282–92.

Pooley, C. And Turnbull, J. (1999b) 'Moving through the city: The changing impact of the journey to work on intra-urban mobility in 20th century Britain', *Annales de Démographie Historique*, vol 1, pp 127–49.

Pooley, C. And Turnbull, J. (2000) 'Commuting, transport and urban form: Manchester and Glasgow in the mid-twentieth century', *Urban History*, vol 27, pp 360–83.

Pooley, C., Turnbull, J. And Adams, M. (2005a) *A mobile century? Changes in everyday mobility in Britain in the twentieth century*, Aldershot: Ashgate.

Pooley, C., Turnbull, J. And Adams, M. (2005b) 'The journey to school in England since the 1940s', *Area*, vol 31, pp 43–53.

Pooley, C., Pooley, S. And Lawton, R. (eds) (2010) *Growing up on Merseyside in the late-nineteenth century: The diary of Elizabeth Lee*, Liverpool: Liverpool University Press.

Porta, S., Crucitti, P. And Latora, V. (2006) 'The network analysis of urban streets: A primal approach', *Environment and Planning B: Planning and Design*, vol 33, pp 705–25.

Porta, S., Crucitti, P. And Latora, V. (2008) 'Multiple centrality assessment in Parma: A network analysis of paths and open space', *Urban Design International*, vol 13, pp 41–50.

Porta, S., Latora, V., Wang, F., Rueda, S., Strano, E., Scellato, S., Cardillo, A., Belli, E., Càrdenas, F., Cormenzana, B. And Latora, L. (2012) 'Street centrality and the location of economic activities in Barcelona', *Urban Studies*, vol 49, pp 1471–88.

Porter, G. (2002a) 'Living in a walking world: Rural mobility and social equity issues in sub-Saharan Africa', *World Development*, vol 30, pp 285–300.

Porter, G. (2002b) 'Improving mobility and access for the off-road rural poor through intermediate means of transport', *World Transport Policy and Practice*, vol 8, pp 6–19.

Porter, G. (2007) 'Transport planning in sub-Saharan Africa', *Progress in Development Studies*, vol 7, pp 251–7.

Porter, G. (2008) 'Transport planning in sub-Saharan Africa II: Putting gender into mobility and transport planning in Africa', *Progress in Development Studies*, vol 8, pp 281–9.

Porter, G. (2010) 'Transport planning in sub-Saharan Africa III: The challenge of meeting children's and young people's mobility and transport needs', *Progress in Development Studies*, vol 10, pp 169–80.

Preston, J. And Raje, F. (2007) 'Accessibility, mobility and transport-related social exclusion', *Journal of Transport Geography*, vol 15, pp 151–60.

Pucher, J. And Buehler, R. (2008) Making cycling irresistible: Lessons from The Netherlands, Denmark and Germany, *Transport Reviews*, vol 28, pp 495–528.

Pucher, J. And Buehler, R. (2010) 'Walking and cycling for healthy cities', *Built Environment*, vol 36, pp 391–414.

Pucher, J. And Dijkstra, L. (2003) 'Promoting safe walking and cycling to improve public health: Lessons from The Netherlands and Germany', *American Journal of Public Health*, vol 93, pp 1509–16.

Pucher, J., Buehler, R. And Seinen, M. (2011) 'Bicycling renaissance in North America? An update and reappraisal of cycling trends and policies', *Transportation Research Part A: Policy and Practice*, vol 45, pp 451–75.

Pucher, J., Peng, Z., Mittal, N., Zhu, Y. And Korattyswaroopam, N. (2007) 'Urban transport trends and policies in China and India: Impacts of rapid economic growth', *Transport Reviews*, vol 27, pp 379–410.

Raje, F. (2007) 'Using Q methodology to develop more perceptive insights on transport and social inclusion', *Transport Policy*, vol 14, pp 467–77.

Reckwitz, A. (2002) 'Towards a theory of social practices: A development in cultural theorizing', *European Journal of Social Theory*, vol 5, pp 243–63.

Redfern, R. (2011) *Evaluation of the cycling city and towns programme*, London: Department for Transport (DfT).

Ricketts, J., Evans, J. And Jones, P. (2008) 'Mobile methodologies: Theory, technology and practice', *Geography Compass*, vol 2, pp 1266–85.

Robson, E. (2004) 'Children at work in rural northern Nigeria: Patterns of age, space and gender', *Journal of Rural Studies*, vol 20, pp 193–210.

Rofique, J., Humphrey, A., Pickering, K. And Tipping, S. (2011) *National travel survey 2010 technical report*, London: Department for Transport (DfT), available at http://assets.dft.gov.uk/statistics/series/national-travel-survey/nts2010-technical.pdf.

Rose, G. (2011) 'E-bikes and urban transportation: Emerging issues and unresolved questions', *Transportation*, vol 39, pp 81–96.

Rose, M. And Parsons, M. (2008) 'High performance Lancashire: Knowledge, skills and mountaineering clothing and equipment before 1953', in J. Wilson (ed) *King Cotton: A tribute to Douglas Farnie*, Lancaster: Carnegie, pp 117–32.

Rose, M., Parsons, M. And Love, T. (2007) 'Path dependent foundations of global design-driven outdoor trades in the north-west of England', *International Journal of Design*, vol 1, pp 57–68.

Ryley, T. (2005) *A study of individual travel behaviour in Edinburgh, to assess the propensity to use non-motorised modes*, unpublished PhD thesis, Napier University.

Sabidussi, G. (1966) 'The centrality index of a graph', *Psychometrika*, vol 31, pp 581–603.

Saelens, B. And Handy, S. (2008) 'Built environment correlates of walking: A review', *Medicine and Science in Sports and Exercise*, vol 40, pp S550–S566.

Saelens, B., James, F., Sallis, J. And Frank, L. (2003) 'Environmental correlates of walking and cycling: Findings from the transport, urban design and planning literatures', *Annals of Behavioral Medicine*, vol 25, pp 80–91.

Sælensminde, K. (2004) 'Cost–benefit analyses of walking and cycling track networks taking into account insecurity, health effects and external costs of motorised traffic', *Transportation Research Part A: Policy and Practice*, vol 36, pp 593–606.

Salmon, J., Salmon, L., Crawford D., Hume, C. And Timperio, A. (2007) 'The science of health promotion: Associations among individual, social and environmental barriers and children's walking or cycling to school', *American Journal of Health Promotion*, vol 22, pp 107–13.

Sangani, K. (2009) 'E-bikes take off', *Engineering and Technology*, vol 10, pp 34–5.

Sankaran, J., Gore, A. And Coldwell, B. (2005) 'The impact of road traffic congestion on supply chains: Insights from Aukland, New Zealand', *International Journal of Logisitics Research and Applications*, vol 8, pp 159–80.

Sanni, T. And Albrantes, P. (2010) 'Estimating walking modal share: A novel approach based on spatial regression models and GIS', *Journal of Maps*, vol 6, pp 192–8.

Schafer, A. (1998) 'The global demand for motorised mobility', *Transportation Research Part A: Policy and Practice*, vol 32, pp 455–77.

Schafer, A. And Victor, D. (2000) 'The future mobility of the world population', *Transportation Research Part A: Policy and Practice*, vol 34, pp 171–205.

Schatzki, T., Cetina, K. And Savigny, E. (2001) *The practice turn in contemporary theory*, London: Routledge.

Scheldeman, G. (2011) 'Beyond A to B', in T. Ingold (ed) *Redrawing anthropology: Materials, movement and lines*, Farnham: Ashgate, pp 129–41.

Scheurer, J. And Porta, S. (2006) 'Centrality and connectivity in public transport networks and their significance for transport sustainability in cities', *World Planning Schools Congress, Global Planning Association Education Network*, 13–16 July, Mexico.

Schmucki, B. (2012) "'If I walked on my own at night I stuck to well-lit areas": Gendered spaces and urban transport in 20th century Britain', *Research in Transportation Economics*, vol 34, pp 74–85.

Shaw, J., MacKinnon, D. And Docherty, I. (2009) 'Divergence or convergence? Devolution and transport policy in the United Kingdom', *Environment and Planning C*, vol 27, pp 546–67.

Sheller, M. And Urry, J. (2000) 'The city and the car', *International Journal of Urban and Regional Research*, vol 24, pp 737–57.

Sheller, M. And Urry, J. (2006) 'The new mobilities paradigm', *Environment and Planning A*, vol 38, pp 207–26.

Shove, E. (2010) 'Beyond the ABC: Climate change policies and theories of social change', *Environment and Planning A*, vol 42, pp 1273–85.

Shove, E. And Walker, G. (2007) 'CAUTION! Transitions ahead: politics, practice and sustainable transition management', *Environment and Planning A*, vol 39, pp 763–70.

Silverstone, R., Hirsch, E. And Morley, D. (1991) 'Listening to a long conversation: An ethnographic approach to the study of information and communication technologies in the home', *Cultural Studies*, vol 5, pp 204–27.

Simmons, J. (1986) *The railway in town and country, 1830–1914*, Newton Abbot: David and Charles.

Simmons, J. (1991) *The Victorian railway*, New York: Thames and Hudson.

Simpson, C. (2007) 'Capitalising on curiosity: Women's professional cycle racing in the late-nineteenth century', in D. Horton, D. Rosen and P. Cox (eds) *Cycling and Society*, Aldershot: Ashgate, pp 47–66.

Sloman, L., Cairns, S., Newson, C., Anable, J., Pridmore, A. And Goodwin, P. (2010) *The effects of smarter choice programmes in the sustainable travel towns: Summary report*, London: Department for Transport (DfT), available at https://www.gov.uk/government/uploads/system/uploads/attachment_data/file/4408/chap1.pdf.

Sloman, L., Cavill, N., Cope, A., Muller, L. And Kennedy, A. (2009) *Analysis and synthesis of evidence on the effects of investment in six cycling demonstration towns*, Report for Department for Transport and Cycling England, London: Department for Transport (DfT).

Solnit, R. (2001) *Wanderlust: A history of walking*, London: Verso.

Southall, H. (1991) 'The tramping artisan revisits: Labour mobility and economic distress in early Victorian England', *Economic History Review*, vol 44, pp 272–96.

Spinney, J. (2006) 'A place of sense: A kinaesthetic ethnography of cyclists on Mont Ventoux', *Environment and Planning D: Society and Space*, vol 24, pp 709–32.

Spinney, J. (2007) 'Cycling the city: Non-place and the sensory construction of meaning in a mobile practice', in D. Horton, P. Rosen and P. Cox (eds) *Cycling and Society*, Aldershot: Ashgate, pp 25–45.

Spinney, J. (2009) 'Cycling the city: Movement, meaning and method', *Geography Compass*, vol 3, pp 817–35.

Steg, L., Vlek, C., and Slotegraaf, G. (2001), 'Instrumental-reasoned and symbolic-affective motives for using a motor car', *Transportation Research-F: Psychology and Behaviour*, vol 4, pp 151-169.

Steinbach, R., Green, J., Datta, J. And Edwards, P. (2011) 'Cycling and the city: A case study of how gendered, ethnic and class identities can shape healthy transport choice', *Social Science and Medicine*, vol 72, pp 1123–30.

Stern, N. (2010) *A blueprint for a safer planet: How we can save the world and create prosperity*, London: Vintage.

Stradling, S. (2007) 'Determinants of car dependence', in T. Gärling and L. Steg (eds) *Threats from car traffic to the quality of urban life: Problems causes and solutions*, Oxford: Elsevier, pp 187–204.

Sustrans Cymru (2012) *Active Travel (Wales) Bill conference: Conference report*, Cardiff: Sustrans, available at www.sustrans.org.uk/assets/files/WalesPolicyDocs/ActiveTravelWalesBill/FINALActiveTravel(Wales)BillConferenceReport.pdf.

Tang, S. And Hong, K. (2008) 'The impact of public transport policy on the viability and sustainability of mass railway transit: The Hong Kong experience', *Transportation Research Part A: Policy and Practice*, vol 42, pp 563–76.

Taylor, E. (2010) 'Evaluating CCTV: Why the findings are inconsistent, inconclusive and ultimately irrelevant', *Crime Prevention and Community Safety*, vol 12, pp 209–32.

Tester, K. (ed) (1994) *The Flâneur*, London: Routledge.

Thaler, R. And Sunstein, C. (2009) *Nudge: Improving decisions about health, wealth and happiness*, London: Penguin.

Thrift, N. (2004) 'Driving in the city', *Theory, Culture and Society*, vol 21, pp 41–59.

Tiwari, G. (2001) 'Pedestrian infrastructure in the city transport system: A case study of Delhi', *World Transport Policy and Practice*, vol 7, pp 13–18.

Tiwari, G. (2011) *Key mobility challenges in Indian cities*, Delhi: International Transport Forum, Discussion paper 18.

Tiwari, G. And Jain, H. (2008) 'Bicycles in urban India', *Institute of Urban Transport Journal*, December 2008, pp 67–76.

Tolley, R. (ed) (1990) *The greening of urban transport: Planning for walking and cycling in Western cities*, London: Belhaven.

Tolley, R. And Whitelegg, J. (eds) (2001) 'Special issue on walking', *World Transport Policy and Practice*, vol 7, pp 1–75.

Tomlinson, J. (1991) *Cultural imperialism*, London: Continuum.

Transport for London (TfL) (2010a) *Cycling revolution London*, London: TfL.

Transport for London (TfL) (2010b) *Delivering the benefits of cycling in outer London*, London: TfL, available at www.tfl.gov.uk/assets/downloads/businessandpartners/benefits-of-cycling-report.pdf.

Transport for London (TfL) (2013) *The Mayor's vision for cycling in London: an Olympic legacy for all Londoners*, London: GLA.

Urry, J. (2000) *Sociology beyond societies: Mobilities for the twenty-first century*, London: Routledge.

Urry, J. (2004) 'The "system" of automobility', *Theory, Culture and Society*, vol 21, pp 25–39.

Urry, J. (2007) *Mobilities*, Cambridge: Polity.

Uteng, T. And Cresswell, T. (eds) (2008) *Gendered mobilities*, Aldershot: Ashgate.

Van Dyck, D., Deforche, B., Cardon, G. And De Bourdeaudhuij, I. (2009) 'Neighbourhood walkability and its particular importance for adults with a preference for passive transport', *Health and Place*, vol 15, pp 496–504.

Van Exel, N., de Graaf, G. And Rietveld, P. (2005) 'Getting from A to B: Operant approaches to travel decision making', *Operant Subjectivity*, vol 27, pp 194–216.

Vaz de Almeida, M., Graça, P., Alfonso, C., D'Amicis, A., Lappalainen, R. And Damkjaer, S. (1999) 'Physical activity levels and body weight in a nationally representative sample in the European Union', *Public Health Nutrition*, 2, 105–14.

Victoria Transport Policy Institute (VTPI) (2012) 'Roadway connectivity: Creating more connected roadway and pathway networks', *Online TDM Encyclopedia*, available at www.vtpi.org/tdm/tdm116.htm.

Walker, M., Whyatt, J., Pooley, C., Davies, G., Coulton, P. And Bamford, W. (2009) 'Talk, technologies and teenagers: Understanding the school journey using a mixed-methods approach', *Children's Geographies*, vol 7, pp 107–22.

Wallman, S. (1984) *Eight London households*, London: Tavistock Publications.

Walsh, M. (2010) 'Still a long way to travel: Gender and mobility in history revisited', in G. Mom, P. Norton, G. Classen and G. Pirie (eds) *Mobility in history: Themes in transport. T2M Yearbook 2011*, Neuchâtel: T2M, pp 255–63.

Walton, J. (2000) *The British seaside: Holidays and resorts in the twentieth century*, Manchester: Manchester University Press.

Walton, J. And Walvin, J. (eds) (1983) *Leisure in Britain, 1780–1939*, Manchester: Manchester University Press.

Warde, A. (2005) 'Consumption and the theories of practice', *Journal of Consumer Culture*, vol 5, pp 131–53.

Watts, L. And Urry, J. (2008) 'Moving methods: Travelling times', *Environment and Planning D: Society and Space*, vol 26, pp 860–74.

Watts, S. And Stenner, P. (2005) 'Doing Q methodology: Theory, method and interpretation', *Qualitative Research in Psychology*, vol 2, pp 67–91.

Webster, W. (2004) 'The diffusion, regulation and governance of closed circuit television in the UK', *Surveillance and Society*, vol 2, pp 230–50.

Weisbrod, G., Vary, D. And Treyz, G. (2003) 'Measuring economic costs of urban traffic congestion to business', *Transportation Research Record*, vol 1839, pp 98–106.

Welsh Government (2012) *Consultation on Active Travel (Wales) Bill*, Cardiff: Welsh Government, available at http://wales.gov.uk/docs/det/consultation/120509a ctivetravelbillv2en.pdf.

Whitelegg, J. And Haq, G. (eds) (2003) *The Earthscan reader on world transport policy and practice*, London: Earthscan.

Whitelegg, J. And Williams, N. (2000) 'Non-motorised transport and sustainable development: Evidence from Calcutta', *Local Environment*, vol 5, pp 7–18.

Whyte, W. (1955) *Street corner society: The social structure of an Italian slum*, second edition, Chicago, IL: Chicago University Press.

Williams, K., Burton, E. And Jenks, M. (eds) (2000) *Achieving sustainable urban form*, London: E & FN Spon.

Wolf, W. (1996) *Car mania: A critical history of transport*, London: Pluto.

Wylie, J. (2005) 'A single day's walking: Narrating self and landscape on the south west coast path', *Transactions of the Institute of British Geographers*, vol 30, pp 234–47.

Websites

BBC website, Election 2010: http://news.bbc.co.uk/1/shared/election2010/results/

Bicycle Association website: http://bicycleassociation.org.uk/

Bike Hub website: www.bikehub.co.uk/

British Cycling website, Transport for London agree to redesign Bow roundabout accident black spot: www.britishcycling.org.uk/travel/article/trav20120112-Transport-for-London-agree-to-redesign-Bow-roundabout-accident-blackspot-0

Campaign for Better Transport website: www.bettertransport.org.uk/home

Campaign to Protect Rural England (CPRE) website, New government safety plan means rural road roulette: www.cpre.org.uk/media-centre/latest-news-releases/item/2057-new-government-safety-plan-means-rural-road-roulette?tmpl=component&print=1

Carbusters website, Groningen: http://carbusters.org/2009/11/03/groningen-the-worlds-cycling-city/

City of Copenhagen website, Cycle statistics: www.kk.dk/sitecore/content/Subsites/CityOfCopenhagen/SubsiteFrontpage/LivingInCopenhagen/CityAndTraffic/CityOfCyclists/CycleStatistics.aspx

Copenhagenize website, Bicycle infrastructure: www.copenhagenize.com/2011/08/case-for-bicycle-infrastructure.html

CTC website: www.ctc.org.uk/

Cycle Training UK website: www.cycletraining.co.uk/index.php?pg=1

Cyclechic website: www.copenhagencyclechic.com/

Cycling Embassy of Great Britain website: www.cycling-embassy.org.uk/

Department of Energy and Climate Change (DECC) website, EU Emissions Trading System (ETS) Phase III: www.decc.gov.uk/en/content/cms/emissions/eu_ets/phase_iii/phase_iii.aspx

Department for Transport (DfT) website, press release, Devolution of local transport, 31 January 2012: www.dft.gov.uk/news/press-releases/dft-press-20120131a/

Department for Transport (DfT) website, press release, High speed trains, 10 January 2012: www.dft.gov.uk/news/press-releases/dft-news-20120110

Department for Transport (DfT) website: www.dft.gov.uk/

Department of Health (DH) website, UK physical activity guidelines: www.dh.gov. uk/en/Publicationsandstatistics/Publications/PublicationsPolicyAndGuidance/ DH_127931

Drivers Alliance website: www.driversalliance.org.uk/

Green Party website: www.greenparty.org.uk/

iConnect (Impact of Constructing Non-motorised Networks and Evaluation Changes in Travel) project website: www.iconnect.ac.uk/

Living Streets website: www.livingstreets.org.uk/about/our-mission1/

London Cycling Campaign website: http://lcc.org.uk/

London Evening Standard website, Westminster in 'war on drivers', 14 November 2011: www.thisislondon.co.uk/standard/article-24009623-westminster-in-war-on-drivers.do

Mairie de Paris website, 2005, Qu'est-ce qu'un espace civilisé? www.paris. fr/politiques/Portal.lut?page_id=5773&document_type_id=7&document_ id=14921&portlet_id=12635

Manchester Evening News website, C-charge a resounding 'NO', 12 December 2008: http://menmedia.co.uk/manchestereveningnews/news/s/1085031_ ccharge_a_resounding_no

Meteorological Office website: www.metoffice.gov.uk/weather/uk/climate.html

National Archives website (a) Delivery of the National Cycling Strategy: a Review: http://webarchive.nationalarchives.gov.uk/+/http:/www.dft.gov.uk/ pgr/sustainable/cycling/deliveryofthenationalcycling5738?page=2

National Archives website (b) Cycling England: http://webarchive.nationalarchives. gov.uk/20110407094607/http://www.dft.gov.uk/cyclingengland/who-we-are/

National Archives website (c) Bikeability: http://webarchive.nationalarchives. gov.uk/20110407094607/http://www.dft.gov.uk/cyclingengland/cycling-england-bikeability/

National Archives website (d) Cycling cities and towns: http://webarchive. nationalarchives.gov.uk/20110407094607/http://www.dft.gov.uk/ cyclingengland/cycling-cities-towns/

National Assembly for Wales website: Active Travel Bill: http://www.senedd. assemblywales.org/mgIssueHistoryHome.aspx?IId=5750

National Atmospheric Emissions Inventory website: http://naei.defra.gov.uk/ overview/ap-overview

National Statistics website: www.statistics.gov.uk/hub/index.html

Natural England website, walking for health: www.wfh.naturalengland.org.uk/

NHS website, walking for health: www.nhs.uk/Livewell/getting-started-guides/ Pages/getting-started-walking.aspx

Raleigh Company website, History: www.raleigh.co.uk/Company/History/

Ramblers' Association website, Benefits of walking: www.getwalking.org/ category/benefits-of-walking/

Royal Borough of Kensington and Chelsea website, Exhibition Road: www.rbkc. gov.uk/subsites/exhibitionroad.aspx

Scottish National Party website: www.snp.org/

Slower Speeds website: www.slower-speeds.org.uk/

Speed Cameras Dot Org website: www.speedcameras.org/

Sustrans website: www.sustrans.org.uk/

Telegraph website, Fair Deal for Drivers campaign: www.telegraph.co.uk/news/ newstopics/fairdealfordrivers/

The Times cycling safety campaign: www.thetimes.co.uk/tto/public/cyclesafety/

The Times Digital Archive (28 March 1934, p 9): http://gale.cengage.co.uk/ times.aspx/

Top Gear website: www.topgear.com/uk/

Transport for London (TfL) website, London Cycling Design Standards: www. tfl.gov.uk/assets/downloads/businessandpartners/lcds_chapter7.pdf

United Nations website, Human Development Reports: http://hdr.undp.org/en/

United Nations website, Universal Declaration of Human Rights: www.un.org/ en/documents/udhr/

Victoria Transport Policy Institute (VTPI) website, Transportation Statistics: www. vtpi.org/tdm/tdm80.htm

Victoria Transport Policy Institute (VTPI) website: www.vtpi.org/

Walk 21 website: www.walk21.com/default.asp

Index